I0754762

THOMAS PHILIPP

ǦURǦĪ ZAIDĀN

HIS LIFE AND THOUGHT

BEIRUTER TEXTE UND STUDIEN

HERAUSGEGEBEN VOM

ORIENT-INSTITUT

DER DEUTSCHEN MORGENLÄNDISCHEN GESELLSCHAFT

BAND 3

ǦURǦĪ ZAIDĀN
HIS LIFE AND THOUGHT

BY

THOMAS PHILIPP

BEIRUT 1979

IN KOMMISSION BEI FRANZ STEINER VERLAG • WIESBADEN

ISBN 3-515-01842-5
ISSN — 0067-4931

Orient-Institut
der Deutschen Morgenländischen Gesellschaft
Beirut/Libanon, B.P. 2988

Mit Mitteln des Bundesministers für Forschung und Technologie
gedruckt in der Imprimerie Catholique, Beirut.

In Memory of our son Karim Werner

ACKNOWLEDGEMENTS

I gratefully acknowledge my obligation to the many who were helpful at one stage or another during the work on this study.

The members of the family of Zaidān in Cairo and Beirut have been most helpful through their own comments and recollections and by giving me access to the collection of Ǧurǧī Zaidān's private papers (now in AUB). I thank especially Emile Saman who gave of his time most generously during my research work in Cairo.

Without involving them in any responsibility for the substance of this study, I would like to express my gratitude to Professor Dr. Nikkie Keddie, Department of History, UCLA, and Professor Dr. S. Wild, Instituut vor het Moderne Nabije Oosten, Universiteit Amsterdam, who read the manuscript and offered their opinion and valuable criticism. I am grateful to Professor Dr. F. Steppat, Institut für Islamwissenschaft, FU Berlin, for his many comments on my work and his continuous encouragement. The initial stage of this study was supervised as a doctoral thesis by the late Professor Dr. G.E. von Grunebaum, Director Near Eastern Center, UCLA, to whom I am deeply indebted for his guidance and inspiration.

I thank Dr. P. Bachmann, Director of the Orient-Institut der Deutschen Morgenländischen Gesellschaft, Beirut, for accepting this study into the series of Beiruter Texte und Studien published by his Institute.

My thanks go to Mr. M. Peeplezadeh and A. Mahmud for their assistance in reading the private correspondence of Ǧurǧī Zaidān. Mr. W. McKie helped greatly in the editing and improvement of the English style of the manuscript. Miss Joan Page showed admirable patience typing the final draft of the manuscript.

I would also like to mention gratefully the financial help provided by the Research Council of Pahlavi University in Shiraz.

Shiraz, May 1975 THOMAS PHILIPP

TABLE OF CONTENTS

PART I

AN INTELLECTUAL BIOGRAPHY

INTRODUCTION

When Ğurğī Zaidān was born in Beirut on December 14, 1861 Lebanon had just emerged from twenty years of severe internal strife. The unrest had stemmed partially from social tensions between peasants and feudal landlords but soon assumed a denominational character which reflected the changing relations between the Druze and the Christian communities in Lebanon. Ğurğī Zaidān's family belonged to the Greek Orthodox community and, although the family apparently was not particularly religious, the awareness of its religious affiliation must have been heightened during this period. The conflict had been mainly one between the Druze and the Christian communities, but it had obtained some Muslim overtones which climaxed in the pogrom of Damascus in July 1860 in which some 5,500 Christians were killed by their Muslim neighbours.[1] These experiences loomed large in the mind of the Christian Arabs for many years and made it necessary to re-think and to re-formulate their relations with the non-Christian environment.

The unrest in Lebanon was not merely an internal affair. It had been intensified by European interference in support of one or other religious community. The French supported the Christian, especially the Maronite community, while the British sided with the Druze community. French troops had landed in 1860 in Lebanon following the massacre in Damascus. The major European powers had then taken an active part in establishing a new political order for Lebanon. Just a few months before Ğurğī Zaidān's birth this new political arrangement for Lebanon as an autonomous province of the Ottoman Empire had been adopted and guaranteed by the European powers.

The introduction of a new order in Lebanon was not limited to the political sphere. With the expansion of European economy and trade, Beirut began to change its face. It developed into a major port in the

1. Salibi 107.

Eastern Mediterranean. Western merchandise began to be widely distributed and Western skills were in demand. Europeans flocked to the city. The old order of society and life began to disintegrate. Ǧurǧī Zaidān's autobiography is an eloquent description of a society in transition.

Already before the European economic impact had gathered any strength in Lebanon, the presence of the West had made itself felt in a very different way: since the beginning of the nineteenth century French Catholic and American and British Protestant missionaries had, often in competition with each other, established schools all over Lebanon in an attempt to attract possible converts from the various religious communities. By and large the missionaries failed in their original purpose - conversion, but in the process of their missionary attempts they laid the foundation for modern education and provided a stimulus for the local communities to establish similar educational institutions. When Ǧurǧī Zaidān was a boy Lebanon had already an extensive number of elementary schools and high schools for boys and girls, and Beirut could boast of at least two very good colleges, the Syrian Protestant College of the American Missionaries and the Université St. Joseph of the French Jesuits. The development of a new educated class is most dramatically portrayed in Zaidān's autobiography. Education was certainly that aspect of change which had the greatest importance for the forming of Zaidān's own personality.

Change under the shadow of the Western presence was not restricted to Beirut. The whole of the Middle East had come to face the same challenge.

The two foci of the contact between the Arab East and Europe during the 19th century were Syria and Egypt. The encounter with the West in the two countries was different in its character and quality. In Egypt the military and political aspects dominated the contact in accordance with her strategic position in relation to Europe for passage to India and access to Africa. Technological progress in the military and economic spheres, centralized and more efficient administration, and political self-awareness were thus the issues of greatest importance to Egypt. In Syria, on the other hand, the Western impact expressed itself mainly in the activities of European and American missionaries who made education and training of the native, and mostly the Christian Arabs, their concern. The various schools and institutions of the missionaries, soon to be supplemented by local attempts to organize education, raised a group of educated people who were interested in the sciences, the literary and cultural products of secular Europe and who did basic scholarly work concerning their own language and literature.

From the forties of the nineteenth century a new factor was added to the military and intellectual ones: the economic role of Europe in the whole of the Middle East began to increase. European economic penetration had obtained its first legal sanction with the Treaty of Capitulations between France and the Ottoman Empire in 1740. But European economic expansionism began in earnest only after the beginning of industrialization. Perhaps the most significant formal recognition of this new economic expansion was the Commercial Convention between Great Britain and the Ottoman Empire. Other European nations soon followed suit with similar treaties. The increasing European domination of the Middle Eastern economy and markets had various social results. On the one hand whole groups of traditional producers disappeared, because they could not compete with the industrial products imported from the West. On the other hand a new social class developed, consisting of people who had frequently been on the margins of the society but now benefitted from European economic and legal protection and were able to take part in the new economic system. The more intensive the knowledge of Europe and its civilization became, the clearer became the idea that a mere adoption of its technical achievements would not be sufficient in order to preserve the status quo of Arab society or to contain the European impact and its dominating position in the Middle East; neither would it be sufficient to restrict to a group of educated specialists whatever changes had to be introduced. The whole society had to participate in the process of Westernization and the adoption of European ideas and institutions. The Middle East, earlier than other non-Western areas, was left with the paradoxical need of having to imitate, and adapt to, Western civilization in order to preserve its own social and cultural identity. « De toute évidence, elles (les sociétés orientales) devront pour échapper à l'Occident, se mettre à son école. Leur faudra-t-il donc, pour survivre, se renoncer? ».[2]

---

2. Berque 24.

At the beginning of the century only isolated products of European technology had been adopted by the Near Eastern society. Even the increasing use of European forms and systems in administration, jurisdiction, agriculture, etc., did not immediately make the society or its rulers aware that the European impact would entail profound changes in the society as a whole. At mid-century the question was still whether the traditional, religiously oriented society could and should accept the concepts and ideas of the modern civilization. Soon, however, there could be no doubt that there was no longer any option to reject or to ignore the Western impact, and the question shifted to whether it would be possible to maintain portions of the traditional society while living in the modern world.[3]

In particular, educated people became conscious of the fact that the whole society was moving towards a new and different phase, increasingly distant from its own past and becoming more closely related to modern Western civilization. This movement was conceived of in "national" terms within the dimension of an increasingly "nationalistic" history, and it became known as the Arab Awakening, *al-nahḍa al-ʿarabīya.*[4]

Derived from the root n-h-ḍ in the classical language, the word *nahḍa* had the general meaning of "a single act of rising, a motion or movement ... also power, ability, strength".[5] In a contemporary dictionary published in 1870, the term *nahḍa* still lacked any abstract meaning of a social, cultural or national awakening.[6] When Ibrāhīm al-Yāziǧī[7] addressed himself in 1868 to the Arabs in an ode, he did not use

3. A. Hourani speaks in particular about the Muslim and his faith when he says of Muḥammad ʿAbduh "He was not concerned as Khayr al-Din had been in a previous generation to ask whether devout Muslims could accept the institutions and ideas of the modern world; they had come to stay and so much the worse for anyone who did not accept them. He asked the opposite question: whether someone who lived in the modern world could still be a devout Muslim"; HOURANI 139. It seems to us that this change of the question held true for the society in the Middle East also with regard to the other not strictly religious but still traditional aspects of life.

4. This expression has to be used with caution because the national aspect, too, was part of the general movement and evolved only with it and through it towards a valid concept of its own.

5. See LANE VIII 2080.

6. See AL-BUSTĀNĪ, B. II 2137.

7. Ibrāhīm al-Yāziǧī (1847-1906) son of Naṣīf Y. Like his father he was a scholar of Arab history and language, published and wrote in various magazines, supervised the Arabic translation of the Old Testament for the Jesuits; DĀǦIR, II 759.

the root n-h-ḍ but said *tanabbahū wa-stafīqū ayyuhā al-ʿarab*, "Arise ye Arabs and awake".[8] During the next twenty years, however, the word *nahḍa* must have become accepted with its particular abstract meaning of a socio-cultural awakening. In 1888 we find it used for the first time in the magazine "al-Muqtaṭaf" in an article about the development of Arab medicine;[9] and since the expression is not further explained, we have to assume that it was already familiar to the reader as an established term. In 1892 an article about "The Latest Egyptian *Nahḍa*" appears in the first year of "al-Hilāl".[10] The term in its modern abstract meaning is usually translated as "renaissance". The Arabs themselves came to designate the European Renaissance with the same term. But one should take notice that the original meaning of the word did not include any notion of a repeated occurrence of a given act or the return to a former situation. Its meaning contained only a change from an inactive position towards a dynamic situation. The abstract term *nahḍa* primarily meant this: a change from lethargy to a dynamic situation of change and progress. This meaning seems to have been the predominant one for the Arab intellectuals at the end of the 19th century. A translation of *nahḍa* as "awakening" or "rise" is, therefore, more appropriate than the usually accepted translations such as "revival", "rebirth" or "renaissance". Only gradually with the development of a historical consciousness towards the past was reference made to the regaining of earlier heights of Arab civilization and culture. Even then it remained questionable whether the actual re-establishment of former institutions and ideas, reaching a similar level of culture but by different intellectual and social means, was intended. Here we find a differentiation between a secular and a religious use of the word. For the Muslim reformer the return to the original institutions and concepts of Islam was the key problem, while for the secular reformer the content of the *Nahḍa* was a more or less camouflaged adaptation of new concepts rather than the revival of old ones. But in either case the use of the term *nahḍa* implies an awareness of the fundamental process of change which the Arab world was undergoing.

---

8. Antonius 54.
9. Al-Muqtaṭaf XII 735.
10. I 123.

In particular, for the secular reformer of Christian background, the quest for a new definition of his own position in society and for the formulation of a cultural identity obtained a pressing urgency. Not only must he try to emancipate himself from his own religious communal background and to determine his position vis à vis Europe, but he also had to re-define his relations with the Muslim Arab environment. Increasingly a new basis for the relations between Christian and Muslim Arabs was found in terms of an Arab cultural and national identity, as a possibility to establish equality between and common identity for all Arabs regardless of their religious background. It is, therefore, not surprising that many of the educated Christian Arabs were in the avant garde of those who gave the Arab *Nahḍa* a national character.

The economic prosperity and greater personal freedom in Egypt on the one side, the increasing limitation of free expression under the oppressive Abdülhamidian regime in Syria on the other during the last third of the century, and especially after the British occupation of Egypt in 1882, caused a migration of many members of the new Syrian intelligentsia to Egypt. In addition, the Syrian Protestant College, one of the most important factors in the creation of a Westernized, educated class in Syria, shifted in the 1880s from Arabic to English as a teaching language and became thus less attractive for the young Arab intellectuals. All these factors led to the development of Egypt at the end of the century as the main centre of Arab *Nahḍa* and of Arab intellectual life in all its different aspects.

The Syrian immigrants, most of them originating from Christian Arab families, constituted a major impetus for the Arab *Nahḍa* in Egypt. They developed and very much monopolized the press in Egypt, the most important instrument for intellectual, educational and political discussion. Such reputable daily newspapers as "al-Ahrām" and "al-Muqaṭṭam" had been founded and were run by Syrians, and among weekly or monthly publications such popular magazines as "al-Muqtaṭaf" and "al-Hilāl" were in the hands of the Syrians. Thanks to their greater familiarity with European literature, they introduced new literary forms in prose and poetry. Through their literary and journalistic activities the Syrians became instrumental in familiarizing the Arab world with Western concepts and modern sciences.

They also engaged themselves in community activities in Egypt such as the foundation of philanthropic societies and the building of hospitals. Their knowledge of languages and their family relations with emigrants to other countries enabled them to play an important role in Egyptian economy and trade. Having experienced Ottoman despotism, they usually were more inclined than the Egyptians to accept the British rule in Egypt. Relations between Egyptians and Syrians were not always free from resentment and prejudices, but on the whole the Syrians proved to be a very fertile element for the Arab *Nahḍa* in Egypt.

Ǧurǧī Zaidān was a typical and important member of this group of Syrian emigrants. Born into a poor Greek Orthodox Arab family he enjoyed very little formal education. His unquenchable thirst for knowledge and learning, however, caused him to use any opportunity to increase his knowledge and to further his education. Very much a self-made man, he did not hesitate to undertake such different activities as founding one of the most important publishing houses in the Middle East, editing and writing his own monthly journal, composing novels and doing research in history, language and philology as well as passing short spells as a military dragoman, a newspaper editor and a schoolteacher. As diverse as these activities and occupations may have been, they all originated from, and were related to, Zaidān's awareness of the Arab *Nahḍa* in which he participated consciously and to the development of which he wanted to contribute.

His influence in the intellectual development of the Arab world was considerable, perhaps not so much as an original and creative thinker but rather as a popularizer of certain ideas and concepts. His magazine and his novels enjoyed great popularity and are even today widely read. His scholarly works set new patterns for historical research and helped develop a new historical and national consciousness amongst the Arabs. Yet, for reasons that we shall discuss later, his role has never been fully recognized and appreciated in the Arab world. It shall be the purpose of this study to analyze and evaluate Zaidān's intellectual contributions to the Arab *Nahḍa* as they were determined by his social background, by the various trends of culture and thought he was exposed to, and by his own life experience.

ǦURǦĪ ZAIDĀN. BIOGRAPHICAL SKETCH

We are very fortunate to possess so much detailed information about the early life of Zaidān. Indeed, no other source gives us such a complete and in general factually correct, description of the young Zaidān as his own autobiography. We have no intention of repeating here the individual events of his childhood and youth, since the translation of the autobiography is part of this study. We would only do injustice to Zaidān's own narrative by paraphrasing it here. Nevertheless, there exist several issues which appear in the autobiography and which demand a closer investigation and more general comment.

Ǧurǧī Zaidān was born in Beirut on December 14, 1861. His family belonged to the Greek Orthodox community, though the religious affiliation does not seem to have played an important role in the daily life of the family. Zaidān described his family as living in "average circumstances", *mutawassiṭ al-ḥāl.*[1] But from the reading one gains the impression that it was a life lived always on the brink of poverty. Put in a nutshell — the boy Zaidān grew up in poor economic conditions; he received only some haphazard elementary schooling, and was put to work early by his father who considered any education beyond simple reading and writing skills a waste. Yet when the boy reached the age of nineteen he passed the entrance examination for the Syrian Protestant College and enrolled as a student of medicine. If we look beyond the period covered in the autobiography we find the mature Zaidān to be a respected well-established member of the bourgeoisie. This brief summary contains one of the motifs of the autobiography and, indeed, of Zaidān's whole life and thought: the motif of the self-made man, the motif of the poor-boy-made-good. The autobiography abounds with terms as "hard work", "perseverance", "awareness of time", "discipline", etc. The key

1. See 135.

event for the youngster Zaidān is his encounter with the book *Sirr an-nağāḥ*, an Arabic translation by Ya'qūb Ṣarrūf[2] of S. Smiles' *Self Help.*[3] Zaidān tells us in his autobiography how reading "about the life of men who reached the top through their own effort and struggle and reliance upon themselves alone" excited him so much, that he was never able to read the whole book through.[4] He felt that the stories in this book reflected exactly his own situation but also, and here the reason for Zaidān's excitement, described ways to escape one's own ignominious circumstances.

S. Smiles formulated in his book just two years before the appearance of C. Darwin's *On the Origin of Species...* some of the concepts that were typical of the *laissez faire* liberalism of the Victorian society at mid-century. Any individual could improve his position in society if he had the talent and the disciplined willpower to use this talent. It was the kind of individualistic social mobility which stood, of course, in complete contradiction to any idea of improvement of whole social classes or class struggle — socialist and marxist concepts which Zaidān was to reject throughout his life as "unnatural".

Smiles' book gave the young Zaidān hope and confirmed the life experience of the mature Zaidān later. It is to books like *Self Help* that one has to turn to find the origin of the social values that Zaidān believed to be of importance. Another book that appealed extremely to Zaidān

---

2. Ya'qūb Ṣarrūf (1852-1927) born in Lebanon. 1870 he belonged to the first group of graduates from the Syrian Protestant College. He taught in various schools of the American Missionaries and from 1873-1884 was an instructor at the SPC. Here he established close ties with Fāris Nimr and Šāhīn Makāriyūs. They all joined the Freemasons, and Ṣarrūf and Nimr began to publish their later famous magazine al-Muqtaṭaf. Inspired by their mentor, Cornelius van Dyck, they were drawn to sciences and scientific theories, and supported the evolutionary theory of Darwin. As natives and believers of questionable faithfulness — even though they had become protestants — they eventually had to resign from the SPC faculty. Ṣarrūf and Nimr then transferred their journalistic enterprise to Cairo, where they later also founded a daily, al-Muqaṭṭam. Ṣarrūf believed that education and scientific thought would open the way for reform and progress of the traditional society; besides many articles dealing with these topics, Ṣarrūf also published various novels and studies: DĀĠIR II 540; DĪ ṬARRĀZĪ IV 124-129; FARAG 74.

3. First published in London, 1856. It went through innumerable editions over the next hundred years. The Arabic translation was published in 1880; DĀĠIR II 542. The translation was characteristically financed by a "Syrian Improvement Committee"; TIBAWI 203.

4. See 164.

was E. Demolin's *A quoi tient la supériorité des Anglo-Saxons* which was published almost forty years after Smiles' book had made its first appearance. Demolin's book was written in the same "popular sciences" manner as Smiles' book, arguing a similar point: the superiority of the value system of British middle class liberalism and entrepreneurship. This time, however, the focus was not upon class differences within one society, but upon explaining the colonial predominance of the British in the world. The book met with the same popular success as did Smiles'. It was translated into Arabic by Fatḥī Zaġlūl,[5] one year after its first appearance.

The appeal of such books that seemingly give conclusive scientific explanation to the ingredients of success is always, and everywhere, tremendous. Demolin's book had the additional attraction for the Arab reader of showing that not only the Arab world was in need of new values in order to rise again, but that as highly civilized a nation as France found herself in a situation in which it apparently would pay to imitate and learn from the British. Many years after its first publication Zaidān would still refer to the book as an authority on what values should be taught to the young generation in Egypt.

Only weeks after the publication of Demolin's book in France Zaidān wrote an article in "al-Hilāl" called "The Eastern Youth", *aš-šabāb aš-šarqī.*[6] Following closely Demolin's main argument of the difference between the French *fonctionnaire* and the British *entrepreneur* as well as the superiority of the latter, Zaidān discouraged the Arab youth from seeking positions within the government bureaucracy: they were insecure (an argument which had more to do, however, with the Syrians' position in Egypt than with bureaucratic positions per se); they hampered private initiative, and offered no possibility for expansion. What was needed to strengthen the country was a concentration of the youth on agriculture, trade and industry. Dedicated, hard work would

5. Aḥmad Fatḥī Zaġlūl (1863-1914), born in Egypt, brother of Sa'd Zaġlūl. He studied law in France, 1884-1887, and worked upon his return to Egypt as a lawyer and judge. He was closely allied with the group of modernists and reformers in Egypt. He became especially famous for his translations of Le Bon's and Demolin's works. The translation of Demolin's book appeared in 1898; Dāġir II 412 and VII 605.

6. VI 333, a somewhat similar argument can be found already in I 271-275.

compensate for the initial lack of money, if a young man wanted to start a career in those fields. These admonitions of the self-made man and the liberal entrepreneur took on a nationalistic quality when Zaidān added that only if the foreigners were eliminated from their dominant positions in these branches of economy would Egypt benefit from its own wealth.[7]

The British middle class *laissez-faire* ideology, later enriched by Spencerian social Darwinism, had found in the Middle East especially receptive ears amongst the Syrian Christians. They recognized in it some of their experience and values and realized that unlimited entrepreneurship would give them the competitive edge over their Muslim compatriots.[8] They, therefore, adopted this ideology wholeheartedly. Zaidān formulated this ideology quite precisely in the introduction to the biography of a compatriot of his, Salīm Ṣīdnāwī.[9] When explaining the purpose of writing this and similar biographies Zaidān observed:

> "There are biographies of people like Disraeli, Rothschild and other men of action and hard work who were born poor and achieved wealth or knowledge or a profession through their efforts and activity. The purpose of such biographies is not so much the immortalization of their memory but rather the emulation of their deeds. The closer their *vitae* are to the needs of the reader, the greater the benefit in publishing their biographies. The biographies of politicians, administrators and soldiers are of no use in our hope for success in our own work. As far as scholars, merchants or professionals who achieved their wealth or greatness through their own efforts and faith are concerned, their biographies set a good example for the young generation — an ounce of example is better than a pound of instruction.
>
> Our writers have this habit of restricting themselves to biographies of scholars, soldiers or politicians, yet we are in greater need of biographies of merchants who are self-made men and who became rich by lawful means befitting the conditions of success. Trade is the most important source of income in our country. Yet it is part of the

7. We find a very similar demand for the avoidance of service in the government bureaucracy and for involvement in agriculture, trade and industry in Muṣṭafa Kāmil's thought; STEPPAT 321.

8. Cf. REID, *Rags to Riches* 359.

9. Ṣalīm Ṣīdnāwī (1856-1908) born in Damascus, sent by his father to learn European tailoring. 1879 he went to Egypt, where he started his tremendously successful career as a business man; ZAIDĀN *Tarāǧim* I, 302-309.

popular phantasies that wealth is not (to be) attained in a legitimate, *ḥalāl*, manner; that the true believer lives in poverty and dies a needy man; so that only liars, cunning people and sly men get rich... is the excuse of those who fail in their efforts".[10]

The above quotation is taken from Zaidān's book *Tarāǧim mašāhīr aš-šarq fī'l-qarn at-tāsiʿ ʿašar*. There existed a long tradition in Islamic Arabic literature to compile biographies of selected groups of important people. But judging from much of the content of this book, Zaidān's immediate model had been Smiles' *Self-Help* rather than the traditional biographical literature. He wanted to show with examples that also in the East it was possible to rise from "rags to riches". It was this desire for self-improvement which Zaidān believed to be most essential for his own society.

In a way his own autobiography was such an example of how a poor boy could rise to fame, if not to wealth. This is perhaps the major qualification the reader of the autobiography should keep in mind. Even though Zaidān was not planning to publish his autobiography just then, he was aware, while writing it, that it contained "many lessons beneficial for the youth".[11] In other words Zaidān projected his belief in self-improvement with all its concomitant values of perseverance, hard work, discipline, etc., into the narration of his early life. Naturally, no autobiography is an account of "objective truth" but the story of a life filtered through the interpretative memory of the author. This does not diminish the value of the autobiography as long as the reader is aware of the tendency and directions of the author's own views and concepts.

Zaidān's autobiography contains many descriptions of the beginnings of Westernization of Beirut in the second half of the century. Zaidān discussed extensively the impact of Western education, the social changes and changes in dress and mores. One particular aspect, though, should be noted here which seems somewhat neglected in the autobiography: the penetration of European economic forces into the Middle East and their importance as a major agent of change and Westernization. This aspect bears especially upon the ideology of the self-made man and the

10. Ibid.

11. *Letters*, Zaidān to Emile, Cairo, Oct. 24, 1908.

entrepreneur, a new socio-economic function which obtained considerable importance amongst the Christian Syrian Arabs in the second half of the nineteenth century. For the Christian Syrian Arab the European economic system with its free competition and profit making offered the first possibility of emancipation from the restricted environment of the religious minority and of obtaining status and influence within society in general. The Christian Syrians were especially favoured by circumstances. Because of their religious background their access to Europeans was easier and often special legal protection could be obtained for them. The positive attitude towards commerce and business which became typical for the Syrian Christian Arabs is well stated in the above-quoted comment of Zaidān about the life of Salīm Ṣīdnāwī "we are in greater need of biographies of merchants who are self-made men and who became rich by lawful means befitting the conditions of success". In this context it is noteworthy that the young Zaidān, when he was to learn a craft, was put in a workshop, where European shoes were made. The owners of the shop had been financially very successful with this new trade.[12] When the parents of Zaidān thought seriously of a career for their son, they decided upon the career of an accountant. This was a new profession and it promised entry to the world of business even for the man without means. Even later, when Zaidān reflected about the kind of subject he should study at the Syrian Protestant College, he was guided in his choice by the financial rewards that the career of a physician seemed to guarantee.

From the autobiography the image emerges of Zaidān the self-made man who had learned already at a tender age that "sitting around without anything to do meant great disgrace", who in spite of his other work, clung with great perseverance to his aim of an education for himself and who finally entered the Syrian Protestant College against the declared wishes of his father. But this image of the self-assertive strong willed youth is somewhat counterbalanced by the description of another characteristic of Zaidān's personality. Zaidān was a timid boy who did not dare to attract the wrath of the teacher and who never participated in the games of the other boys. In the company of the young

12. See 140.

toughs of the city he felt inferior and believed himself to be a total failure. He did not dare to speak out in the company of others and even in the College he was tormented by his insecurity and felt ill at ease with his classmates. This shyness or timidity never seems to have left him completely: "I like to avoid the cause of enmity — from my childhood I noticed this natural disposition in me — therefore, I would avoid anything that would infuriate the teacher or would cause him to rebuke me or beat me".[13] The fear to expose himself and his shyness with people are a factor which we should keep in mind when we try to find the reasons for his hesitation in later years to participate actively in political life and for his preference for the role of the writer to that of the teacher.

In the fall of 1881 Zaidān succeeded — thanks to his own intellectual perceptiveness and the help of a friend who prepared him for the entrance examinations — to fulfil his boyhood dream and enroll as a student of the medical school of the Syrian Protestant College. He succeeded greatly during his first year of studies. He was the best in his class and ended his course work by receiving awards for distinction as a student in chemistry and Latin during the commencement festivities. During this period Zaidān participated in quite a number of social activities. He had long walks with friends through the parks and at the shore of Beirut, he frequented literary salons, he attended gatherings with friends and classmates. But he always seemed to have been rather shy and introverted, moderate and balanced in his opinions.[14] After Zaidān's first year at the Syrian Protestant College had passed peacefully enough, the College exploded at the beginning of the next year into a deep crisis. Zaidān dedicated a large part of his autobiography to a detailed description of the events of this crisis, which eventually forced him to leave the College. The background, the actual events and implication of this crisis have been competently described and analyzed in other places.[15] Here we shall restrict the discussion, therefore, to the meaning this event had for Zaidān himself.

---

13. See 137.

14. ḎĀK 36, 42.

15. Cf. for instance TIBAWI "History of the SPC" 279 ff, FĀRIS. A very lucid interpretation of the events can be found in FARAG.

The Syrian Protestant College had been founded in 1866 in Beirut by American missionaries.[16] It quickly became a centre for the intellectual life just starting to develop in Syria. Fāris Nimr,[17] Ya'qūb Ṣarrūf and Šiblī Šumayyil[18] belonged to the earliest graduates of the College. Buṭrus al-Bustānī's[19] *al-Madrasa al-waṭanīya*, the patriotic school, served as a preparatory school for the college. Even "the first organized effort in the Arab national movement" has been traced to a group whose members had all been educated in the Syrian Protestant College.

Soon after the foundation of the College a discussion had begun about the introduction of English as the language of instruction. By 1879-80 English was introduced throughout the College with the exception of the Medical School. The faculty was divided over the question of the language of instruction into a liberal and a conservative camp, the latter demanding the elimination of Arabic as a teaching language. But the divisions between liberals and conservatives were not restricted to the language problem alone. It included also the more basic question as to the role Protestant Christian doctrines should play in the education provided by the College. This discussion came to a head over the issue of the validity and admissibility of Darwin's recently formulated theory of evolution. The liberal camp centred around Cornelius van Dyck,[20] his son,

16. For history of missionary education activities in Syria see especially Tibawi.

17. Fāris Nimr (1857-1951) born in Lebanon, was educated in missionary schools and taught at the SPC. Together with his fried Ya'qūb Ṣarrūf he not only ventured into journalism but initiated various scientific and literary societies first in Beirut and later in Cairo. He is best known for his journalistic activities but was also famous for his translations of European books and his own literary attempts; Dāģir III 1352; dī Ṭarrāzī IV 138-142. Cf. also *supra*, ftnte 2.

18. Šiblī Šummayyil (1860-1917) born in Lebanon had studied medicine in the SPC and became one of the first and most outspoken protagonists of Darwinism in the Arab world. In 1885 he settled in Egypt where he continued his work as a physician and writer; Dāģir II 497; Reid "*Syrian Christians ...*" 183-185.

19. Buṭrus al-Bustānī (1819-1883) born in Lebanon. Scholar of Arabic language and literature. Collaborated with Eli Smith in the translation of the Bible into Arabic. After the turmoil in 1860 between the Christian and the Druze communities he founded in 1863 his *al-Madrasa al-waṭanīya*, which was one of the first attempts to provide secular national education. He wrote the first modern Arab dictionary, *Muḥīṭ al-muḥīṭ*, and began an encyclopaedia, *Dā'irat al ma'ārif.* He founded also several shortlived magazines; Dāģir II 180, GAL II 495; Suppl. II 767; Suppl. III 390.

20. Cornelius van Dyck (1818-1895) born in the U.S.A. had come to Beirut in 1840 after finishing his medical studies. He was the only non-theologian among the American missionaries in Syria. Besides his work as a physician, he helped to establish

William,[21] Edwin R. Lewis,[22] their colleague in the Medical School, and Fāris Nimr and Ya'qūb Ṣarrūf, who were both at the time teaching in the Syrian Protestant College and had been publishing for five years their magazine "al-Muqtaṭaf".

In 1882 E. Lewis gave the commencement speech in which he mildly praised Darwin and his theory. This provided the occasion for the conservative camp to take action against the liberals amongst the faculty. E. Lewis was dismissed. Students who went on strike in response to his dismissal were locked out from the campus. Eventually C. van Dyck and some liberal colleagues resigned. After a lengthy exchange of letters, protests and declarations, most of the expelled students refused to return to the College and tried to finish their studies independently.

It is noteworthy that during the whole dispute between faculty and students the real issues were hardly ever mentioned; the theory of biological evolution and closely connected with it in this case the problem of freedom of speech and thought at the College. Only once the students explicity denied that E. Lewis was a protagonist of Darwinism. Their whole argument for the re-employment of E. Lewis did not touch upon the validity of the evolutionary theory or of E. Lewis's right to discuss this theory, but was based on a legalistic point, namely that the students joined the school and paid their fees with the understanding that Lewis should be their teacher in chemistry, a contract, so to say, which the school had broken by dismissing E. Lewis. In the same manner the faculty never argued that E. Lewis did an objectionable thing by speaking favourably about Darwinism. It was simply claimed that the students had no right whatsoever to interfere with hiring and firing policies of the faculty.

Unequivocal proof can be found that the real issue was Darwinism and the attempt to suppress the teaching of evolutionary thought

---

village schools, collaborated in the translation of the Bible into Arabic, wrote Arabic textbooks for his students, etc., 1867 he joined the faculty of the SPC as a teacher of medicine; ZAIDĀN *Tarāǧim* II 40-53; cf. also ḪŪRĪ.

21. William van Dyck, third son of Cornelius van Dyck, joined the faculty of the SPC in 1880. He held evolutionary views and brought Darwin's books with him to Beirut; FARAG 75. Her spelling van Dyke is erroneous.

22. Edwin R. Lewis (d. 1907), ordained minister and physician, he taught in various missionary schools and from 1881-1882 in the SPC, from where he was forced to resign because of his commencement speech; TIBAWI 244.

at the College, if one reads in the Annual Report of Syrian Protestant College,[23] that since January 1883 the Board of Trustees required each teacher appointed to the Syrian Protestant College to sign a Declaration of Principles. This declaration was a manifesto of Protestant religious dogma which implied the incompatibility of supporting any part of the theory of evolution with teaching at this Protestant institution. In 1884 the appointments of Fāris Nimr and Ya'qūb Ṣarrūf after E. Lewis, the most outspoken protagonists of Darwinism, were terminated.[24] With this last step, the Syrian Protestant College finally lost its role as a centre for the rapidly developing indigenous intelligentsia of the Arab World at the end of the 19th century.

For Zaidān this crisis at the College was of crucial importance. For him it meant a total change in his planned career, the premature termination of his medical studies, and eventually his leaving Beirut for Cairo. But it was not only for personal reasons that he gave this crisis so much space in his autobiography. He saw in it a more general importance. He called it, obviously quite proudly, though not correctly — since student unrest had already been a typical feature even in the traditional education institutions — "the first time in the East that students united to demand their rights".

Concerning his own participation in this strike, Zaidān wrote that Iskandar al-Bārūdī[25] was one of the main leaders in the protest action and that "perhaps I was more devoted to Iskandar al-Bārūdī during these events than anyone else because I believed him, just like any student believes his teacher".[26] It is more than doubtful that his personal devotion to his former teacher was the sole reason for his active participation in this conflict. In the first meeting of the protesting students he was

23. *Annual Reports* 80.

24. PENROSE 69 tries to explain the dismissal "to have been based on well-founded suspicion that the two young men were playing too active a part in dangerous politics. There is no question that they both were leaders in a secret Arab society ..." If that were the case they should never have been appointed teachers in the first place, cf. ANTONIUS 81; not to mention the proposal made in July 1882 to raise their salary and make them eventually adjunct professors; TIBAWI "History of the SPC" 283.

25. Iskandar al-Bārūdī (1856-1921) born in Sidon, obtained M.D. degree from SPC in 1882, worked as a physician and writer. 1894-1914 editor of the magazine, aṭ-Ṭabīb, contributed many articles to al-Hilāl and al-Muqtaṭaf; DĀĠIR II 157.

26. See 181.

made chairman of the meeting. However, Zaidān hastened to explain this was only for one meeting and the only reason why he was chosen was that he was on friendly terms with all students, thanks to his conciliatory nature. This was certainly partially true, but it implies somewhat of an understatement of his own role. He was strongly enough involved as to emerge as one of two students of his class that never gave in to the demands of the faculty and left the Syrian Protestant College for good.

As much as Zaidān discussed the problems of freedom of thought and equality before the law, he remained rather silent about the issue that constituted the test case for the application of freedom of thought in the Syrian Protestant College and which created the crisis in the school. True, he mentioned that Lewis gave a lecture on Darwinism, adding that Lewis did not oppose in any way the Christian religion but that theologians saw in it a threat to the foundation of Christianity. But this rather non-committal mentioning of Darwinism does not do justice to the importance the theory had for Zaidān's contemporaries and indeed Zaidān himself. The role of Darwinism in modern Arab thought has yet to be investigated adequately. Darwinism was more than just one particular scientific theory. It promised the key to a scientific explanation and analysis not only of nature but of human society and its historical development as well. The importance of science in general and Darwinism in particular for the Arab intelligentsia was that it seemed to provide a secular rational answer to tradition and to religion: "... the religion of science was a declaration of war on older religions".[27] Šiblī Šumayyil, an early graduate of the medical school of the Syrian Protestant College was to become one of the main protagonists of the evolutionary theory in the Arab World. Ya'qūb Ṣarrūf and Fāris Nimr had published in their magazine "al-Muqtaṭaf" articles about Darwin and the theory of evolution already before the speech of E. Lewis which triggered the crisis at the College. "Al-Muqtaṭaf" also later dealt with the concepts of evolutionary theory. The autobiography does not tell us whether Zaidān at the time had already become an adherent of the evolutionary theory. Zaidān himself actually claimed that his participation in the strike was caused by his loyalty to his former teacher.

27. Hourani 250.

Judging from his close contact with Cornelius van Dyck, E. Lewis, Ya'qūb Ṣarrūf and Fāris Nimr, not only at the College but also at such places as *Šams al-birr*[28] and the Freemason Lodges, we may assume that at that time he was not only already familiar with Darwinism but also sympathetic towards it.[29] In his very first book which appeared in 1886, Zaidān applied the evolutionary theory to the phenomena of language. Over the years Darwinism attained an increasingly important position in his thinking. We shall deal with this development when discussing Zaidān's approach to history and his concepts of society.[30] The origins of this trend in his thought are to be found in the period of his affiliation with the Syrian Protestant College.

The same belief in science and rationality that led the Arab secular intelligentsia to adopt Darwinism with such enthusiasm caused a great number of them to join the organizations of the Freemasons. Here, as in the case of Darwinism, we are still lacking any serious evaluation of the role of the Freemasons in the Middle East.[31] In the Middle East even more than in Europe their organization represented the belief in an enlightened universal rationality by which the Freemasons tried to replace the irrational dogma of specific religions. This rationality was to unite man beyond the petty limits of his own religious background. The importance of Middle Eastern Freemasonry was its aim to provide a framework in which members of various religious communities could meet and co-operate in the same rational spirit.[32] The Masons are comparable in this function to the early scientific and literary societies which flourished

28. *Šams al-birr* founded 1869 as a branch of the British YMCA by Fāris Nimr and Šāhīn Makāriyūs. Many of the students from the SPC were its members. Zaidān, too, became a member; ZAIDĀN *Ta'rīḫ ādāb* IV 70.

29. Cf. the speech he gave according to *Ḏāk* 72 ff in which Zaidān developed, however, a more Lamarckian argument: if women were given the opportunity to use their brain more, it would develop to the same size as that of man.

30. See 55 ff.

31. The works of Šāhīn Makāriyūs, Zaidān, the anti-Mason writings of Cheikho and lately such somewhat confused works as those of Abī Rašīd can be considered in the best case as a primary source of information.

32. This idea is already expressed by one of the earliest active Freemasons, Ya'qūb Ṣarrūf: "There was nothing in it [Masonry] that contradicted the Christian religion... but it unites the hearts of the Christians and the Muslims"; letter Ya'qūb Ṣarrūf to Louis Cheikho, Cairo, June 14, 1911, also amongst the unpublished papers of Zaidān, Collection AUB.

in the nineteenth century in Beirut, Cairo and other cities. "Freemasonry and free thinking seem to have been closely linked at that time in the Middle East. To be a Freemason was to show one's dislike of orthodox traditional religion, the power it gave to the ecclesiastics and the hatred and division it promoted and perpetuated in society".[33] The first Freemason Lodges had been founded in Beirut in 1862 and 1869.[34] In Egypt the first one existed already in 1832.[35] Zaidān mentioned in connection with the student strike that many of the students belonged to the Freemasons. But he remained silent with regard to his own membership. Nabīh Fāris assumed that Zaidān was associated with one of the Lodges in Beirut which also helped him to make his way later in Cairo.[36] But there is no unequivocal proof for this assumption. Fāris Nimr, Ya'qūb Ṣarrūf and Šāhīn Makāriyūs[37] belonged to a Lodge in Beirut. It can be considered likely that Zaidān, too, had joined one of the Lodges. In Cairo Zaidān belonged definitely to the Freemasons Organization. In 1888 he was made Secretary of one of the Lodges that belonged to the organization of the Grand Patriotic Lodge of Egypt.[38] At the time Zaidān felt so strongly committed to the cause of the Freemasons that he composed an apologetic book about the history of the Freemasons. Zaidān's active interest in the Freemasons seems to have coincided more or less with the period in which he co-operated most closely with Fāris Nimr, Ya'qūb Ṣarrūf and Šāhīn Makāriyūs. Soon, however, he lost interest in the Freemasons. In his later works one finds hardly any reference to the Masons and in his private life his membership in the Freemasons' Lodge seems not to have played any important role.[39]

---

33. Keddourie 20.

34. Steppat "*Eine Bewegung unter den Notabeln Syriens*" 644.

35. Rašīd 174.

36. Fāris 349.

37. Šāhīn Makāriyūs (1853-1910) founded together with Fāris Nimr *Šams al-birr* in 1870. He was the first editor of al-Muqtaṭaf and in 1882 he became editor of aṭ-Ṭabīb. A close friend of Fāris Nimr and Ya'qūb Ṣarrūf, he went together with them in 1884 to Egypt and continued to participate in their journalistic enterprises as well as editing his own newspaper. He also wrote a history of the Freemasons; Dāġir III 1271, Zaḫūrā 417.

38. Documented in collection of unpublished papers of Zaidān.

39. Cf. comment by his daughter Asmā, quoted in Ware 78.

After the strike at the Syrian Protestant College had come to its unfortunate conclusion, Zaidān refused to accept the conditions the College had set up for the re-entry of the striking students and preferred to look elsewhere for an opportunity to continue his studies. The Medical School of *'Ain šams* in Cairo seemed to offer this opportunity. Equipped with letters of recommendation Zaidān arrived in Egypt in 1883. He soon was discouraged from continuing his medical studies. The decision was probably not only motivated by his lack of financial resources but also by his decreasing interest in medicine itself which made him less willing to invest additional years in medical studies.

In Cairo he soon took over the editorship of "az-Zamān", a daily newspaper.[40] He remained its editor until 1884. The reasons for leaving this job are not evident. Neither are his motives clear as to why with his friend Ǧabr Ḍūmiṭ[41] he joined Wolsely and his expeditionary corps that was to relieve Gordon in Khartoum. Zaidān was attached to this army as a dragoman, and guide. We may catch a glimpse of his life with the British Army in the description by Nasīb 'Abdallāh Šiblī al-Lubnānī:[41a] tension developed between the British Officers and the Syrian dragomans. An English officer tried to command Zaidān to do some menial servant work which Zaidān refused with the answer

> "Know then that we have the position of dragomans not that of servants, and if you thought that any one of us would give in to your tyrannical orders, you should know that we are Ottoman Syrians and Syrian blood flows in our veins. We will never submit without law to any human being even if he came straight from heaven."[42]

---

40. Az-Zamān founded 1882 by the Armenian 'Alksān Ṣarafyān. It appeared twice weekly. It was closed down when it criticized the al-'Urābī government. Reopened after the British occupation it supported the British presence in Egypt as a contribution to the progress and modernization of that country. Some years later — probably 1888 — it was closed down again by the Ḫidīw because of anti-Ottoman statements; Dī Ṭarrāzī III 22, Zaidān *Ta'rīḫ ādāb* IV 58.

41. Ǧabr Ḍūmiṭ (1859-1930) born in Lebanon, attended SPC 1872-1874. 1884 he went to Egypt joining his friend, Zaidān. After his return to Beirut he was made professor for Arabic Language and Literature at the SPC in 1889; Dāġir II 553. Ḍūmiṭ remained a very close friend of Zaidān even after their ways had parted and they had settled in Beirut and Cairo respectively.

41a. See 240, n. 11.

42. Ḏāk 164.

It came to blows between the officer and Zaidān until a high-ranking officer and friend of Zaidān re-established order. As with other events Nasīb Šiblī reported, we have no way of establishing the veracity of the story, but as an anecdote it illuminates the characteristics of a certain situation, namely the overbearing manner of the British officers and the sensitivity of a Syrian like Zaidān who already in his student years in the Syrian Protestant College experienced some doubt whether the Westerners would be willing to relate to the people of the East with the same justice as to their own.

After the Wolseley expedition, sent too late, had been unable to save Gordon, it returned to Egypt. Zaidān took his leave of the army and returned in 1885 together with Ǧabr Ḍūmiṭ to Beirut, where they both started studying languages, especially Hebrew and Syrian.[43] Here Zaidān was made a member of *al-Maǧma' al-'ilmī aš-šarqī*,[44] a scientific society whose leading members were C. van Dyck, Ya'qūb Ṣarrūf, Fāris Nimr, Buṭrus and Salīm al-Bustānī[45] and Ibrāhīm al-Yāziǧī. Zaidān's language studies were brought to fruition in his first book

43. DĀĠIR II 554.

44. The history and relations of the various scientific societies at that time in Beirut is somewhat confused. The oldest societies seem to have been *al-Ǧam'īya al-'ilmīya* founded in 1847 by Buṭrus al-Bustānī, Nāṣīf al-Yāziǧī, Eli Smith and Cornelius van Dyck; and *al-Ǧam'īya aš-šarqīya* founded in 1850 by the Jesuits. Membership was restricted to local and foreign Christians; ANTONIUS 51-54. Zaidān gives the former society under the name *al-Ǧam'īya as-sūrīya*; *Ta'rīḫ ādāb* IV 68. Out of these two societies was formed the *al-Ǧam'īya al-'ilmīya as-sūrīya*, which included also Muslims and Druze (e.g. Muḥammad Arslān, Ḥusain Baihum); *Ta'rīḫ ādāb* IV 69. According to DĪ ṬARRĀZĪ II 172 this society was already founded in 1852 by Buṭrus al-Bustānī, Naṣīf al-Yāziǧī and Salīm Naufal. ANTONIUS 53 gives 1857 as the founding date of this society. He attributes to it a definite national political character and credits it as the cradle of the Arab national movement. For an opposing interpretation see HAIM « The Arab awakening; a source for the historian?". The *Maǧma' al-'ilmī aš-šarqī* was a successor organization to the by then defunct *Ǧam'īya al-'ilmīya as-sūrīya*, according to *Ta'rīḫ ādāb* IV 73 it was founded in 1882. The membership lists supplied for both societies in the latter source indicate one important difference between them: in contrast to its predecessor the *Maǧma'* included also American and European, i.e. non-Arab members. The character of this organization is, therefore, not quite clear. In both places Zaidān indicates his own membership without, however, giving a date. If 1885 is correct, cf ḤASAN 11, he was only for a very short while a member since this society dissolved when Fāris Nimr and Ya'qūb Ṣarrūf left for Egypt.

45. Salīm al-Bustānī (1848-1884), son of Buṭrus al-Bustānī. One of the first to attempt to write novels and historical novels in Arabic. He collaborated on many of his father's projects; DĀĠIR II 186.

al-Alfāẓ al-ʿarabīya wa'l-falsafa al-luġawīya. On the merits of this work Zaidān was made a member of the Royal Asian Society of Italy.

In the summer of 1886 he travelled to London, again accompanied by his friend Ǧabr Ḍūmiṭ, and Zaidān spent most of his time in the reading rooms of the British Museum. It was there that he first became familiar with the works of the European orientalists. It seems that he and his friend were planning originally on a long stay but with the approaching winter Zaidān's health became very poor and he left London to go back to Cairo which became his permanent residence. Fāris Nimr and Yaʿqūb Ṣarrūf offered him a job as administrative manager and assistant editor of "al-Muqtaṭaf". His contract shows that he was to be responsible for every aspect of administration: finances, organization of subscriber lists, mailing, the library of "al-Muqtaṭaf", personnel, etc. As far as these tasks would permit, he was also to participate in editorial work.[46] During the next fifteen months he worked for "al-Muqtaṭaf", in spite of the strong disapproval of his father who suggested that he should return to Beirut and learn a "decent" profession such as physician or lawyer.[47] The arrangement with "al-Muqtaṭaf" did not please Zaidān in the end. Perhaps he was disappointed with his small say in editorial policies;[48] perhaps he felt he needed more time to concentrate upon his own writings. He left "*al-Muqtaṭaf*" perhaps dissatisfied, but certainly richer for the valuable experience of managing the publication of a magazine. This experience came in conveniently when he later started his own magazine. With Fāris Nimr and Yaʿqūb Ṣarrūf, however, he remained on the best of terms.

His independent work as a writer produced the historical study of Freemasonry and a book about the history of Egypt, *Ta'rīḫ miṣr al-ḥadīṯ*, published in 1889. But his work as an author evidently did not suffice to support him financially. It was probably for this reason that in 1889 he accepted an offer of the Greek Orthodox School, *al-Madrasa al-ʿubaidīya al-kubrā*,[49] to be its head teacher for the Arabic language.

46. The contract of Zaidān's employment is amongst the unpublished papers in the AUB collection.

47. *Letters*, Zaidān to his father, Cairo, August 28, 1887.

48. WARE 67.

49. *Al-Madrasa al-ʿubaidīya al-kubrā* was founded 1860 by Raphael and Ananias Abet, two naturalized Greeks who originated either from Syria or Egypt. Teaching

His main interest, however, remained history and the next book he published, in 1890, was a history of the world, *at-Ta'rīḫ al-'āmm*, with the equally presumptuous sub-title "From Creation Till Today". In fact it was a rather thin collection of historical facts and events of Asia and Africa, dealing mainly with the Middle East.

In 1891 Zaidān expanded his activities to the more practical aspects of publishing when he founded, together with Naǧīb Mitrī[50] a printing press which they called *Maṭba'at at-ta'līf*. It was a small affair in a few rooms with a hand-driven press and a few boxes of letters and their joint enterprise came to an early end a year later. While Zaidān kept the *Maṭba'at at-ta'līf*, which he re-named in 1896 *Dār al-hilāl*, Naǧīb Mitrī opened a new publishing house which he called *Dār al-ma'ārif*.

Sometime during the year 1891 Zaidān came out with his first historical novel, *al-Mamlūk aš-šārid*, which met with so much success that he felt encouraged to quit his job as a teacher.[51] From that time on he remained an independent writer, working as a journalist, novelist, linguist and historian, but always on his own.

With his resignation from teaching, the establishment of a publishing house and the publication of his first historical novel, the year 1891 constituted a turning point in his professional life. His personal life also took on a new dimension when he married, in early 1891, Maryam Maṭar from Beirut. Maryam had grown up as an orphan. According to one source, she had been educated in a convent school.[52] But her daughter Asmā

---

language was Greek and French. Since 1866 a special section in Arabic was attached to the school; for the history of the school see Politis I 442-448. Achille Sekaly, *Les Syriens Orthodoxes en Egypte. La question de l'Ecole Ebeid*, Cairo 1920, p. 53 *et passim* makes it a point to prove that the founders were Greek Orthodox of *Syrian* origin. He traces the family back to the grandfather of the two founding brothers, a certain Ya'qūb 'Ubaid, who supposedly had immigrated with his father at the beginning of the 18th century to Cairo from Baalbek. Since Sekaly's whole pamphlet is a bitter attack on the predominant *national Greek* influence on the affairs of the Greek Orthodox community in Egypt, his claim of Syrian origin for the founders may not be totally reliable. Zaḫūrā 457, indicates 1889 as the year Zaidān began to teach there, Ma'lūf 470 indicates 1888.

50. Naǧīb Mitrī born 1865 in Lebanon, went to Egypt in 1884 where he worked in various printing presses. In 1891 he founded, together with Zaidān, *Maṭba'at at-ta'līf*. One year later he left Zaidān to found his own printing house, *Maṭba'at al-ma'ārif*; Ṣābāt 248, the same source 237 also gives 1889 as the founding of *Maṭba'at-ta'līf* which seems less likely.

51. Zaḫūrā 457.

52. Ma'lūf 473.

asserts that she had attended the American School for Girls in Beirut.[53] Maryam had come to Cairo in 1887 in order to find a teaching job at one of the American missionary schools. Zaidān and Maryam met the same year. Their decision to marry met with violent opposition from Zaidān's parents who did not think the girl proper and wealthy enough for their son. A drawn out and bitter correspondence between Zaidān in Cairo and his father in Beirut began. Friends interceded on both sides, but finally consent for the marriage was obtained. Some of Zaidān's experience during this difficult time found fictional expression later in the only non-historical novel he wrote, *Ǧihād al-muḥibbīn.*[54]

Maryam and Zaidān had four children: Farīd, Emile, Asmā and Šukrī, born in 1891, 1893, 1895 and 1900 respectively. The first-born died at the age of two, while the other three are still alive — Emile and Asmā living in Cairo, Šukrī in Beirut. From Zaidān's letters to his son, Emile, and from the reminiscences of Zaidān's surviving children, expressed in many conversations with this author, one gathers the impression that the family must have been very close and loving.

The change in Zaidān's professional and personal life in the early nineties meant that he had now definitely settled in Cairo where he was to stay until his death. It is impossible to obtain a clear picture of his economic situation during these years. For his major enterprise, the *Dār al-hilāl* and the publications that appeared there we have no financial records, with the exception of some very fragmentary notes in his private papers. It seems Zaidān never owned a house in Cairo and, in fact, was worried about rent increases.[55] On the other hand, he could afford to send his son to college in Beirut and he himself travelled, especially in the later years, extensively during the summer months. He frequently went to Beirut. Shortly after the Young Turks' Revolution, he visited Istanbul in 1909. Three years later he made an extensive journey to Europe and the following year he visited Palestine. One source[56]

53. Ware 68.

54. For a very detailed description of the affair of Zaidān's engagement and marriage see Ware 68-77. According to Ware the parents of Zaidān gave their consent already in 1888. He does not explain why it then took another three years before the marriage actually took place.

55. *Letters*, Zaidān to Emile, Cairo, March 20, 1909.

56. Amīn 129.

emphasizes the financial success of Zaidān's enterprises. Perhaps what is meant there is the simple fact that he could support his family with his writings and/or his publishing house. He certainly never lived in great wealth.

After Zaidān had established himself permanently in Cairo he began to bring his parents, brothers and his sister to Cairo. Two of his brothers, Mitrī and Ibrāhīm[57] worked with him in the *Dār al-hilāl*.

Work, indeed, must have become the keynote of Zaidān's life. Since his early childhood it had been impressed upon him that one never should waste one's time. Zaidān's capacity for work remained astounding. In 1892 he started his single most important project, the publication of his magazine "al-Hilāl". A large part of his time must have been consumed by this magazine, for which he was for a long time not only the sole author but also manager, editor, sales agent all in one. With great regularity, starting in 1891, he also wrote one historical novel each year. After a certain routine had established itself and after he had delegated much of the administrative work to his two brothers, Zaidān found enough time and energy left to write scholarly works. From 1899 until his death he wrote a volume almost every year, dealing usually with topics from Arab history and literature.

What time was left from his work Zaidān spent with his family and friends, of whom he had many in Cairo. Salāma Mūsā describes him during this time as an "extrovert, stout, jocular man with a great many friends".[58] In the letters Zaidān wrote to Emile between 1908 and 1912 one finds the names of a stream of friends and visitors who came regularly to his house. Once a week, on Tuesdays, a *soirée* was given at the Zaidāns', attended by people from the cultural elite of Cairene society: journalists, writers, historians and sometimes even a teacher from *al-Azhar*. European orientalists visiting Cairo would join. Zaidān did lead a rather

57. Mitrī (born approximately 1870) and Ibrāhīm (born 1879) grew up in Lebanon. Ibrāhīm attended there the school "Les Trois Docteurs" (see 138 n. 26). Both came around 1896 to Egypt and worked for their brother in the printing press *Dār al-hilāl*. Mitrī became its director and remained so after Zaidān's death. Ibrāhīm was made a member of the St. George Society of the Greek Orthodox Syrians in Egypt and remained active in Syrian community affairs in Egypt; ZAHŪRĀ *As-Sūrīyūn* 327, 349.

58. MŪSĀ, translation, 154.

active social life in Cairo. Most of his friends, however, belonged to the circle of Syrian emigrants in Egypt.

It suited Zaidān's temperament to work as a private writer. He shied away from active participation in political organizations and from public appearances. For a while he had been an active member of the Freemasons. He belonged also to a short-lived literary and scientific society, *Ǧam'īyat al-i'tidāl*, which had been founded in 1886 by Ya'qūb Ṣarrūf, Fāris Nimr and other emigrants from Syria.[59] Zaidān became an enthusiastic supporter of the Young Turks' regime in Istanbul. Yet when friends asked him to run as a candidate in the elections for the new Ottoman parliament, he refused claiming others were better suited.[60]

The one time he was prepared to accept a more public task was when he was offered in 1910 a position at the newly founded Egyptian University to teach a course about Islamic history.[61] He hesitated to accept the offer, apparently, because he was aware of possible Muslim opposition to his appointment. Still the offer was flattering because it was the first official recognition of his scholarly merits in Egypt. Having been one of the first to demand the establishment of a university in Egypt his appointment also seemed to be a confirmation of his own educational ideas. Finally, Zaidān accepted the offer but the affair ended in disaster. Before he had even begun to teach, he was unceremoniously dismissed by the university, which found itself under pressure from Muslim quarters to cancel his appointment.[62]

This humiliating experience confirmed what Zaidān must have felt before: he had never been accepted by the educated Muslim as a qualified scholar of Islamic and Arabic history. He had never succeeded in breaking down the barrier of religious prejudice.[63] The affair of his aborted university appointment cast a shadow over the last four year of his life. "The incident left a stain of bitterness in his heart and he (Zaidān)

---

59. *Ta'rīḫ ādāb* IV 83.

60. *Letters*, Zaidān to Emile, Cairo, Dec. 23, 1908.

61. See also 66, 67 for a detailed discussion of this affair.

62. XIX 178-181 and Zaidān to Emile, Cairo, Oct. 12, 1910. For translation of this letter see 210-214.

63. For Muslim opposition to Zaidān and his work see 62-65.

always mentioned it with grief"[64]. Zaidān spoke about this incident lengthily in his letters to Emile. When two years later Rašīd Riḍā[65] published some vitriolic attacks against his works, Zaidān's bitterness increased. He felt misunderstood and ungratefully treated by his contemporaries. In a somewhat emotionally loaded letter he wrote to Emile "... it was I who revived Arab literature by what I wrote and by the influence my books had upon the feelings of envy of (other) writers, inducing them to compete... Today they begin to write in a reflective and explanatory manner. All this they got from my works".[66] The lack of recognition embittered him and he hinted in the letter that he would turn his interests away from this nation, *umma*, to totally different and Syrian topics.[67]

In spite of the great success of his novels and the popularity of "*al-Hilāl*" he had failed to eliminate the objections of religious prejudice and had not been acknowledged by the educated Muslims of his time. It is significant that he should have taken a new interest in "Syrian topics". It is the same mood that caused him, during the last four years of his life, to take such a lively interest in the Ottoman Empire of the Young Turks and give it his full support. His letters to his son, Emile, who studied at the time in Beirut, are full of longing for his son and his hometown. When he began to write his autobiography in 1908, he was certainly stimulated by the thought of Emile studying at the same institution that he himself had attended some thirty years earlier. But the preoccupation with his own childhood and his hometown, Beirut, also shows that he felt more clearly than ever that he had not succeeded in becoming a fully accepted member of the society in which he had chosen to live. When

---

64. Mūsā, translation, 154.

65. Rašīd Riḍā (1865-1935), born in Syria, he went to Egypt to attach himself to the Muslim reformer Muḥammad 'Abduh. He followed the latter in his modernist approach to Islam, but inclined later to a more fundamentalist approach to Islam. His revivalist interpretation of a purist Islam brought him eventually close to the Wahhābī Movement. Since 1898 he published the magazine al-Manār which remained until his death the main platform for his ideas. He also wrote an extensive biography of Muḥammad 'Abduh; Dāġir II 396; for his political and reformist ideas see Kerr 153 ff; for his role in Arab nationalism see Haim 19, ff.

66. *Letters*, Zaidān to Emile, Cairo, March 28, 1912, for translation see 219.

67. *Ibid.*

he died totally unexpectedly in Cairo on July 21, 1914, he had already become established as one of the most prolific and most widely read contemporary Arab authors. But, despite this, he had felt isolated. He was disappointed and bitter about the reaction of his Muslim compatriots to his work and apparently willing to give up his preoccupation with the Islamic Arab past and culture.

THE EDUCATION OF SOCIETY

The close contact between modern Western civilization and non-Western people resulted in profound challenges to the traditional patterns of society everywhere. The traditional societies had to attempt to adapt to an increasing degree to Western patterns of life and systems of thought. In order to participate in the modern civilization it was necessary to acquire new skills, knowledge and attitudes. Education became essential on the path towards modernization. People who acquired Western skills and knowledge came to occupy key functions within the transitional society. A new class of intelligentsia with a secular education developed. There were no inherent reasons that a secular education should be restricted to any particular social strata. The intelligentsia was recruited from various parts of society and secular education tended to become universal.

Education appeared to Zaidān as the most important factor for the progress and development of a people and especially if the people had not yet fully participated in the modern civilization of Europe. He was aware of the fact that the Arab people were in the midst of an awakening, striving towards new levels of development and progress. These goals could be reached in Zaidān's opinion only by internal reform of society and modernization of all its aspects. He was critical of political activists like Aḥmad 'Urābī[1] and Muṣṭafā Kāmil.[2] The best he could say for

1. Aḥmad al-'Urābī (1841-1911) born in Egypt. He became one of the first native Egyptians to join the officer corps of the Egyptian Army. Under his leadership the army together with the constitutionalists took over actual power in Egypt, defying European financial and power interests. The revolt led eventually to the British occupation of Egypt in 1882; Cromer I part 2; Blunt; *Tarāǧim* I 211 (al-'Urābī's memoirs).

2. Muṣṭafā Kāmil (1874-1908) born in Egypt. Egyptian nationalist and politician. He studied law in Egypt and France. On his return to Egypt he concentrated upon journalistic and political activities aimed at a national unity between Muslim and Coptic Egyptians and the complete independence of Egypt from Britain; Steppat 241-341; *Tarāǧim* I 289; Dāǧir II, 649.

them was that their actions and programmes were premature. Inner reform had to precede political independence. Far more frequently we find in his works references to such people as Ǧamāl ad-Dīn al-Afġānī[3] and Cornelius van Dyck. Zaidān opposed thoroughly al-Afġānī's political Pan-Islam, but, nevertheless, appreciated him for having introduced, especially in Egypt, a number of people to modernist trends of thought and attempts to reform society. Zaidān often compared the role of al-Afġānī in the Arab *Nahḍa* to that of Cornelius van Dyck. Zaidān was most impressed by the educator Cornelius van Dyck. When he as a young student met C. van Dyck for the first time in the Syrian Protestant College, van Dyck had spent already some forty years in Syria. During this time he had been engaged in establishing schools, teaching, translating and working as a physician. He had himself composed many textbooks in Arabic on chemistry, internal medicine, trigonometry, astronomy, etc. C. van Dyck let his scientific work never be influenced by his religious beliefs. He had become the personal friend and mentor of many of the young Arab intellectuals in Beirut. He had encouraged them in their work, helped for instance Fāris Nimr and Ya'qūb Ṣarrūf to publish their magazine "al-Muqtaṭaf" and defended the cause of the students in the Syrian Protestant College. For Zaidān C. van Dyck remained the educator *par excellence* who, by his teaching, writing and personal example, gave guidance to many of the new educated class. Zaidān conceived also of his own role in the Arab *Nahḍa* as that of the educator and reformer. In his eyes this was the task of the moment, more important than political agitation or military action.

Education had been the key to Zaidān's own success and had shaped his life more than any other factor. One should not forget, however, that he had enjoyed only very little formal training; some years in traditional elementary schools and hardly two years in the

3. Ǧamāl ad-Dīn al-Afġānī (1838-1898) born in Persia. He insisted that a reformed and purified Islam offered to the Muslim people a genuine alternative to Western civilization. His main aim was political Pan-Islam, i.e. the creation of political unity between all Muslim countries; a unity which he believed could stave off the European encroachement upon the Muslim world. Promoting this idea he collaborated at times with constitutionalists and modernists in the Muslim world such as Muḥammad 'Abduh in Egypt but also frequently with absolute rulers such as the Šāh of Persia and the Sultan of the Ottoman Empire; *Tarāǧim* II 55 ff; DĀĠIR II 126; KEDOURIE; KEDDIE; et al.

Syrian Protestant College. Most of his knowledge was self-taught. According to his own statement Zaidān had been aware of the need for education already as a boy.[4]

Although Zaidān saw himself very much in the role of the educator, he spent a suprisingly short period of time as an actual teacher in a school. We are not sure of the reasons that motivated him to accept such a position in the first place, but when we regard the multitude of subjects that attracted his interest, his prolific production as a writer, journalist and scholar, and the wide range of people who came into contact with his writings, we can imagine that it must have been extremely unsatisfying for Zaidān to spend his time teaching Arabic to a small number of high school students. He never denied the great importance of the role of the school teacher, but he must have felt that he, personally, could be more efficient and successful as an independent writer.

All his works, beginning with his first attempt to develop a "philosophy of language" in 1886, had the explicit purpose of informing, enlightening and educating. He criticized the traditional writers who wrote about topics that could be of interest for a small audience only, and who used a style more suited to show off their own linguistic abilities than to facilitate the understanding of the subject matter. A different type of writer was necessary, one who would write for a general audience, *al-kātib al-ʿāmm*,

> "He is the servant of the community, *umma*, and he is in charge of its guidance. It is his duty to exert himself for its welfare. He should have no doubt about three stipulations for his writing: (1) he should choose a subject for which he sees the nation has a need; (2) he should cast it into a form that can easily be comprehended; (3) he should display truth and frankness without inclining towards any affiliation or party".[5]

This definition of the writer and his task has a strong educational colouring. Usefulness for the community, *umma*, easy comprehensibility, objectivity and truth are demanded from him and his work. The writer is the educator of the *umma*. It is disputable whether Zaidān referred her

4. See 160.

5. *Taʾrīḫ ādāb* II 5.

to *umma* in a national sense[6] but he certainly meant society as a whole, not only its elite.

The question of who was actually addressed in Zaidān's writings bears some closer scrutiny. Frequently Zaidān himself stated in the prefaces to his books what audience he had in mind.

According to Zaidān himself the whole project of his historical novels was guided by the idea of familiarizing the common people, *al-ʿāmma*, with their own past in an easily comprehensible and entertaining manner. Already in his first book, *al-Alfāẓ al-ʿarabīya waʾl-falsafa al-luġawīya*, Zaidān had emphasized that this book should be of use to the general public, *maṣlaḥat al-ʿāmma*. He justified the efforts to write his book *Taʾrīḫ miṣr al-ǧadīd*, by pointing to the absence of any history book about Egypt which was "close to the understanding of common people and yet pleasing to the elite".[7] Zaidān's castigation of writers who write only for their own entertainment or that of a small esoteric group bears out his intention to spread education as widely as possible within the society.

We should, however, be extremely careful with this term *ʿāmma*, common people or masses, which Zaidān used so frequently and, one gets the impression, loosely. Zaidān's ultimate aim seems to have been the education of the common people. In 1898 he declared:

> "The teaching of the elite alone, which is the situation with most nations, is not enough. The aim is the teaching, educating and training of the common people, because they constitute the public of the nation. No nation will succeed in its plans as long as its common people are ignorant."[8]

This enlightened belief in the universality of education and knowledge remained a strong feature in Zaidān's thinking and connected later with his support for constitutional government. Yet this trend never did become exclusive or totally convincing in his thought. We must, therefore, differentiate between his declared educational intentions towards the common people and the social group he actually addressed and could possibly attract with his writings. One should bear in mind that

6. For a discussion of Zaidān's usage of this and other terms see 86.

7. *Taʾrīḫ miṣr* introduction.

8. VII 10.

at Zaidān's time 10% of the men and 0.5% of the women in Egypt were literate.[9] Even if we take into account that a literate person would read aloud in the family circle or in a café to those who could not read themselves, the people who came into actual contact with Zaidān's works could have constituted only a very small sector of society. The use of the expression *'āmma* then is certainly misleading if we think in terms of the masses of society as a whole. Zaidān's educational efforts were clearly limited to that small section of the population that was literate.

The traditional education had put a strong emphasis on religious learning and on such subjects as were directly relevant to religion. The style and terminology of the scholarly language was highly specialized and esoteric and not accessible to one who had a command of the spoken Arabic only. Towards the end of the nineteenth century a new group of educated people had developed next to the traditional educated class. The process of modernization had demanded new skills and different types of knowledge. Recently established secular schools and, to a certain extent, Western missionary schools had produced people whose training and education responded more to the new needs of society. The members of this new intelligentsia, as this group is often called, usually had had as children some elementary training in the traditional subjects of learning without, however, becoming educated men in the traditional sense. Because of their Western training neither the form nor the content of traditional learning and education could satisfy their intellectual interests.

It appears then that it was Zaidān's purpose to break out of the esoteric terminology and language of the traditional Muslim scholar and to extend the range of knowledge beyond that of traditional learning. He intended to supply this new intelligentsia with secular and contemporary information which he deemed essential for a modern education.

"Al-Hilāl" perhaps best indicates that Zaidān wanted to appeal with his writings especially to this intelligentsia, the nucleus of a newly developing bourgoisie in the Arab society. The wide variety of subjects in "al-Hilāl" dealt with any aspect of civilization relevant to the educated bourgoisie. Its own past and Western contemporary civilization were the two sources from which the new class tried to forge its own identity and

9. Luṭfi al-Sayyid, 159.

norms. "Al-Hilāl" provided almost encyclopaedic information about the own history and culture and about the new Western civilization. It did not specialize in a professional manner in any particular subject, and whatever subject it dealt with, it did so in a fashion intended for the comprehension of the layman. With its special section about health and the hygiene of the family, it addressed itself explicitly to the emancipated woman who, in Zaidān's time, was only to be found, if at all, in the more secular Westernized bourgoisie.

Zaidān's frequent use of the terms "common people" and "elite", his reiteration that the masses need a lighter literary diet, and phrases such as "the spreading of knowledge among the people in accordance with the difference of their comprehension and variety of knowledge" [10] leads one to assume that Zaidān indeed was differentiating between various parts of society.[11]

A different light is shed on Zaidān's use of the terms "elite" and "common people" when we relate them to a time dimension of which Zaidān himself was conscious. He realized that the intellectual *Nahḍa* was only at its beginning, that the indigenous writers were still very weak.[12] The historical novels were not written because a sociologically static *'āmma* wanted to be entertained. They were written to arouse in the ignorant reader an interest in history and to enable him to read eventually more serious works in history. After having serialized his historic novels for a decade in "al-Hilāl" he began to publish scholarly works about history as annual supplements to the magazine for its subscribers. That is to say, the same readers who were provided with the historical novels were now also exposed to more scholarly works about the same subjects. This does not imply that these readers advanced suddenly from a social *'āmma* position to that of a *ḫāṣṣa* but that in Zaidān's opinion the very same public which he always had addressed, the predominantly secular bourgoisie had improved with regard to its education and intellectual perception. In the introduction to the *Ta'rīḫ at-tamaddun al-islāmī* Zaidān spoke about the need of such history books for the Arab reader and continued:

10. VII 491.
11. IX 149-151.
12. XIX 19.

"We stated to prepare the mind of the readers — in accordance with the different levels, variety of knowledge and perception — to read such history with the help of the Islamic historical novels, which we published in serialized form in "al-Hilāl" since the reading of sheer history is difficult for the literate public, *ğumhūr al-qurrā'*, especially in our country where learning is still in its infancy."[13]

We can say, therefore, Zaidān addressed himself in fact over the years to one and the same audience, the developing bourgoisie.

It is almost impossible to make any estimates about the actual number of people who read the works of Zaidān. In order to obtain at least some idea about the size of his audience it seems most fruitful to turn for a moment to "al-Hilāl" and the historical novels which were both explicitly designed to appeal to the largest possible reading public.

During the last quarter of the nineteenth century the press had become for the Arab *Nahḍa* the most important instrument of expression. Almost everyone of the new intelligentsia in the Arab world was at some time in his life involved in editing, publishing, or writing for a magazine or newspaper. When Zaidān began the publication of his magazine, some 170 magazines and newspapers had been published in Egypt.[14]

Zaidān's work as an administrator and part-time editor for "al-Muqtaṭaf" had given him the practical experience for producing his own magazine later. The example that "al-Muqtaṭaf" set for Zaidān's own magazine is undeniable, not only in the general layout and its divisions into sections, but also in the abstaining from any direct political involvement, and its secular interest in anything concerning culture and modern civilization. Not without reason did "al-Hilāl" declare itself a "scientific, historical and literary magazine", while "al-Muqtaṭaf" was sub-titled a magazine for science, craft and agriculture. "Al-Muqtaṭaf" was far more oriented towards the sciences and technology than "al-Hilāl" which emphasised historical, literary and social questions. This rather general statement and the fact that almost all the main articles had a cultural or historical character should not mislead us about the vast variety of topics offered in every issue of "al-Hilāl".

13. *Ta'rīḫ at-tamaddun* I 12.

14. *al-Kitāb aḏ-ḏahabī* 154.

The emphasis was clearly on historical, cultural and social issues, but the scope remained, nevertheless, almost encyclopaedic. This, indeed, was one of the roles of "al-Hilāl" as well as "al-Muqtaṭaf" with different emphasis: to give the Arab reader information about anything and everything pertaining to modern secular civilization and its origins.

The success of the magazine was great. Seven years after its beginning, Zaidān had to reprint the first volume, so strong was the demand for it.[15] Reprints of certain volumes occurred also later on.[16] The magazine spread quickly not only over Egypt and Syria but over the whole world. In 1897 it could be found already in Syria, Iraq, Persia, India, Japan, the Maghreb, West Africa, Zanzibar, Transvaal, Australia, New Zealand, the West Indies and South and North America.[17]

In the conclusion of the volume XX, Zaidān claimed that the number of readers had doubled every year. Apparently he did not deem it necessary to make any records of the sales of his magazine. At least no such records could be traced. It is, therefore, difficult, if not impossible, to estimate the actual number of readers of the monthly circulation of "al-Hilāl". One source[18] estimates the number of readers for 1897 to be around 10,000 without, however, giving any indication on what this estimate is based. In the same year Zaidān claimed to receive every month about one hundred letters to the editor.[19] This also does not help us since we have no way of knowing what percentage of readers would respond to the magazine by writing. In 1902 Zaidān stated that "al-Hilāl" is "of all Arab journals the most widely spread in the civilized countries, and tens of thousands of people read it".[20] This seems to be a very rough estimate, and it is not clear upon what evidence Zaidān based this judgement. All this, however, again says very little about the actual number of copies printed. The fact that it was "widely spread" may well mean that a few copies reached each country and were accessible in the social center of the Arab immigrant community. In the "Letters to the Editor"

---

15. VIII 512.
16. XVII 561.
17. At-Ṭanāḥī 148.
18. Zaḫūrā 457.
19. V 23.
20. X 8.

people refer sometimes to articles which were printed a year or even longer before. This means that each copy of the magazine went through many hands. Certainly the actual circulation must have been much smaller than any estimated number of readers.

The same lack of records leaves us absolutely in the dark as to the financial aspects of this enterprise. Whether the magazine was self-supporting, whether other printing jobs done in the *Dār al-hilāl*, the publishing house of Zaidān, helped to finance the magazine or whether even outside financial support was involved, we do not know.

Aside from the question of the exact number of readers and the financial aspect, we still can say that "al-Hilāl" was a great success in terms of a growing and responsive audience. It appealed to all those who searched for new answers in the secularized civilization of the West, encouraged to do so by the simultaneous assurance of their own civilizing and cultural achievements. It appealed alike to the Muslims and the Christians who had already felt the impact of the modern civilization. It is interesting in this context that people would subscribe to "al-Hilāl" as well as to "al-Muqtaṭaf", apparently feeling that they were complementing each other. Its success and impact upon the Arab reader can certainly also be felt in the foundation of magazines that appeared in similar form, such as "al-Mašriq" of the Jesuit Louis Cheikho[21] in Beirut and "al-Manār" of Rašīd Riḍā. "Al-Mašriq" was founded in 1898 and Cheikho emphasised in his introduction the need of the Catholic reader for such a magazine. If one adds the frequency with which "al-Mašriq" attacked both "al-Hilāl" and "al-Muqtaṭaf", especially on religious and philosophical issues, one can feel the threat the Jesuits saw in the impact of these secular magazines.

Zaidān himself saw the main reason for the success of his magazine in the close contact it kept with its readers. The audience grew in size, in knowledge and in sophistication thanks to the impact of modernism and the *Nahḍa* movement, which created a whole new stratum of educated people. Together with them, "al-Hilāl" grew. Zaidān's fine journalistic

21. Louis Cheikho (1859-1928) lived in Beirut where he joined the Jesuit Order. He was a teacher, philologist, historian. He wrote various works about Arab Christian and Muslim history. A history of Arab literature in the nineteenth century of his remains until today an important source of information. In 1898 Cheikho founded his magazine al-Mašriq; DĀĠIR II 515.

sense and his close contact with the readers allowed him to make the magazine attractive by balancing historical matters with contemporary subjects and offering a change of pace in items like notes on health and hygiene. He offered also mildly sensational topics like "The Wonders of Creation".

One of Zaidān's ideas to make the magazine more attractive was the introduction of serialized historical novels. Repeatedly, too, he gave credit to these novels for the popularity of his magazine.[22]

Zaidān's immediate precursor as author of historical novels in Arab literature was Salīm al-Bustānī. He published his first novel *Zenobia* in 1871. Al-Bustānī's aim was to write for the education and edification of the reader and to familiarize him with his own social and political ideas, aiming mainly at a Syrian-Arab nation. Written in a simple Arabic style plot, historical background and message of al-Bustānī are more often than not integrated. The romantic story, the invented intrigue take the predominant place in al-Bustānī's novels; the historical account is secondary and the historical accuracy suffers somewhat from this.[23]

Zaidān struck a more successful balance between the fictitious narrative and the historical elements in his novels. But he himself had declared that the fictional element of his novels was only of secondary importance for him, indeed so much so that he was willing to change the plot according to the demands of the readers.[24]

---

22. V 9; VI 936. Throughout Muslim Arab literary history there existed a certain genre of historical tale or epic dealing either with early Muslim conquests, called *al-futūḥ* or with biographies of historical heroes, called *as-siyar*. This genre was not really accepted as part of the classic literature and was, because of its simple style and frequent use of local dialect, popular with the lower classes. Since the end of the Middle Ages no more historical tales were created but a passive interest in them remained alive; cf. F. ROSENTHAL 165-167. It seems, however, that the writing of historical novels in Arabic, which started at the end of the nineteenth century, was directly stimulated by European examples, rather than the traditional historical tales. The artistic form, the attempt to deal with historical material in a scholarly fashion and the stylistic means speak for such a European impetus. But the fact that the historical novel should take such a large place in the general novel writing in Arabic at the time is probably related to the still existing popularity of the traditional historical fiction of *al-futūḥ* and *as-siyar*. Zaidān himself was familiar with these tales from his childhood.

23. NAǦM 140-156.

24. In Zaidan's first historical novel. *al-Mamlūk aš-šārid*, a devoted servant finds a cruel end when he is killed by his own master who does not recognize him under the particular circumstances of their encounter. When Zaidān was criticized for this by his readers, he answered, « « I do not conceal from the distinguished readers that I

The function of the fictional narrative was to attract the reader and to give Zaidān an opportunity to familiarize him with history and with his own past. According to his own remarks, Zaidān was familiar with the works of Scott and Dumas. His realism places him closer to the French than to the English writer.[25] But Zaidān also criticized Dumas sharply. He attacked him for his willingness to bend history for the sake of the story and to use history only as a dressing, which in Zaidān's opinion was harmful and without educational value for the reader.

Zaidān's novels can be placed somewhere between the historical novel proper and the "Professorenroman". They rarely succeed in dramatizing historical processes in the life of individual characters. The novels consist on the one hand of a rather stereotyped fictional story of love and adventure and on the other of some introductory historical remarks and lengthy paragraphs of elaborate accounts of historical places, costumes and inventory in general. The connection between the historical facts and the narrative tends to remain artificial and forced. The action and thought of the persons in the story rarely reflect the historical background. Zaidān's historical interests and educational purposes are usually too strong and his narrative talent too weak to make his novels a well balanced and integrated combination of historical knowledge and artistic imagination.

We find ourselves very much in agreement with Arasili when he says that in order to do justice to Zaidān's novels and to understand their success in spite of their artistic mediocracy, one has to compare them to the existing entertaining literature which consisted of the *siyar* and the *futūḥ*. In comparison to them Zaidān's novels appeared to be full of realistic action and life.[26] Perhaps more important is the fact

---

tried several times to revive this servant, but I was afraid of what befell Sir Walter Scott when he resurrected a nobleman from his grave upon the demand of his publishers and exposed himself to criticism and disapproval. When I saw myself exposed to rebuke at any rate, I chose the lesser evil and contradicted the printing press not nature, *muḫālafatan aṭ-ṭab'*, *lā muḫālafatan aṭ-ṭabī'a*. But if the distinguished readers prefer his resurrection, then I will resurrect him for them in the second edition, if God wills"; al-Muqtaṭaf XVI 404. Indeed we find in the following edition a rather incoherently added chapter in which the servant appears in good health.

25. Krachkovsky 51-87.

26. Arasili 14.

that Zaidān had made historical fiction in the form of historical novels a literary genre acceptable also to the educated class.

The novels were educational and informative, yet at the same time, entertaining. They offered suspense and intrigue together with the moral edification of the victorious fight of good against evil, and information about a past which was becoming increasingly important to a public whose search for its own identity was growing. Ṭāhā Ḥusain may serve here as a witness to the attraction these novels held:

> "I shall not forget that in the days of my youth I used to start reading one of the historical novels of Ǧurǧī Zaidān; I would hardly have proceeded with the reading when I was enthralled by it and it would keep me from my al-Azhar lessons until I had finished it; and it would be still on my mind a long time after finishing it. The critics may say what they want, but about one thing here there is no doubt: the historical novels that Zaidān published were of the most important impact which enabled this *Nahḍa* to bear the novelistic fruit still enjoyed by readers of Arabic today."[27]

Zaidān found an eager and responsive audience. For instance, after having let his novel *Al-'Abbāsa uḫt ar-Rašīd* come to unhappy end, his readers reacted strongly and protested. They not only wrote him but even sent telegrams from Syria almost immediately after the last part of the novel had been published.[28]

A more objective criterion for the success and popularity of his novels is the fact that by the time of his death almost all of them were in their second, third or even fourth printing.[29] Even though we have no way of establishing the numbers of copies involved in each printing, the fact remains that the increasing demand made it worthwhile reprinting each novel time and again.

Zaidān's success was also reflected in the fact that he was imitated. 'Abd al-Masīḥ Anṭākī Bey,[30] for instance, editor of the newspaper

---

27. Ṭ. Ḥusain "*Aṯar al-hilāl*" 133.

28. VII 18.

29. The latest editions of the novels appeared in the 1960's in Cairo and Beirut.

30. 'Abd al-Masīḥ Anṭākī Bey (1875-1922) born in Aleppo of Greek-Orthodox religious background. He became a writer, journalist, novelist. He made several attempts at publishing magazines and newspapers in Aleppo and Egypt. He was especially interested in the Christian communities of Syria and Lebanon. With his historical

al-'Umrān, published in 1903 the first novel of what was supposed to become a series about Christian history.[31] It also seems that Rašīd Riḍā intended since 1905 to publish a series of historical novels about Muslim history, an intention which Zaidān felt was an attempt to imitate his own work.[32]

Another aspect of the success and attraction of his novels was their almost immediate translation into Persian, Turkish, Urdu, Azerbaijani, sometimes even into Malay and Kurdish.[33]

Zaidān's favourite medium of education was the written word. This preference, however, did not imply that he overlooked the importance of schools and higher educational institutions. "Al-Hilāl" reported consistently about schools in Egypt and Beirut. It was over the issue of education that Zaidān uttered his only open and direct criticism against the British rule in Egypt. On the one hand, the British were not willing to develop the educational system in Egypt; on the other, they claimed the Egyptians were not yet prepared for self-government. How, Zaidān asked rightly, can they be prepared if they are not provided with the proper education.[34]

There was no doubt in Zaidān's mind that the British occupation brought many benefits to Egypt, but the school system, definitely deteriorated in comparison to the pre-'Urābī time. Schools were not free any more, the use of Arabic as a teaching language was limited severely and the general level of teaching deteriorated.[35]

Zaidān felt he could not really blame Cromer[36] for serving the

---

novel *Šahīd al-galgala*, Cairo 1905, he planned to begin a series of historical novels about the most important Christian personalities; Dāġir III 145.

31. Krachkovsky 75.

32. *Letters*, Zaidan to Emile, March 28, 1912.

33. XIII 38; XIV 135, 182; Krachkovsky 76. Attempts were made to publish the novels also in European languages. A certain C.N. Tabet from Beirut not only translated some of the novels but also got in touch with French and American publishers; *Letters*, Tabet to Zaidān, Boston, April 15, 1904. But most of these projects failed. In the end only two novels were ever translated into European languages, one into German, one into French, without however raising any great response; see bibliography.

34. XV 451.

35. XV 393.

36. Evelyn Baring 1st Lord Cromer, as the Consul-General of Britain in occupied Egypt, he practically ruled that country in an autocratic way from 1883 to 1907; Marlowe; Lutfi al-Sayyid; see also Cromer's *Modern Egypt*, et al.

interests of his own nation, but he believed that it was the responsibility of the Egyptians to establish their own educational system. He appealed especially to the rich to donate money and to institute schools on their own. Zaidān lauded those few Egyptians who donated land for building schools.[37] In the same manner as he had used statistics on education to prove that only after education has spread could political aims be pursued successfully, he used statistics from various countries to show that investment in education was correlated to progress and pointed out how little Egyptians were actually investing in education.[38] Schools should be free for everyone and, of course, the teaching language should be Arabic, so that all could benefit from education. Zaidān's emphasis on a school system being established by private initiative and not by government agencies was certainly to a great extent due to his liberalism. But just as Muṣṭafā Kāmil,[39] Zaidān, too, realized that leaving construction and management of a school system in the hands of the government meant leaving it under the control of the British whose attitude, in his opinion, was extremely detrimental to Egyptian education be it on the elementary, high school or university level.

Zaidān's special interest was focused on the establishment of a college or university.[40] He claimed repeatedly that he was the first, in February 1900, to demand in an article the establishment of an Egyptian college, while the Egyptians themselves really started to think about it only after the incident of Dinšawāi.[41] The British were not in favour of such a plan because "they feared that a university would be

37. VII 540, 610; VIII 378.

38. XVI 201; XXI 36.

39. Steppat 318

40. VIII 264, XII 18, XIV 18, XV 67, XVI 512, XVII 272, XXII 563.

41. XVII 337, XXII 563. Dinšawāi is a village in Egypt in which in 1906 a hunting party of British officers entered into an altercation with villagers. One of the officers died later, possibly as a result of the beating. In any case the British authorities chose to consider this to be the case and they punished the villagers by executing several of them publicly. This overreaction of the British created for the first time a widely spread nationalist protest of the Egyptians, the demand for national independence became now popular with all classes of society. Zaidān's claim to have been the first demanding an Egyptian university seems doubtful. Apparently Muṣṭafā Kāmil came out publicly with a demand for a university practically at the same time as Zaidān did; Steppat 318.

just another form of nationalist sentiment and a threat to British rule".[42]

The British supported the project of a multitude of elementary schools that would instruct the people in some elementary skills without creating any native intelligentsia. Zaidān's concern with education in terms of values and qualities of character caused him to criticize severely any such project. In his eyes it was useless to transmit merely information, *ta'līm*, unless a whole style and new attitude towards life and society went with it. It was essential that, together with the subject matter taught, an example was given by the teacher to induce the student to strive for his personal freedom, independence of thought, love for the fatherland, progress and other noble traits. More important than many small schools were a few exceptional teachers who would set an example by their own personal qualities. To produce such teachers, however, it was necessary to send qualified people to a higher institution of learning where factual knowledge was taught as well as the new values. Only a university or college could achieve this. After a sufficient number of teachers had been trained and motivated in such a fashion, it would be useful to set up a large system of elementary schools.[43]

Again we see that generally and somewhat vaguely Zaidān displayed an interest in general education. But the main issues for him were the educational needs of the bourgeoisie. The establishment of a local university would answer the needs of the Egyptian bourgeoisie, which was forced otherwise to send its children to Beirut or Europe for a higher education. The masses certainly could not derive any direct benefit from such an institution in the near future.

Discussing the various forms and means of education we have mentioned so far Zaidān's use of the journal, his purposes when writing historical novels and his concepts about educational institutions. By far the most important vehicle of education, however, was the Arabic language itself. The regeneration of the Arabic language was an intrinsic part of the *Nahḍa* movement. In the Lebanon it was especially under the influence of the Protestant missionaries that people like Buṭrus al-Bustānī searched for a new style in Arabic. The translation of the Bible by the

42. Tignor 337.
43. XIV 18 ff.

missionaries and, even more, the translation of Western textbooks for schools made the need for a renewal of the language even more evident. Zaidān's close intercourse with van Dyck and the early members of the *Nahḍa* in Beirut must have made him aware of the problem of the regeneration of the Arabic language. At the time that Zaidān attended the Syrian Protestant College, all the subjects in the Medical School were taught in Arabic. An Arabic style, sober and easy to comprehend, modernized enough to discuss Western scientific subjects, had already advanced in its development. Zaidān himself never had enjoyed any profound education in the Arabic language and literature. In spite of this lack, or perhaps just because of it, he realized the need for modernization and change in the language if it was to be used as a tool for modern education.

Language was the subject of Zaidān's first work. His main thesis was that language developed according to the laws of natural evolution. He rejected the idea of a "classic" stage of language, which would remain the only pattern worth imitating in later generations. With the proposition of continuous development and change of language, he achieved several things: he established that Arabic was a living language; he freed it from the suffocating obligation to follow a given set of "classical" patterns; and he legitimized changes in its style and vocabulary as a natural permanent phenomenon. In fact, demanding changes in it according to the needs of modern civilization seemed only to follow the very laws of its own development.

In order to translate and integrate Western knowledge into Arabic it was necessary to develop new expressions and terms. Zaidān appreciated every attempt in this direction, suggested obligatory use of new Arabic terms in magazines and other publications,[44] and eventually demanded the establishment of a language academy.[45] At the same time, he was not a fanatical purist who tried to arabize *par force* every Western expression but pointed out that already in the Koran and in pre-Islamic times words from other languages had penetrated the Arabic language.[46] In fact, he criticized the concept of purity of a culture or language because it is

44. I 221-228.
45. XXI 101.
46. I 306-316.

always influenced by and mixed with elements of neighbouring cultures. He, himself, however, rarely made use of direct transliteration of European terms. Sometimes when he felt that particular European concepts, such as "communism" and "socialism" had not yet found an equivalent Arabic term, he would add the English or the French word in brackets after the Arabic term.[47]

On many occasions Zaidān stressed the need for simplicity and clarity of style. They were essential for his intention to spread education as far as possible within society. The content had to be clearly understood and was certainly more important than stylistic elaborations and niceties, "since we see the nation in greater need of facts and truth than of elaborate expressions".[48]

In his plea for simplicity of style, Zaidān argues — as he always did when discussing education purposes — that in order to be effective and useful the language must be within the "comprehension of the common people". There cannot be any doubt that he meant the somewhat educated "common people" because in the discussion about the merits of the high Arabic, *al-luġa al-fuṣḥā*, and the spoken Arabic, *al-luġa al-ʿāmma*, he rejected any attempt to elevate the spoken language to a medium of literature and education.

It seems that the permanent discussion about the merits of the literary and the spoken language arose periodically to a special intensity, often stimulated by some remark of a European official in the administration whose own inability to master the literary Arabic language convinced him of the impracticality of adhering to a "dead" language, which in any case nobody actually used in conversation. Such was the case with an Englishman William Wilcox, a high ranking irrigation engineer, and ten years later with Wilmoor, one of the British judges. In both cases Zaidān's answer was based on similar arguments, the national-cultural aspect of which we will discuss in more detail later. He claimed that only the literary language had the wealth and linguistic capability to create and adapt all the expressions and words which had become

---

47. Cf. for instance XVI 265, where Zaidān tried to establish the term *iǧtimāʿīya* for socialism and *ištirākīya* for communism. For a discussion of these terms see REID "*The Syrian Christians*", 190.

48. *Ta'rīḫ ādāb* II 7; XX 530.

indispensable with the growing participation of the Arab world in modern civilization. Zaidān hastened to add that if one wanted to maintain literary Arabic as an instrument of thought and culture, one would have to introduce to it greater simplicity and clarity.[49]

Zaidān's attitude towards the Arabic language is, therefore, clearly circumscribed. On the one hand he belonged to the modernists who did not shy away from any effort to free the language from its traditional rule and stifling patterns and to adapt it to the needs of the new civilization. On the other, he never attempted to elevate the spoken language to the level of a literary language. He never even used it for the dialogues in his historical novels, something that some Egyptian authors such as 'Abdallāh an-Nadīm[50] and James Ṣanū'[51] tried occasionally. When Zaidān published in "al-Hilāl" a letter in which 'Īsā Iskandar al-Ma'lūf defended the proposition to use the spoken language exclusively, Zaidān did this only with the pointed comment that this was a very rare and unusual position among Easterners, *ahl aš-šarq.*[52]

National-cultural and socio-educational arguments were also intertwined in Zaidān's approach to the use of Arabic as a teaching language. After the British occupation

> "the British were naturally inclined to foster the study of English... As English became the dominant foreign language of the bureaucracy, educated Egyptians were increasingly interested in having their sons learn English in the government schools... The British were not reluctant to relegate Arabic to a secondary position, as many of the British officials regarded Arabic with ill-concealed contempt... Neither was Arabic considered a language of science; it was felt to be imprecise and lacking in the necessary vocabularly. If Western

49. I 176-180; X 279 ff.

50. 'Abdallāh an-Nadīm (1844-1896), journalist, nationalist, active in the al-'Urābī movement. He went underground after the British occupation, emerged in 1891 when he was caught and exiled. He wrote one of the earliest plays in Arabic, called "*al-Waṭan*"; Hourani 196; *Tarāǧim* II, 94.

51. James Ṣanū' (1839-1912), born in Egypt of Jewish religious background. Author of theatre pieces, published various magazines and was active in the nationalist movement. He belonged to the group around Ǧamāl ad-Dīn al-Afġānī and Muḥammad 'Abduh and opposed the policies of the Ḫidīw Ismā'īl. He introduced the political satire to Arabic literature; Dāġir II, 554, Gendzier, Moosa.

52. X, 373.

science was to be taken up it should be done in European languages the British argued."[53]

English and French were used to an increasing degree as teaching languages in the Egyptian schools. Zaidān saw the obstacles which the use of Arabic as a teaching language might entail: insufficient numbers of textbooks,[54] difficulty of keeping up with translations from Western languages, shortcomings of the Arabic language as far as technical terms were concerned, etc. All these appeared to him as minor difficulties which he was willing to endure rather than let the Arabic language die as a literary and cultural language, and restricting education ot a small elite able to acquire the knowledge of foreign languages. Even those Arabs who did receive a modern education would be disqualified to pass on this education and knowledge to their compatriots, because they would be unable to do so in any other language than the one in which they received their education.[55] For this reason he repeatedly deplored the introduction of English as the language of instruction in the Syrian Protestant College.[56] He believed that with this act the Syrian Protestant College had renounced voluntarily its role as a center of and main stimulant for the Arabic *Nahḍa*. Neither did Zaidān miss any opportunity to attack the Egyptian government for letting English and French take over as teaching languages in the Egyptian schools.[57] For all his criticisms of *al-Azhar* as a traditional institution, Zaidān nevertheless praised it because it was the only institution throughout the centuries of decay that kept the literary Arabic language alive.[58]

Education was useless even if its standards were comparatively high unless given in Arabic. Only the use of Arabic as a teaching language would guarantee that the whole society would benefit from education which otherwise would remain restricted to a small elite. Zaidān conceived here of education as a universal process extending eventually to

53. Tignor 325-326.

54. A problem which Zaidān himself tried to tackle with such books as *at-Ta'rīḫ al-'āmm* and *Ta'rīḫ miṣr al-ḥadīṯ*.

55. XV 393 ff.

56. XII 18.

57. I 270, VII 610, XV 393.

58. XV 131.

the whole society. The use of Arabic as a teaching language was essential for such a concept of education.

Zaidān saw his own task as that of the educator and he considered education as the key factor for the progress of society and the advancement of the individual within society. Zaidān had often spoken of the necessity to educate the "common people" and occasionally he made it quite clear that the whole society or nation had to be the object of education. His concern with universal education was most pronounced in his insistence that Arabic should be the medium of teaching and learning. Only through the use of a simplified and modernized Arabic could the whole Arab society participate in the process of modernization, which would eventually lead the Arab people to take its place as an equal amongst the other advanced nations. Here the question of education bears already strong national overtones. We shall discuss in another place[59] at length the importance which Zaidān attributed to language as the source of national identity. Obviously, though, when education becomes "national education", the object of it must be the whole society.

The notion of universality of education and knowledge, however, was not really borne out by the sum total of Zaidān's educational efforts. We have observed that his intention to simplify and dramatize historical material in order to familiarize the "common people" with it, found its definite limitations through the very question of literacy. "Common people" who could read at all were few. Zaidān's concern when writing historical novels or his journal had not been with all members of society but with the reading audience of the new bourgeoisie. This point is driven home even more forcefully in Zaidān's discussion of educational institutions. He had very little to say about elementary education but spent much effort to promote the establishment of a university, an institution which clearly served foremost the educational needs of the new elite.[60]

The concept of universal education essential for the progress of the nation as a whole was counterbalanced in Zaidān's thinking by his ideas about the origins of the elite, the new bourgeoisie. These ideas were the result of Zaidān's own experience as a self-made man and his

---

59. See 97-99, 103.

60. See WARE 104 ff to which the last part of the above discussion is indebted.

adoption of social Darwinism as an explanation for social structure. Anybody could become a member of the bourgeoisie but he had to do so through his own efforts in self-improvement. Education should be universally available but certainly nobody should be forced to learn (nowhere did Zaidān promote the idea of obligatory education). The individual had to show by his own motivation and intellectual capability that he himself was able to acquire education and that by this he proved to have been selected by nature to be part of the new elite, the bourgeoisie.

RELIGION AND POLITICS IN SOCIETY

Zaidān was born shortly after the critical clashes in the Lebanon between the Maronites and Druzes in 1860. He grew up in a climate of relative political stability. His attention was drawn towards modern sciences and theories, and he was willing to risk his educational career in the fight over the acceptability of a particular scientific theory. In Beirut he belonged to circles that saw as their main purpose the spread of enlightened education and culture, but we never read of any political association that Zaidān might have joined or of any political opinion that he nurtured as a young student. For him the key to progress and emancipation was education of the individual and knowledge of the sciences, not the political activism to attain collective rights.

When he came to Egypt in 1884, he still could see the traces of the 'Urābī revolution, but he never experienced the tension of that period itself. In the wake of the collapse of the 'Urābī movement and the British occupation, a mood of political exhaustion and apathy had settled over Egypt which only started to change towards the end of the century when a younger generation, for which the failure of the 'Urābī movement was history and not personal experience, began to question the justification for the British occupation. Zaidān belonged to an in-between generation for which the participation in active politics seemed no longer possible or not yet promising of success. In Zaidān's opinion it was necessary to lay the scientific and educational foundations before one engaged again in political action.

It was not only his emphasis upon education and his reliance upon the rationality of science which kept him from participating actively in politics. The second political awakening in Egypt was centred primarily around the question of Anglo-Egyptian relations and Egyptian independence and, secondarily, on a more general level, around the quest for a more inclusive political identity, which very often had clearly Muslim overtones. On both counts the Christian Syrian Zaidān had to remain an outsider. As was the case for most of his Christian compatriots, Zaidān's motivation and opportunity for political action were restricted. His interest in political thought and theory, therefore, remained for a long time rather secondary. But dealing, as he did, with Islamic history, with modern civilization, and with the role of modern science in it, he could not avoid but take a position with regard to religion and its various functions in society.

Zaidān's attitude towards religion was formed by the contact with religion at home and at school, by his own increasing tendency to see at the basis of the modern secular civilization scientific principles, and last but not least, by the awareness of his own marginal position as a Christian in a predominantly Muslim society.

In the autobiographical description of Zaidān's childhood and youth the religious aspect in daily life and education is notably lacking. The family was Greek Orthodox, but it seems that Zaidān's parents rarely went to church, either because they had to work Sundays and holidays in order to make a living[1] or because they did not feel the need to participate in a religious community life. Nor do we read of any religious life at home, such as praying or the display of religious objects. The only contact Zaidān seems to have had during his childhood with the Greek Orthodox Church was during the first two years as a schoolboy when he had to learn the hymn book by heart under the supervision of a rather uneducated priest.

His first and only intensive confrontation with religion happened in the Syrian Protestant College. Here conformity with a strict Protestant ritual was demanded from the students, and the teaching of the Protestant tenets was part of the course work of every student. The teachers, however, to whom he felt most strongly drawn — Cornelius van Dyck, E. Lewis, Fāris Nimr and Ya'qūb Ṣarrūf — were rather liberal in their views and more interested in their scientific work than in theological discussion and the display of religiosity. Perhaps the time Zaidān spent in the Syrian Protestant College had been too short to evoke from him a definitive reaction formulating his own position towards religion. Neither did he

1. See 135.

convert to Protestantism like Fāris Nimr and Ya'qūb Ṣarrūf (their professional alliance with the College might have made such a conversion desirable), nor did he turn violently anti-clerical and atheistic like Šiblī Šamayyil, one of the earliest graduates of the College. He remained Greek Orthodox, but we never hear that membership in his community was of importance for his personal life.

Interpretations of history based on traditional religious thought play a varying and over the years decreasing role in Zaidān's works. His very first book *al-Alfāẓ al-'arabīya wa'l-falsafa al-luġawīya* dealt already with the development of language in strictly evolutionary term. But when he discussed some years later in his book *at-Ta'rīḫ al-'āmm* the creation of the World, Zaidān adhered completely to the Biblical story. However, the problem of the origin of man presented itself again and again to Zaidān. Gradually he moved away from the Biblical story of creation to an evolutionist interpretation of the origin of man. The change of his approach can be well traced in various of his articles in "al-Hilāl". [2] From the claim that the Biblical story must be closest to the truth because it is the oldest written evidence, he shifted soon to the assertion that man existed already long before the time which the Bible indicates as the time of creation. In a further step Zaidān explained the method of determining the age of the earth by geology and other sciences and expounded the Darwinist theory about the development of living beings without, however committing himself explicitly to this theory. In his book *Ṭabaqāt al-umam* which appeared in 1912, he finally dealt with the question of the origin of man solely according to the theory of evolution. The congruence with the Scripture is established by reinterpretation of the text, e.g. each day of creation should be understood as a period of many thousand years. But questions such as whether a common ancestor existed for all human beings were answered with the results of bone finds in Java not with Biblical statements. Zaidān's emancipation from the Bible had become complete and he tried to give a totally scientific and secular interpretation to man's history.

Even on the rather rare occasions at which Zaidān entered such theological discussions as the proof for the existence of God or the veracity

2. cf. XI 72; XV 308; XX 309, 538.

of the prophetic revelation, we find him to an increasing degree discussing the metaphysical world in terms of ratio rather than of revelation, of law rather than of divine will. In a similar spirit of secularism, Zaidān solved the problem of the relation between science and religion. By sciences Zaidān meant the systematical knowledge based upon data collected from observation and controlled experimentations which when repeated always render the same results. In order to differentiate sciences in this modern senses from *'ilm*, learning in general, he often used the term *al-'ulūm al-ḥaqīqīya* "the true sciences".

He was cautious in his statements and did not openly construct a hierarchy establishing sciences above religion. This would have opened him too easily to attacks from the Muslim as well as the Christian side. When he credited every religion with containing some scientific (and, therefore, relevant) truth, this might appear as a rather tolerant attitude that prefers no religion over the other. But Louis Cheikho, for instance, recognized very correctly that the equal ranking of religions by Zaidān had not so much to do with tolerance as with a totally a-religious attitude.[3]

Indeed, it becomes obvious that for Zaidān science was the decisive criterion, not religion. The development of modern society is based in his opinion upon the scientific insights into the law of nature and its evolution. The compatibility between any particular religion and modern society was to be achieved according to Zaidān, by the re-interpretation and one-sided adaptation of religion to the requirements of civilization. He mentioned in this context Qāsim Amīn and Muḥammad 'Abduh who recognized the "duty" to interpret the Koran in such a fashion as to bring it into agreement with modern science".[4]

Especially in the latter he saw the foremost representative of a trend to re-interpret the Muslim faith in the light of that scientific knowledge which forms the basis of modern society. He praised him and believed his task as a reformer of religion at least as important, if not more so, than that of the founder of a religion. Muḥammad 'Abduh's method of teaching and slow reform at the spiritual centre of Islam, *al-Azhar*,

3. Cheikho in al-Mašriq XV (1912) 714.
4. XVI 432.

was the only way that would promise success to a Muslim *Nahḍa*. The only possible way in which Zaidān could foresee such a revival of Islam was an adaptation of Islam to the secular civilization in which government is separated from religion. A re-interpreted Islam may provide the individual with an emotional and intellectual basis from which he can participate in modern civilization, but one gains the impression that "re-interpretation" remained for Zaidān mainly a throwing off of the traditional shackles of religion, rather than the reconstruction of a positive religious identity.

As we saw, Zaidān himself adopted this very attitude towards the Bible. It was the ultimate subjection of religion to science when Zaidān predicted that religion, even though it would always exist, would develop along the lines of natural evolution. He foresaw "a change of its aspects, ramification of denominations, of which some will overcome others in line with the general evolution".[5] If religion can be understood and explained in terms supplied by the natural sciences, it is clear that religion cannot be sufficient any more as a basis for a value system of society.

Zaidān's treatment of religion was also determined by the awareness that he was living in a society in which religious affiliation was still of utmost importance and in which his position as a Christian writing about Islamic topics was, to say the least, precarious.

It is not accidental that from the beginning he felt free to discuss the history of language in evolutionary terms. This approach may have hurt some traditional Muslim Arab sentiments which considered pre-Islamic poetry together with the language of the Koran, the absolute and inimitable apex of Arabic language. But it did not directly contradict any tenet of the Muslim let alone Christian creed. As we saw, Zaidān was far more cautious to apply the concept of evolution to the creation of man. Here the veracity of the Bible and the Koran were directly put into question.

Very often Zaidān would try to avoid sensitive religious issues altogether. In his four volumes of *Ta'riḫ ādāb al-luġa al-'arabīya* in which he discussed extensively the pre-Islamic and ancient periods he dedicated

5. XVI 310.

only a total of twelve pages to the description of the origin and development of Islam before the Umayyad period, thus preventing any profound discussion of the person of the Prophet, of the revelation, etc.[6]

When Zaidān dealt with the particular relationship between Islam and Christianity he tried persistently to play down any historical tensions between the two. He emphasized that throughout most of the history of the Islamic Empire, the Christians lived in harmony with their Muslim compatriots and that in the golden age of the Abbasid Empire religious tolerance was greatest. This harmonious symbiosis was only rarely disturbed by rulers such as al-Mutawakkil (842-847 A.D.) and al-Ḥākim (996-1021 A.D.), but such rulers were not typical and their persecution of the Christians was motivated by personal reasons. The blame for this kind of persecution could not be put upon the dynasty or the nation to which those rulers belonged.[7]

It is remarkable that in the voluminous *Ta'rīḫ at-tamaddun al-islāmī* hardly a paragraph deals with the Crusades.[8] Zaidān considered this time the darkest period of European civilization, a period of religious fanaticism. Its outcome, the Crusades, "history is ashamed to remember".[9] Even in his novel *Ṣalāḥ ad-dīn*, which takes place at the height of the conflict, the Crusaders play only a very peripheral role. Zaidān's sympathies were on the side of the Muslim hero,[10] and it is the intrusion of the European Christians which carries the blame for the disruption of the good relations between Muslims and Christians in the Islamic world:

> "...after the Crusades, which did much to stir up fanaticism on both sides. The Christians recollected how the Muslims had been preferred to themselves, and how their rulers had persecuted the Christian religion; and the Muslims' irritation against their Christian subjects was increased by the secret support which the latter gave the Franks."[11]

---

6. This lack of balance was already perceived and criticized by Ḥusain Haikal. He is aware of Zaidān's inhibitions which he feels are unjustified, because also the thinking Muslims recognize the role of the Koran in the development of Arab language and literature; HAIKAL 234 ff.

7. *Ta'rīḫ at-tamaddun* IV 172.

8. *Ibid.*, 282 ff.

9. *Ta'rīḫ al-'āmm* 141.

10. II 610; XXI 641.

11. *Ta'rīḫ at-tamaddun* IV 172.

But in spite of all his caution and effort not to occupy too exposed a position in his writings, and despite his emphasis upon the desirability of religious tolerance, it was unavoidable that his essentially secular approach should create him enemies amongst the Christians as well as the Muslims. Zaidān was well aware of this animosity. Speaking about the reaction of the reading public to his *Ta'rīḫ at-tamaddun al-islāmī*, he wrote:

> "... Secondly, we expected the Muslim scholars and the Arab intelligentsia, *ḫāṣṣat kuttāb al-'arabīya*, to look into this book with great interest and to examine its topics because it is an investigation of the exploits of their ancestors. Thirdly, (we expected) that the masses would think ill of us because we are aware of differences in denominations and schools of thought, especially since we, as a Christian, write about the history of Islam..."
>
> "Our third expectation, however, was confirmed two-fold. Both the Christians and the Muslims loathe us, only because we strove for the truth as it is, disregarding personal interests and likings. This truth is burdensome for those who hear it. It is unavoidable that Islamic civilization should have good and bad aspects. If a Muslim reads it, he will disregard what good aspects of Islam we mention and be only conscious of the negative aspects and accuse us, the author, of fanaticism. If a Christian reads it, he only sees the good aspects and accuses the author of disloyalty towards Christianity. But neither the one nor the other affect us. We strive for the truth and our aim is evident in every line and word of our works. We are not, God forbid, claiming infallibility. Mistakes have penetrated many of our works. Therefore, we would like to read the opinions of scholars in order to correct our works as far as possible."[12]

Amongst Christian groups people who were otherwise on rather friendly terms with Zaidān criticized him for his secularism. Father A. Karmeli,[13] who in general reviewed Zaidān's works most favorably regretted Zaidān's claim that mankind needed millions of years for its evolution. This claim was misleading, he explained, since Zaidān did

12. XIII 48-49.

13. Anastās Marī al-Karmalī (1866-1947) born in Bagdad of Lebanese origin, educated in Bagdad and France, joined the Carmelites. He was a scholar of the Arab language and history. His magazine Luġat al-'arab appeared in Bagdad 1911-1914 and 1927-1931; Dāġir II 664.

not add that this was the materialistic concept of history which differed widley from the "correct" historical concept.[14]

His main critic and antagonist in this respect was Louis Cheikho, the Jesuit scholar in Beirut and founder of "al-Mašriq". He was suspicious of Zaidān's attitude towards religion and attacked him for his secularism and Darwinian approach.[15] For Cheikho the Protestants and the members of the Syrian Protestant College were a natural object of wrath. He was perhaps even more antagonized by the secularism displayed by the Freemasons who mainly recruited themselves from the ranks of the Protestants and members of the Syrian Protestant College. His writings attacking the Freemasons, speak for themselves, and both "al-Hilāl" and "al-Muqtaṭaf" were the objects of much the same antagonism displayed by Cheikho in "al-Mašriq".[16]

The first attack from the Muslim side came after the publication of Zaidān's *Ta'rīḫ miṣr al-ḥadīṯ* in 1889. A certain Amīn al-Ḥulwānī al-Madanī published in 1890 a pamphlet[17] in which he accused Zaidān of 101 mistakes in his book. The essence of his attack was the attempt to disqualify the Christian Zaidān as a writer about Islamic history. Al-Ḥulwānī claimed that Zaidān was a teacher in a Jesuit school in Cairo and accused Zaidān of being part of a Christian Syrian conspiracy aimed at controlling — with the help of the Europeans — the Egyptian nation. In his own published answer,[18] Zaidān stated that the main purpose of this attack against his book had been to belittle the Syrians and praise the Egyptians. Conscious of the real tensions existing between the two communities in Egypt he hastened to point out that the pamphlet of al-Ḥulwānī was published in India because, as Zaidān believed, no Egyptian publishing house was willing to print this drivel. It was the only time that Zaidān ventured to answer publicly such criticism. He was just beginning his career as a writer and probably felt the

---

14. Luġat al-ʿarab II (1912) 582-595.

15. al-Mašriq XV (1912) 714.

16. cf. his *al-Ḫulāṣa al-māsūnīya.*

17. Amīn al-Ḥulwānī al-Madanī (d. 1898) came from Cairo to Bombay where he worked as a teacher and writer. Zirkilī I 357 in Cairo 1954 edition. Title of the pamphlet is *Nabš al-hadayān min ta'rīḫ ǧurǧī zaidān,* Bombay 1890.

18. *Radd rannān ʿalā nabš al-hadayān.*

need to defend himself because his own reputation was not yet firmly established.[19]

This mixture of anti-Christian sentiments and some not yet elaborated nationalist feelings became typical of the later Muslim criticism of Zaidān's works. The sharpest criticism appeared in 1912 in "al-Manār" authored by the Indian *'ālim* Šaiḫ Šiblī an-Nu'mānī.[20] The criticism was limited by the religious views of its author and attacked the personal integrity of Zaidān.[21] Šiblī an-Nu'mānī accused Zaidān of a consistent effort to belittle the Arabs and to abuse them. He tried to demonstrate that Zaidān had expressed himself about the Umayyads solely in a negative manner because they were a fully Arabic dynasty and government and that he related only positive aspects about the Abbasids because he, Zaidān, considered them non-Arabs. Zaidān did not dare, an-Nu'mānī claimed, to attack openly the Four Righteous Caliphs and the Prophet since he was interested in marketing his book profitably. It is certainly true that Zaidān did not hesitate to depict negative aspects in Arab Muslim history as well, and perhaps he had inherited a certain bias against the Umayyads from early European scholarship, which in turn had been influenced by the works of the historians of the Abbasid period. It is also true that Zaidān allocated extremely little space to dealing with the period of the Prophet and the Four Righteous Caliphs, feeling obviously uneasy about discussing, as a Christian, the period so decisive for the forming of Islam. But it is an outright fabrication of Šiblī an-Nu'mānī to claim that Zaidān considered the Abbasid Empire as non-Arabic and that he had only positive things to report about it.

The basic issue of contention between Zaidān and Šiblī an-Nu'mānī is the following: Zaidān, the Christian Arab, was mainly interested in the cultural and literary achievements of the Arabs at this time and was, therefore, especially concerned with the period of the Abbasid Empire

---

19. For a discussion of al-Ḥulwānī's pamphlet see Ware 196-198.

20. *Šaiḫ* Šiblī an-Nu'mānī (1869-1914). Member of the *Salafīya* movement in India. He belonged to a Brahmin family which had converted to Islam. He studied at Aligaṛh University in India, was a collaborator of Aḥmad Ḫān and followed Ǧamāl ad-Dīn al-Afġānī's trend of thought concerning the rejuvenation of Islam. He founded in 1898 the *Nadwat al-'ulamā' al-hindīya*, a learned society in Lucknow, and was one of the first to write in Urdu; Dāġir III 1503. al-Ǧundī 137-145.

21. al-Manār XV (1912) 58 ff.

when, in close co-operation with educated people of various creeds, Arab-Muslim culture reached its peak. Šiblī an-Nuʻmānī, the Muslim from India, was mainly concerned with the reputation of the Arabs as good Muslims. When Zaidān, for instance, observed that the Arabs, especially during the rule of the Umayyads, considered themselves better Muslims than the non-Arab Muslims, an-Nuʻmānī countered that the Prophet himself had said that there was no difference between Arabs and non-Arabs — therefore, Zaidān's claim must be wrong. This point exemplifies well Nuʻmānī's traditional paradigmatic way of argument which he sometimes used against Zaidān's secular historical approach. Often, however, he applied his considerable scholarly knowledge to show that Zaidān had used sources in highly selective fashion and often falsified them.

Zaidān had considered *Šaiḫ* Šiblī an-Nuʻmānī for twenty years as a friendly colleague.[22] We have found no indications for the motives that caused an-Nuʻmānī to furnish his criticism with such a personal attack upon Zaidān, insinuating cowardice and commercial purpose as Zaidān's guidelines for writing. Looking at the criticism itself it appears as if the accusations of *Šaiḫ* Šiblī an-Nuʻmānī concentrated on the anti-Arab attitude that he believed to perceive in Zaidān's work. It is, however, difficult to see what stake the Indian Muslim scholar would have in nationalist defense of the Arabs[23] or why he should take such pains at all to show that Zaidān was led by anti-Arab feelings, when it must have been clear to him that on the whole Zaidān identified very strongly with Arab history and its achievements — in spite of critical remarks about the Umayyads. Šiblī an-Nuʻmānī's preoccupation with the Umayyads' attitude towards Islam and his repeated attempt to provide evidence for the piety of the Umayyads and their abidance by the religious law, seems to point not so much to a nationalist pro-Arab interest as to the concern of the Muslim scholar over the secular interpretation of early Islamic history by a non-Muslim.

But perhaps the role of Šiblī an-Nuʻmānī and his criticism is not as important as that of Rašīd Riḍā. After all, he had published Šiblī

22. *Letters*, Zaidān to Emile, Cairo, March 28, 1912.

23. Ende suggests cautiously the possibility of a relation between Indian Muslim enthusiasm for Muslim Spain and a general pro-Umayyad attitude; Ende 41.

an-Nu'mānī's criticism in "al-Manār" and he deemed it necessary in the same year to reprint the *Šaiḫ's* article in a booklet together with some other reviews of Zaidān's works.[24] In the contribution of Aḥmad 'Umar al-Iskandarī[25] to this book the main line of argument was Zaidān's lack of qualification to write about Islamic history since he never had studied the Muslim sciences. Rašīd Riḍā had succeeded in giving his booklet a wider basis by including a review article by the Jesuit, Louis Cheikho. The latter took issue — as he usually did — with Zaidān's secular interpretation of history and Darwinian approach in analyzing the development of society, language and religion.

In the introduction to this collection of criticism Rašīd Riḍā explained his reasons for publishing it. The reasoning reflects well his identification with Islam increasingly interwoven with pro-Arab national sentiments; a mixture that was typical for Rašīd Riḍā's thinking.[26] In his opinion Zaidān was not qualified to write about Islamic history because as a Christian he never studied the Muslim sciences and was therefore, intellectually not equipped to understand the meaning of Islamic history. To this religious argument, repeated by Aḥmad 'Umar al-Iskandarī in his article, Rašīd Riḍā added a different one, namely he admitted to being concerned that the translation of *Ta'rīḫ at-tamaddun al-islāmī* into Turkish might add fuel to the fire of Young Turkish chauvinism. The weaknesses of this book and the falsifications and fabrications that appear in this book had, therefore, to be pointed out and criticized.

Indeed, if one looks at the timing of the publication of Rašīd Riḍā's booklet, it appears that for him this second reason was the most important one: the last volume *Ta'rīḫ at-tamaddun al-islāmī* had been published in Arabic in 1906. But it was only six years later when the work had been translated into Turkish that Rašīd Riḍā saw fit to come out with a major effort to criticize Zaidān's work.[27]

24. *Kitāb intiqād ta'rīḫ at-tamaddun al-islāmī* Cairo, 1912.

25. Aḥmad 'Umar al-Iskandarī (1875-1938) studied at *al-Azhar* and *Dār al-'ulūm*, where he also taught. 1933 he was made professor of Arab Literature at the Egyptian University. He also worked for the Ministry of Education in Cairo; Dāġir II 121. Dāġir gives as his name Aḥmad 'Alī al-Iskandarī, cf. Ware 200.

26. See for instance Haim 20 ff.

27. See Philipp 331, Ende 37.

Rašīd Riḍā had been concerned that the Turkish translation might be misused for chauvinistic purposes against the Arabs. This notion was, in a fashion, promptly borne out, as can be seen from some letters to Zaidān from Maġāmiz[28] who was responsible for the Turkish translation of *Ta'rīḫ at-tamaddun al-islāmī*. He complained to Zaidān that the illustrations in the book showed too much superiority of Arab civilization. With regard to the history of the transfer of the Caliphate to the Ottomans, he wrote that he had changed Zaidān's description in such a manner as to leave no room for any possible claim of the Arabs to the Caliphate. It sounds almost sarcastic when he adds "because our aim is history, not politics".[29] It is an irony of the two conflicting national ideologies that Maġāmiz should have seen too positive a description of the Arabs where Rašīd Riḍā feared too negative a picture.

If Zaidān had been in need of any solid proof of the antagonism he had aroused against himself in Muslim religious circles, he had received it already in 1910 when he was unceremoniously dismissed from his position as professor of Islamic history in the recently founded Egyptian University in Cairo — before he had even begun to teach there. In June 1910 he had been invited to teach a course in Islamic history in the coming academic year. Zaidān hesitated to accept the offer, not only because of his own workload, but also because of the difficulties that might arise if a Christian taught this subject. Such an arrangement might have been feasible in Abbasid times when, he believed, religious tolerance prevailed "but we know from much evidence that their situation is not ours".[30] He finally was convinced by the appointment committee that no difficulties would arise since he would not be teaching the religion of Islam. In spite of his hesitations Zaidān must have been flattered by this appointment which confirmed his position as a scholar. However, five months later, in October 1910, Zaidān had to learn from a notice in the Islamic daily newspaper "al-Mu'ayyad"[31] that the university had

28. Maġāmiz, there seems to be little information available about this somewhat strange personality. A Christian Arab from Aleppo he developed strong anti-Arab feelings. He went to Istanbul where he worked for 18 years as editor of various pan-Islamic publications.

29. *Letters*, Maġāmiz to Zaidān, no date, no place.

30. XIX 177.

31. Al-Mu'ayyad was founded 1889 by 'Alī Yūsuf as a daily newspaper repre-

cancelled his appointment. Only a day later he was informed officially that the university "intended to change its first decision in consideration of the sentiments of the nation".[32] A university delegation sent to him explained that "in view of the sentiments of the uneducated Muslim masses, the university thought it proper to turn to a Muslim professor to lecture about the history of Islam".[33] Zaidān suspected that here, too, Rašīd Riḍā had a hand in opposing his appointment.[34]

The attacks from Muslim and Christian religious quarters never caused Zaidān to waver in his own pronounced secularism. But also because of this very experience, he did not fail to recognize the importance of the social and political functions religion had in the past and still had in the present.

Frequently Zaidān's ideas about society resembled those of the mediaeval Muslim philosophers: society was divided basically into two groups, the elite, *al-ḫāṣṣa*, and the common people, *al-ʿāmma*, and one should not expect too much intelligence and reason amongst the common people. Therefore, the truth that is accessible to the educated, thanks to their intelligence, has to be presented to the masses in the form of revelation and belief. Throughout the years Zaidān's emphasis on the special dependence of the common people upon religion, remained the same.[35] Of course, such a concept of society also made any political system inadmissible that would let the masses participate in the political power. Nay, the ruler had to be vested not only with political but also with religious authority in order to exert control over the masses. Drawing mainly on his knowledge of Islamic history, Zaidān believed to see a close relation between the successful connection between religion and political power on the one hand and the longevity of a dynasty on the other hand. Religion gained here a very important role as the basis of stability and solidarity within society.

---

senting a pro-Islamic pro-Arab point of view. It was founded partially in response to the daily al-Muqaṭṭam which was founded in the same year by Fāris Nimr and Šāhīn Makāriyūs and which usually took a pro-British stand.

32. XIX 180. For Zaidān's account of this controversy see XIX 178-181 and *Letters*, Zaidān to Emile, Cairo, Oct. 12, 1910.

33. *Letters* ibid.

34. *Letters*, Zaidān to Emile, Cairo, March 28, 1912.

35 cf. XII 222, XVI 310, XIX 241.

The "pessimism about the masses" of the mediaeval philosophers had found a strong echo in Zaidān's time in the thought of Ǧamāl ad-Dīn al-Afġānī who insisted on the need of religion for the common people.[36] Whether Zaidān was directly influenced by Ǧamāl ad-Dīn al-Afġānī's writings cannot be determined with certainty. He did praise Ǧamāl ad-Dīn al-Afġānī, though, for re-introducing the thought of the Muslim philosophers into the contemporary intellectual development of the Middle East,[37] and called him "the philosopher of Islam in our time."

The traditional simplistic division of society into elite and common people is a pattern which Zaidān frequently used. Often, however, we find this concept presented in an up-dated form using for its description the terminology of social Darwinism. The ruler or the elite still retained the same position and powers, but now thanks to the survival of the fittest and the rule of the strong over the weak. In this context Zaidān's interpretation of the role of religion obtains a somewhat different connotation. He argued that especially the weak will cling to religion because it promises to the weak for the next world what he cannot achieve in this world. Therefore, the common people are, in Zaidān's opinion, more susceptible to the religious appeal. Zaidān approved of this role of religion because it seemed to constitute a kind of safety valve for social frustration.

One profound change, however, occurred in Zaidān's analysis of society when he used the social Darwinist terminology. He introduced the factor of social mobility. The survival of the fittest meant for him as it did for the social Darwinists, that any individual regardless of his original social position, could rise in the social hierarchy by hard work, self-discipline and perseverance. Zaidān, himself, made the point explicitly when writing in his autobiography about the impression the book *Self Help* had made upon him.[38] The same belief in the self-made man and his required qualities is a recurring theme in his letters to his son, Emile.[39] A number of the biographies Zaidān wrote for his *Tarāǧim mašāhīr aš-šarq fi'l-qarn at-tāsi' 'ašar* read as if they were taken from

36. Keddie *An Islamic Response* 46.

37. *Tarāǧim* II 61.

38. See 12, 164.

39. cf. *Letters*, Zaidān to Emile, Nov. 12, 1908, 207.

S. Smiles' *Self Help*. The belief in this kind of social mobility certainly was strengthened by the fact that his own life was one of the best examples for the career of a self-made man.

The attempt to apply the laws of Darwinism to human society encounters the inherent difficulty of determining what exactly constitutes the basic unit that is fighting for its survival. Zaidān saw on different occasions either the individual or the whole society as the basic unit fighting against similar units for its own survival. However, he never saw this struggle taking place between the various classes of society. Any kind of socialist or communist concept envisioning an egalitarian society after a final class struggle contradicted what Zaidān believed to be natural, i.e. hierarchical order of human society, and provoked his sharpest criticism.[40]

With the exception of the concept of social mobility, Zaidān's application of Darwinism did not essentially contradict the mediaeval political and social thought in the way he made use of it. The implications were in each case almost the same for him. Society had to be hierarchically organized and would be controlled by the elite in the traditional understanding or the fittest in a Darwinistic terminology. Political power rested always with a restricted group, while in both cases religion was mainly of importance with regard to the masses.

A third approach to society, which Zaidān used increasingly in his later years, contradicted, however, clearly the above-mentioned ones. It originated from the assumption that modern society was based upon rationality and the insights obtained from sciences. In truly enlightened fashion Zaidān believed that education and the spreading of scientific knowledge amongst all members of society would guarantee the progress of society and the betterment of its members. In due time all members of society could be educated and improved. The condition for this was, of course, that any irrational, unscientific principle was refused as the guideline for the modern society. It is this enlightened attitude which caused Zaidān to consider Ǧamāl ad-Dīn al-Afġānī's proposition of a political Pan-Islam useless because it did not help the Muslim to adapt to modern civilization, but rather excluded him from it.[41] Zaidān's

---

40. IX 425 ff, XVI 276, XIX 195 ff.

41. XV 405-406.

opposition to any political Muslim movement, however, was not motivated by reason and logic alone but also by the emotionally unacceptable implication that a political community based on Islam — and Islam would have to be the religious basis in the Middle East — would carry with it the perpetuation *sine die* of Christian minority status in the Muslim world. Or perhaps one has to turn around the logical sequence of Zaidān's thought. An emphasis on the religious aspects in society would have automatically stamped Zaidān as a member of a less privileged religious minority. Therefore, he preferred a theoretical approach to society which gave religion only secondary importance as compared with the sciences and a general secular outlook which Zaidān could fully share.

The universality of education and knowledge, politically expressed in a constitutional system guaranteeing equal rights and political participation to all, contradicted directly Zaidān's earlier political concepts, which had emphasized the role of the ruler and the necessity for obedience of the common people. Nevertheless, we can observe that after the Young Turk Revolution, Zaidān spoke more and more in favour of a constitutional political system which implied for him a secular society based on modern sciences and universal education — not of religion.

One of his first discussions of constitutionalism appeared in connection with the Russo-Japanese War when he pointed to the progressiveness of the Japanese who had a constitutional government.[42] Later Zaidān considered it a positive result of this war that Russia adopted a constitutional government.[43] The Russo-Japanese War attracted the attention of the Middle Easterners not only because for the first time a non-European power defeated a European power, but also because the outcome of the war seemed to prove the superiority of a constitutional political system over absolute rule. It may well be that this event first drew Zaidān's attention to contemporary political thought.

In October 1906, the first full-length article about constitutional government appeared in "al-Hilāl" and referred especially to the Persian constitution granted two months earlier by the Šāh Muẓaffar ad-Dīn (1896-1906). It was not until the Young Turk Revolution that Zaidān took a lively interest in problems of government and its various forms.

42. XII 338.
43. XIV 8.

For the following six years until his death, Zaidān published many essays regarding questions of constitutional government. Zaidān supported the new government implicitly by showing the advantages of constitutional government in general. The advantages were obviously the greater participation of the people in the government and the equality of all, regardless of religion or nationality, before the law.

But even when discussing constitutional rule, Zaidān showed a strong inclination towards authority; absolute authority, which in the last analysis could not be harmonized with constitutional concepts and an enlightened belief in the effect of universal education. In his first article concerning constitutionalism in 1906 when he compared monarchy, aristocracy and democracy, he already claimed that monarchy was the original form of government — the most natural one — because it developed from the patriarchalism in the family.[44] But modern civilization especially as exemplified in English society, showed that constitutional government was superior. Looking at the map of the world and seeing where monarchies were concentrated, Zaidān assumed that the Easterners had perhaps a natural inclination towards monarchical rulership, a notion he quickly denied after the Young Turk Revolution.[45] At the same time, he insisted that a constitutional government headed by a king, whose position is hereditary within the family, was preferable to a republican government.[46] This proposition Zaidān might have put forward out of respect for the Ottoman dynasty (and the *Ḫidīw's* as well). It appears from later eassys that the argument is more profoundly based than on mere sympathy for the Ottomans. Zaidān discussed the difference between a republic and a constitutional monarchy. This difference was so important because for him the monarch bound by a constitution was not yet a mere figurehead without any political importance and influence. It seems that Zaidān invested him with powers similar to that of the American President, for example, who is controlled and guided by a constitution but on whom this very constitution confers decisive political power. Therefore, the question whether republicanism, *ǧumhūrīya*, is preferable to constitutional monarchy, *al-ḥukūma al-malakīya*

44. XV 18.
45. XVII 41.
46. XVII 321.

ad-dustūrīya, is of importance. Zaidān conceded that both forms are good because in each case a constitution and parliament control the action of the ruler, i.e. the president or the king. Nevertheless, he explained why he thought the constitutional monarchy preferable:

1. This form is closer to the natural form of rule — the patriarchalism in the family.
2. Republicanism worked only in small societies like Athens or Rome, but with the expansion of the society people preferred a monarch. Zaidān relied here solely upon the example of Rome.
3. The king is interested in his throne and country over a longer period of time, while the president is interested in the country only for the specific time that he is in office. He is interested in short range success without considering the possible long-range implications.
4. "The elections for the president of the republican government are a great burden which demand great expenditure. Dissent and corruption are involved in the competition between the parties for the nomination of that president, whom they believe to be in agreement with their desires, but their desires are not congruent with the welfare of the nation, *umma*. In the constitutional monarchy there is no need to spend this kind of money and no need for the nation to go through the suffering during this time of elections".[47]

If elections are such an unnecessary burden and a waste of money, and if monarchy is so much closer to the natural form of government, one is slightly at a loss to explain in which way the whole society is participating and why it should participate in the government. In fact, Zaidān never believed[48] that the whole society is participating in rulership:

> "The supporters of republicanism desire that every single individuals of the nation participate in legislation and in the election for the president. But this is a futile phantasy because the rule lies, in any case, in the hands of the elite, consisting of the politicians, the nobility or the wealthy people. These people just as in ancient Athens are today the masters of power and influence, and with their influence in newspapers and speeches direct the movement of

47. XIX 83.
48. XXI 94-95, where he spoke about the masses in Europe.

the elections among the masses. The wretched masses only imagine that they do what they want. The truth is they do what their elite wants them to do, and they elect who this elite desires to be president or deputy or whatever else. The elite consists of parties, each of which has its own goal. The individual considers it, or the association, but not the whole nation as the ultimate orientation".[49]

Three years earlier in an article about the history of political parties, Zaidān made the following two statements:

> "When modern civilization came to shine in the light of science, when schools were founded for the popularizing of teaching among the masses and the elite, and when the government exerted itself to awaken an interest for science in the people and almost forced them towards it, then the democratic principles reappeared; and this time they established themselves firmly and grew because they were based on true sciences. The masses attained a voice that was heard and an opinion that was of consequence. The reins of government returned to their hands...

Three pages later, however, he wrote:

> "We do not deny that even in the most civilized nations the people lean towards a party without knowing a thing about it, and they support an aim towards which they strive by example, dedication and imitation without understanding it. They do this supported by the opinions of men they trust whom they made their representative in their elections, and they feel that he is responsible to help them and guide them materially and spiritually. The representative, on the other hand, feels responsible for the welfare of those who made him their representative and for considering their feelings".[50]

Zaidān displayed here on the one hand a firm belief in biological laws: all men are born different, the strong will rule the weak, and the elite will, therefore, always rule the masses whatever the political system of government. Even under a democrate system the ruling elite will do as it pleases, and the common people will only have the illusion of participating in the government.

On the other hand, Zaidān saw a clear difference between earlier civilizations and modern civilization because of the changed role of

49. XIX 84.
50. XVI 145, 148.

the masses in the latter. For the first time a civilization was based on scientific knowledge, and with the increased spread of knowledge and education, more and more people would be able to participate in the government of the nation.

An attempt to solve the contradiction was the introduction of the time factor between innate inequality and the equalizing tendency of education, which is not really a solution to the problem but rather an avoidance of it because a decision whether the lower classes are mature enough at any particular point in their history to participate equally and fully in society does not have to be made, since more education can always be postulated, and the decision postponed into the distant future.

Zaidān demanded a long period of preparation, *isti'dād*, for every social or political change so as to adapt the people to new circumstances and demands. When comparing the French and the English constitutional development, he pointed out how many centuries it had taken in England to establish a stable constitutional government, while in France the abruptness of the change[51] resulted in much bloodshed which, however, failed to establish the new order firmly.[52] The preparation of the people had not been sufficient. This idea of preparation achieved great importance in Zaidān's thinking. A gradual evolutionary preparation was necessary for any change. A sudden change in the form of a revolution could not be of much use because it lacked a basis among the population. Preparation meant for Zaidān education, which implies not only the transmission of scientific knowledge but also the forming of the people into responsible modern citizens.

Zaidān refrained from any public political stand. Since for him preparation was the *conditio sine qua non* for political action towards the achievement of a constitution or of independence, the education demanded by Zaidān received itself a certain political connotation. Zaidān was a-political in the sense that he avoided direct participation in contemporary political life and transferred political issues to a cultural level of education and knowledge. The implication in this attitude was the

---

51. Zaidān used the term *inqilāb* for the French as well as for the English case. The term had not yet attained here the specific meaning of revolution but simply meant change.

52. XXI 526.

acceptance of present political circumstances and, for an undetermined point in the future, the expectation of political change and reform, thanks to the gradual preparation of the people. Possible pressure that might develop by a total submission to the present political situation, could find an outlet in the expectation for the future.

We never hear just how much preparation would be necessary or how long political activity should be restricted to education and the spread of knowledge, and whether all strata of society, including the masses, needed the same amount of preparation. Perhaps it is just this very vagueness which makes the idea of preparation a key concept for Zaidān's analysis of the political history of various modern nations. Thus, the lack of preparation of the population was a major cause in foiling 'Urābī's attempt to establish a constitutional government in Egypt.[53] Shortly after the Young Turk Revolution, Zaidān was, *post factum*, convinced that the new regime would be successful because a long time was spent in preparing the population before the takeover. Years later, after the attempted counter-revolution, interference of foreign powers and increasing centrifugal tendencies within the Ottoman Empire, Zaidān believed that the government of the Ottoman Empire should retain some absolute powers because the people were not yet familiar with the meaning of a constitution. The constitution itself was good, but it was given all of a sudden to the people when they were not prepared for it.[54]

Perhaps it is in the discussion of national independence that this concept of preparation played the most important role. In 1897 Zaidān reported about the risings in India which started in June of the same year in the Tochi Valley. His analysis of the reason for the failure of this revolt outlined already the basic argument Zaidān would use in all future discussions of the independence issue:

> "The Indians did not gain anything but trouble from this revolution because they have not yet reached that stage of civilization which would permit their independence. Not its rage and not its efforts towards independence will be of any use to the oppressed nation

53. XV 18.
54. XXI 526.

> if it has not attained a sufficient knowledge of science and administration in order to teach the common people their duties and rights and the meaning of independence and unity. When the nation has reached that point, it is easier for it to decide whether it is preferable to remain in the same situation or to risk the status quo by demanding independence. No importance can be given to the great numbers (of people), since the mind overcomes the body. But if it has not reached this stage, its situation is like that of a child not yet of age, who does not know what is good and what is bad for him. Obedience and submission are the first demands".[55]

Two years later Zaidān felt that the increasing demand for independence in Egypt necessitated a contribution of a more general nature to this discussion. He insisted that it was futile to turn to another nation for help. If a stronger nation had occupied a weaker one, the weaker nation, wanting to regain its independence should not ask a third nation to liberate it — such would only imply a change of masters, not the achievement of true independence. Without mentioning any names, Zaidān here obviously attacked Muṣṭafā Kāmil and all those who believed at that time — the *entente cordiale* between England and France had not yet been forged — that France would deliver Egypt from the hands of the British. In order to achieve true independence, Zaidān continued, one had to start from within:

> "We declare that today we are more in need of an intellectual, *adabī*, independence than of a political independence, which means we need an education towards the independence of thought."[56]

On the eve of the Young Turk Revolution, and after the granting of a constitution in Persia, Zaidān dedicated a great many articles in "al-Hilāl" to the issues of constitution and independence. Taking as an example the fight for independence of the American colonies, Zaidān again made his point that this war only was successful after the Americans were sufficiently prepared for it. To prove their preparedness, he described in detail the educational system and the number of colleges existing in the colonies before the war of independence.[57] However

55. VI 109.
56. VII 298.
57. XVI 5.

he added that Britain, too, matured considerably and that today she would not go to war over the issue of independence of one of her colonies if this colony had advanced to a level of education comparable to that of the British and if she was satisfied with regard to preferential trade conditions. Australia was for Zaidān the example of such maturity of the British.[58]

In the case of India the demand for independence failed because the Indians refused to accept the new culture and education and to learn from the British.

> "It is not enough that we imitate the civilized nations and demand independence. It is our first duty to imitate them in their quest for science because this is the basis of true civilization, the source of administration and politics, and the foundation of society."[59]

In another essay written in the same year, Zaidān addressed the Egyptians directly. He criticized the many discussions about independence, constitution and personal freedom, and the discussions about the means and methods by which to achieve these things. He suggested that it would be better to concentrate all efforts and energy upon education. The masses first had to understand what the meaning of "freedom" and "fatherland" was before genuine constitutional government could be introduced. The Persian constitution, for instance, rested on very weak foundations because only the elite participated in it. Once the general level of knowledge and education had been raised, it would become evident whether political independence was really necessary and, if so, whether it should be achieved by the force of arms or by other means.[60]

From the preceding discussion it becomes evident that over the years Zaidān advanced a variety of ideas and concepts concerning political theory. At least four different trends of thought can be identified:

a. The traditional concept of Muslim political theory which differentiated between the common people, *al-'āmma*, and the elite, *al-ḫāṣṣa*, postulating the obedience of the common people to the rule of the elite.

58. XVI 67.
59. *ibid.*
60. XVI 24.

b. The interpretation of social and political structure in terms of social Darwinism, by which natural differences would establish a hierarchy of the strong over the weak. The concept of the "survival of the fittest" permitted social mobility of the individual. The rule of the "fittest" had, however, in Zaidān's opinion to be acknowledged by the weaker members of society.

c. The complete rejection of any socialist or communist form for society because total equalizing and levelling would "contradict the natural laws of society."

d. The enlightened trust in rationality and the belief in the universality of education and knowledge. This would enable every member of society to participate in political rule through the constitutional channels of elections, representations and parliamentary control fo the government.

The contradictions created by these various concepts are obvious. Perhaps it is still possible to understand Zaidān's application of social Darwinism as an attempt to update the mediaeval political theory. In both cases political authority remained permanently vested in a small elite which could either by divine or natural law demand the obedience of the masses. In the same vein Zaidān's opposition to socialism and communism can be explained by his defence of stable social hierarchies with clearly defined and exclusive political authority. But the concept of a constitutional government giving equal rights to everybody and general participation in the political decision-making could not be brought into harmony with the above-mentioned view of permanent social hierarchies and exclusive political theory. Zaidān's feeble attempt to bridge the gap by the concept of "preparation" only begged the question. Its very vagueness avoided the problem rather than solving it.

Zaidān's inability to find a solution to the questions of the functions, extent of, and participation in, authority demands some explanation. L. Ware has made a valuable point by bringing the psychological dimension into the discussion of authority. There can be no denying the usefulness of the psychological approach for the better understanding of the acts and behaviour of a person. But there are some definite limitations to this method which are determined by the amount of relevant information available about the person. This factor becomes especially serious in the case of people who lived in the past. In the case of Zaidān we are fortunate to have an autobiography — a report biased by his own motivation for writing it — and a collection of letters written to his son. It is the kind of material that can yield a great amount of information for a psychological interpretation.

L. Ware writes: "In personal terms, this problem (i.e. authority) had been posed during Zaydān's childhood and had never been successfully resolved. The demands that Ḥabīb Zaydan made on Jurjī — and which Jurjī would make on Emile — concerning life choices did not produce a spirit of rebellion but increased sublimation of conflict, almost a denial of conflict with authority".[61] Without doubt Zaidān, the boy, had serious conflicts with his father. Even later when he was already living in Cairo his father tried to interfere with his professional ambitions and marriage plans.[62] At the same time, however, we learn from the memoirs — the sole source at our disposal — that Zaidān did defy his father when he went to study at the Syrian Protestant College. His father's reaction seems to have been one of resignation.[63] After having participated in the student strike against the faculty of the SPC, Zaidān preferred to leave the school rather than knuckle under the authority of the professors. Later he married the girl he was determined to marry and followed a professional career which was distasteful to his father. In other words we would maintain that Zaidān had had his clashes with authority and had fought them out. It remains doubtful, to say the very least, whether his childhood experience formed his later concepts of political authority.

What can be said, though, is that his total life experience, especially his professional success as a self-made man and his social ascendance to respected membership in the bourgeoisie — developments that for him occurred within the existing order — made him inclined to accept established hierarchies and authority.

Two other factors contributed in our opinion far more to the contradictions in Zaidān's political and social thought — the general intellectual climate in the Middle East of the time and the actual political events. The people in the Middle East were caught in the middle of a most

61. Ware 149.

62. *Letters,* Zaidān to his father, Cairo, August 28, 1887.

63. See.

profound transformation under the shadow of the dominating presence of Europe. It would not be sufficient to describe this transformation as a change from "old" to "new" or from "religious" to "secular" or Eastern to Western patterns of life. In short it was not a transition from one well defined situation into another. One's own past could perhaps still be perceived as one wholesome entity. But Europe did not offer a unified picture. Its own identity was torn by internal contradictions. The fragmentized image of Europe seemed to offer different and often contradicting answers. A Šiblī Šumayyil could turn from Darwinism to socialism, a Muṣṭafā Kāmil could promote Egyptian nationalism, a Nimr, Ṣarrūf or Zaidān could believe in the powers of rationality, knowledge and education, Luṭfī as-Sayyid could agree with Muḥammad 'Abduh on the need for internal reform, though they disagreed on the objects of the reform, or one could seek to develop Islamic political powers in order to resist European imperialism as Ǧamāl ad-Dīn al-Afġānī attempted to do. Under the overpowering presence of Europe, even the view of one's own past began to lose its homogenous character. One could conceive of the past in religious terms of a purified Islam or in national terms of a cultural identity or a geographical belonging; one could find in the past democratic and constitutional experiences of the early Caliphs or absolute rulership of later rulers; one could see examples of wordly activism or pious withdrawal from this world. The possibilities were numerous and their combinations almost unlimited.

Zaidān's thought, like that of many of his contemporaries reflected this diversity and *Zerrissenheit* in the often unsuccessful attempt of an eclectic synthesis. His eclecticism certainly had been enhanced by his own heterogeneous educational experience which had known only fragments of formal education — traditional as well as modern — and had consisted mainly of autodidactic efforts.

Finally, the political events of Zaidān's time made themselves felt in the development of his thought. There exists, for instance, an obvious correlation between the triumphs of constitutionalism in the non-European world — beginning with the Russo-Japanese War — and Zaidān's preoccupation with the subject of constitutionalism and the inherent questions of rationality and universality of education and knowledge.

Zaidān's unwavering support of the Young Turk regime, however, cannot solely be explained by his belief in the constitutional system, a belief which, as we saw, had never been totally convincing. In order to explain his adherence to the Young Turk cause, we have to look beyond his political theories and social thought into the problems of Zaidān's minority background, cultural identity and nationalism.

CULTURAL AND NATIONAL CONSCIOUSNESS *

Zaidān's concept of the internal structure of society had originally been guided by a mixture of traditional social thought and social Darwinism. A concept, that put great emphasis on the authority of the "most deserving" according to religious law or the "fittest" according to the law of nature. Later he had turned more to an enlightened concept in which all members of society could be equal because of universally accessible education, and in which all members of society could participate in authority. Yet this left unanswered the question as to what criteria identified individuals as members belonging to a specific group or society and by what means a group coherence could be created.

In Zaidān's opinion the formation of a group and the means by which it unified its members could change according to needs. Any acquired or inherited characteristic could be used as a means to create solidarity if it promised to be useful to the members of the group. Not only does each society, in the opinion of Zaidān, have a choice of means of solidarity in the course of time, but there exists the availability of various means of solidarity at the same time. The Egyptians, for instance, could belong to and promote an Arab cultural identity while political usefulness would create also a feeling of solidarity with the Ottoman Empire as a whole.

The relative value of the means of solidarity and identification, such as fatherland, kinship, religion and language and the relative value of any moral ethic system, respectively, is one of the most remarkable features in Zaidān's thinking. It is necessary to keep this in mind in order to understand his own attempts to forge an identity for his society.

---

* Some of the observations and ideas expressed in this chapter have been adapted from two earlier articles by the author "Language, History and Arab National Consciousness in the Thought of Jurji Zaidan", *IJMES* IV (1973) 3-22; "Approaches to History in the Work of Jurji Zaydan", *Asian and African Studies* IX (1973) 63-85.

He rejected all absolute values, assuming only the individual's insistence on the usefulness of the group to him. The meaning of this usefulness beyond the fulfilment of the basic existential needs again could change with human desires. This concept of the relativity of all values made him a far more radical modernist than, for instance, Muṣṭafā Kāmil who replaced the absolute values established by religion with the absolute value of the fatherland, or Šiblī Šumayyil who promoted a universal "socialist" patriotism as an absolute value, from which all other values would be derived. That Zaidān attributed only relative value to the various means of solidarity certainly had much to do with his own life experience. He had grown up in Lebanon but lived most of his life in Egypt. He belonged by religion to a minority. He lived in Egypt at a time when it was theoretically a part of the Ottoman Empire, but was for all practical purposes under British control, and when it had even started to develop demands for its own independence. Zaidān's education had been a mixture of traditional primary education and modern college education combined with a good deal of self-educational effort.

But the belief in the relativity of values does not mean that Zaidān was lacking a definite opinion as to which values could provide his contemporary society with the most useful, i.e. effective solidarity and coherence. For him the most important fundaments of group solidarity throughout history were kinship relations, common religious identification and national identity. The basis of kinship had become obsolete in Zaidān's opinion because it could not unify effectively groups larger than the tribal association.

Zaidān's approach to religion has been discussed in the preceding chapter. He did not underestimate the appeal it had had in the past as a sentiment for solidarity. But at the same time he de-emphasized its importance in the contemporary context. This approach had been determined by his own ambivalent position as a Christian living in a Muslim society. Clearly an emphasis of religious identity would have meant the emphasis of a Muslim identity and would have threatened the marginal position of the Christian Zaidān. Zaidān shared the awareness of this marginality with a large group of Syrian Christian Arabs. It is characteristic for their position that they should be among the earliest and most outspoken protagonists of an Arab national identity. But their secularism and search for a new identity was not only a reaction to the felt danger of Muslim domination. It was also an attempt to emancipate themselves from the social and intellectual narrowness of the life in their own Christian minorities.

With the expansion of European economy and the eventual economic domination of the Middle East by Europe, the first avenue that opened itself for such emancipation from the minority status had been a career in business. Many of the Syrian Christians, often protected and privileged by one or other of the European powers, availed themselves of this opportunity. But the security and status which material wealth and economic success could provide were in the best case precarious. A more profound attempt of emancipation aimed at the change of the very basis upon which the differentiation between the Christian minority and the Muslim majority rested. This implied not only the rejection of a Muslim identity but also the negation of the power that the Church wielded over the members of the Christian minorities. We find, therefore, the attacks of a Šiblī Šumayyil or a Faraḥ Anṭūn[1] as often directed against the Christian clergy as against the Muslim religious establishment.

From Zaidān's memoirs one obtains the impression that the membership in the Greek Orthodox Church never played a dominant role in the life of his family. Nevertheless, Zaidān's criticism of the spiritual and intellectual narrowness of the community is apparent when he speaks about the family priest or his first school years.[2] Later he refused to bend to the religious dogmatism of the Syrian Protestant College. Unlike other Syrian Christian writers Zaidān avoided any outright attack against the Greek Orthodox community or against its clergy, just as he had always been extremely cautious not to attack directly Islam and its institutions. But he was quite aware that his secularism and reliance on scientific truth had created for him enemies amongst the Muslims as well as the Christians. The insistence upon his secularism was not only a defence against Muslim religious encroachment, but also a sign that the

1. Faraḥ Anṭūn (1874-1922) born in Lebanon of Greek Orthodox religious background. He settled in 1897 in Egypt. He wrote several books dealing with secularism in society and the separation of religion from government; Dāġir II 147, Hourani 253 ff, Reid "*Syrian Christians*" 180-183.

2. See 136.

framework of the Christian religious identity had become meaningless for him. In his search for a new and more inclusive identity he became more and more involved in the prevailing tendency of his time to forge a new identity for society on a national basis. The most obvious criteria for a secular national identity were the sharing in a common history, language and territory.

It is perhaps best to introduce the analysis of Zaidān's ideas about national consciousness and identity with a discussion of the Arabic terms he used to describe a national entity or society in general. For contemporaries of Zaidān the attempt has been made to define the meanings that they attributed to certain terms.[3] A similar analysis of the usage of terms in Zaidān's works leads only to limited results. He used *umam* and *šuʿūb* alternately for describing the various people that became part of the Islamic Empire and spoke at the same time of one *al-umma al-islāmīya.*[4] *Umma* also might occasionally mean the people in the separate Arab territories such as Syria, Iraq and Egypt.[5] The term *umma* when used to describe the Arab or the Egyptian nation seems to have lost its traditional religious connotation and attained a national colouring, but then again Zaidān also used the term in connection with the Ottoman Empire and spoke of *al-umma al-ʿuṯmānīya*;[6] and the term is also used in the widest possible sense of "people". The Egyptian nation, *al-umma al-miṣrīya*, constitutes a national association, *ǧāmiʿa qaumīya*, an expression for which he sometimes substituted *ǧāmiʿa ǧinsīya.*[7] *Ahl al-waṭan*, *al-umma*, *aš-šaʿb*, *ǧāmiʿat al-muwāṭinīn* may all describe the inhabitants of Egypt, in addition to such expressions as *al-bilād al-miṣrīya* describing the Egyptian nation.[8] On the other hand, the term *umma* is used in connections as *al-umma al-islāmīya*, *al-umma al-miṣrīya*, *al-umma al-ʿarabīya* or *al-umma*

3. Cf. Wendell for the concept of *umma* in Luṭfī as-Sayyid's thought; also Zolondek for the term *aš-šaʿb*; Steppat 256 comes to negative results as far as Muṣṭafā Kāmil is concerned: "überall sonst verwendet er *umma*, *šaʿb* und dazu gelegentlich noch *qaum* also austauschbare Synonyma, die er abwechselnd als 'peuple' und 'nation' übersetzt".

4. *Taʾrīḫ at-tamaddun* III 51.

5. X 279.

6. VII 9.

7. XV 405.

8. VII 11.

al-'uṯmānīya designating a religious, territorial, ethno-cultural and political entity respectively.

The terms *waṭan* and *waṭanīya,* fatherland and patriotism, however, need a closer examination — *waṭan* designated originally only the dwelling place. With the penetration of European ideas and concepts into the Arabic language, *waṭan* was used to translate the concept of fatherland, a defined territory to which the individual was related in a way that determined his social, political and moral behaviour.[9] Zaidān used the term *waṭan* very often in the second, the modern, meaning. Thus, he spoke of the *Ḫidīw* Taufīq as

> loving the Egyptian fatherland (*waṭan*), intending to further the cause of its inhabitants, because he strengthened the patriotic (*waṭanī*) education which was unspoiled by any foreign spirit.[10]

Often Zaidān would speak of a patriotic education which is demanded in order to teach the youth dedication to the fatherland. Then again he gave to the term *waṭan* the traditional meaning when he, for example, discussed the solidarity that is generated among people who share a common territory:

> For instance, the inhabitants of Cairo are united by Cairo, but they unite with those of Alexandria against the non-Egyptians and with the people of the East against the people of the West.[11]

In each case he spoke of *al-'aṣabīya al-waṭanīya.* Here again we find an example of the relativity of values, this time the territorial solidarity which is an attitude defined only in relation to other factors and changing according to the varying of these factors.

Indeed Zaidān never delineated exactly the territory that constitute a particular *waṭan.* He mentioned the Egyptian and Syrian fatherlands. On several occasions he explained that usually each particular fatherland is defined by the language common to all its inhabitants, and he cited

9. It seems, however, that the term was first used in Turkish in a modern meaning. Handjieri translates *vatan* as 'patrie' cf. LEWIS 329. MARDIN 326 claims that the term *vatan* had already been established in its modern meaning in Turkish at the beginning of the nineteenth century.

10. V 42.

11. XV 13.

the European countries as an example.[12] But we never find him using the concept of an "Arab fatherland." If he spoke of the love for the fatherland, *ḥubb al-waṭan,* he would usually enumerate various Arab areas such as Iraq, Syria, Egypt and the Arab Peninsula. Asked what the meaning of the love for one's fatherland is, Zaidān answered that the fatherland is the place where one grows up. One longs for it even as a grown-up because one is most deeply impressed by one's surroundings as a child. The relation to one's fatherland is also determined by how much positive and negative experience one absorbed there. He continued:

> The reasons for the love of one's fatherland are habit and familiarity, and we do not think that the love is natural in the sense that man loves the country in which he was born even if he does not live there. If one was born in a city and then was taken somewhere else still as a little baby when one cannot yet comprehend one's visible surroundings, one does not long for it and does not love it and in reality this is not one's fatherland, because one does not live there.[13]

A later definition of *waṭan* indicates clearly the social and moral implications that the modern meaning of the term carries:

> The fatherland is the country in which people establish their interests in a collective fashion and establish mutual laws.[14]

On the whole Zaidān's concept of a territorial entity constituting a *waṭan* remained vague, and for him it was certainly not the most essential foundation on which to base a modern society.

This much was certain for him: Egypt and Syria belong to the East, *aš-šarq,* different and separated from the West, namely Europe.[15] The Mediterranean constitutes a dividing line rather than a unifying element as it did later, for instance, for Ṭāhā Ḥusain[16] who, being more assured

12. XV 292.

13. III 504.

14. XIII 17.

15. I 46; XXII 403.

16. Ṭāhā Ḥusain (1889-1974) born in Egypt studied 10 years at *Al-Azhar,* belonged to the group around Luṭfī as-Sayyid. 1915-1919 he studied in France. Upon his return to Egypt he became a teacher and administrator of educational institutions. He wrote a variety of novels, articles and scholarly studies, in which he promoted the idea of a westernized secular culture in a liberal society for Egypt which he wanted to reconstitute as a part of the Western World; HOURANI 324-240; CACHIA.

in his secular approach, claimed a common legacy of classical antiquity for all areas bordering the Mediterranean. What does *aš-šarq* comprise, and who are the *ahl aš-šarq*, the people of the East whom Zaidān mentioned so frequently? In his *at-Ta'rīḫ al-'āmm*, written in 1890, Zaidān had intended to set forth a history of the whole World and had started with the history of the East, namely Asia and Africa. However, the history of these two continents was narrated only insofar as its Biblical and Islamic parts were concerned.

In the magazine "al-Hilāl" Zaidān frequently included in the News Section reports about China and Japan, but this did not imply a particular interest in "the East", since he wrote with the same regularity about countries in other continents. However, when he established a section in the magazine about "the kings and the rulers of the East", he did appeal to a vague identification with the East.

> We are in the midst of an Eastern awakening participated in by the Easterners in India, Persia, Afghanistan and Turkistan, in addition to Iraq, Syria, Egypt, the Arab countries. The means for these countries to learn about each other, their different regions, people and creeds, is the Arabic language, and the Arabic press is the instrument for their contact with each other.[17]

He meant here all Arabic countries and those Muslim states in which Arabic plays a role as the religious language. It seems that he overestimated its role as the means of communication for the secular intelligentsia of these countries. Certainly Annam, which he includes in this series, is beyond the realm of either the Arabic language or the Muslim creed. With the beginning of the Russo-Japanese War this section in "al-Hilāl" was interrupted by several articles about Russia and Japan, and also Korea and Tibet. This, however, was done more because of the importance of current events in that area than a particular identification with it since, as Zaidān put it, "but the Chinese, Japanese and the rest of the people of the Far East are separated from the people of the Near East by great distance in religion and language".[18]

A similar concept of the East is found in his *Tarāǧim mašāhīr aš-šarq fī'l-qarn at-tāsi' 'ašar* published in 1907. The large majority of personalities

17. XI 98.
18. XII 537.

whose lives are described here are Arabs or at least Arabic speaking. Some Persian and Turkish personalities are included. All these people belong to that area which Zaidān sees united by either language or religion. The Emperor of Abyssinia, the Empress of China, the Prime Minister of Japan are people beyond the unifying realm of one language or religion. Nevertheless, Zaidān included them as "Easterners". One could argue here the case for a vague feeling of identity with all non-Westerners.

Three years later, in 1910, Zaidān proposed to subdivide world history into an Eastern and a Western portion, which would make possible an independent periodization of the history of each part. Thus, Zaidān suggested an "Eastern Antiquity" terminated with the period of Alexander the Great, an "Eastern Middle Ages" which was transformed into the "Modern Age of the East" with the rise of Islam.[19]

Zaidān achieved several things with this separation between Eastern and Western history:

a. A periodization which should be more adequate for the history of the East. It should be noted, however, that Zaidān was guilty of the same "culture-centric" misconception for which he reproached the conventional partition of history which spoke of World history and meant European history. He spoke of history of the East but meant only the Near East. Chinese and Japanese, not to mention sub-Sahara African, history had no place in his scheme.

b. An emphasis upon the greater age of Eastern history which starts before the corresponding period of Western history.

c. Islamic history gains a new role: in spite of the division of history into Eastern and Western, Zaidān did not give up the concept of their close interrelation and he emphasized in the same article again the mediating role of Islamic civilization between antiquity and modern Western civilization which was of vital importance for the shaping of the modern civilization. This interpretation meant the maintaining of Zaidān's original partition of history into antiquity, Islamic and modern Western civilization.

At the same time, however, the division into Eastern and Western history enabled Zaidān to depict Islamic civilization also as a modern

19. *Miṣr al-ʿuṯmānīya* 4 ff.

civilization which still has not come to its termination, an idea which could be sensed already when he said "history of Islam is tantamount to the modern history of the East."

As long as Zaidān had talked about only one World History with its three stages of antiquity, Islamic and modern civilization, the role of Islamic civilization in history had been an honourable and important but also a definitely terminated one. Confusion arises, however, when he now ascribed to Islamic civilization the two-fold role of being the mediating force between antiquity and modern Western civilization and also of constituting the modern period of a separate Eastern historical development maintaining its own vitality. Zaidān attempted a periodizing of Islamic history itself, which shows an ambiguity in the use of historical concepts perhaps reflecting Zaidān's undecidedness as to whether Islamic civilization had yet fulfilled its functions in the evolution of history. He divided the Islamic period, the modern phase of the Eastern history as follows:

a. Period of formation and growth, *takawwun, numū'*, starting with the appearance of the Prophet and including the fall of the Umayyads.
b. Period of maturity, *bulūġ*, which consists of the Abbasid period until the Turks gain control of the Empire in the middle of the 9th Century.
c. Period of ramification and diversification, *taša''ub, tafarru'*, which ends with the fall of Baghdad in 1258.
d. Period of the Islamic Middle Ages, *al-qurūn al-islāmīya al-wusṭā*.
e. The latest *Nahḍa*, which begins with the invasion of Egypt by Napoleon.

The first three terms — formation, growth, maturity — remind one strongly of the comparison with the biological development of the living organism. Taken together with the next two terms — ramification and diversification — they could describe one circle of evolutionary development. Then, however, Zaidān saw the need to protract the life of Islamic civilization in order to explain the *Nahḍa* as a part of it. He, therefore, had to add after the period of ramification and diversification, which actually should lead to new and different evolutionary developments, a "Middle Ages" connecting the original Islamic civilization with the modern development of the *Nahḍa*. The latter two categories have nothing to do with the concept of evolution but substitute for it a rather formalistic periodization of "old" (or "classic"), "middle" and "new" in a fashion similar to the division of the histories of the East and the West. He achieved with this rather incoherent and forced periodization a continuation of Islamic civilization in World history until this day.

The ambivalence about the continuity of Islamic civilization appears to grow if we read his comment about the *Nahḍa*: "It is borrowed, *muqtabasa*, from the modern Western civilization".[20] Perhaps it is, however, possible to reduce this confusion somewhat when we realize that with the term "Islamic civilization" Zaidān actually meant the history of the Arabs since the appearance of Islam. His whole division of the Islamic history suggests that he had Arab history in mind and not that of any other Islamic people let alone that of all the other "Eastern" people. When he for instance, terminated the period of highest maturity with the gaining of control by the Turks in the Abbasid period, he disregarded totally later contributions of the Turkish or Iranian people to the Islamic civilization. As far as the Arab period of Islamic civilization is concerned, it indeed came to an end in the middle of the 9th Century. For the Arabs then follow "Middle Ages", a term which for Zaidān always has a highly negative connotation of lacking civilization and culture. The *Nahḍa*, again, he allowed to begin with an event more meaningful for Egypt than for the whole Ottoman Empire. Zaidān's unclear use of the term "Islamic civilization" leads to confusion here. But if we understand that actually he spoke of Arab history, we realize that for him "Islamic civilization" in its conventional meaning had come to an end, while the Arabs were now beginning a new development within a new and different civilization.

The terms "East" and "Easterner" then do not imply a systematic incorporation of the whole non-Western world. Zaidān did not even mean always the whole Muslim world because Muslim states in India, East Africa and Persia remained rather marginal in his thinking. Most frequently "East" stands for all those areas that are inhabited by an Arabic-speaking population. The historical perspective of Zaidān also

20. XIX 157.

included all people who previously inhabited these areas, such as Jews, Phoenicians and ancient Egyptians.[21]

Zaidān must have remained closely attached emotionally to Syria (he rarely differentiated in his terminology between a particular Lebanon and an inclusive Syria). He spent many a summer in Lebanon where he met old friends and members of his family. Krachkovsky reports that Zaidān actually had tears in his eyes when he, Krachkovsky, addressed him in his own *Šāmī* dialect.[22] Zaidān wrote once, rather naively, that Syrian emigrants actually have a stronger longing for their home country than other emigrants, and he pondered occasionally about the greatness Syria could achieve if all her emigrants were able to return.[23]

In a time of more pronounced national attitudes in Egypt, the Syrian emigrant Zaidān felt somewhat defensive about his own relation to Syria. He explained that emigration has actually been one of the national characteristics of the Syrians ever since the time of the Phoenicians.[24] He meant in particular the Christian Syrian emigrants, whom he defended against accusations of lacking patriotism and national feelings. They are not given, he claimed, a real part in the Ottoman entity, *al-ǧāmi'a al-'uṯmānīya*. They do not fight in the Ottoman army and they do not speak the language; the Syrian fatherland, in its poverty, does not need them. They are forced to emigrate in order to make a living. He asserted that from the ethnic point of view the Syrians are not Arabs but a mixture of many different peoples. As far as their culture and language are concerned, however, they are fully Arab.[25] This identity they should try to preserve when emigrating to non-Arab countries. Zaidān, true to his own concept that values and solidarities were interchangeable and without any absolute value of their own, realized, however, that the North American culture had an overwhelming impact upon immigrants and that a Syrian identity could not persist in this *milieu*.[26]

---

21. XXII 403.
22. Krachkovsky, *Manuscrits Arabes* 19.
23. XIII 14.
24. I 275; XIII 14.
25. XVII 425.
26. XIII 13.

Zaidān continued that there is more to the national character of the Syrians than emigration and trade. Throughout history they played the role of the transmitter of knowledge and learning; they were the link between one culture and another.[27] Zaidān traced this role back to the Phoenicians, recognized it also in the activity of the translators of Greek philosophy and learning into Arabic at the time of the Abbasides, and believed that this role has not changed even in modern times. Clearly Zaidān identified his own work here with the historical function that he ascribed to the Syrians as a national characteristic. Zaidān put the blame for the backwardness of Syria, which existed in spite of the many positive qualities of the Syrians, upon the religious strife and dissent in the country first incited, as he believed, by the European interference and later cultivated by the regime of Abdülhamid in order to safeguard its own interests in the area. The result is that now the political order is "built upon religious divisions, and this is not in harmony with the spirit of this age".[28]

If emigration was a national characteristic of the Syrians, immigration was the distinguishing characteristic of the Egyptian society. In order to prove this theory Zaidān used examples from the Egyptian history starting from Pharaonic times: wave after wave of immigrants came to Egypt and it was always only a question of time until they were considered Egyptians.[29] One cannot help but notice how neatly Zaidān and the other Syrians living in Egypt combined both the national characteristics of the Syrians and the Egyptians thanks to this definition. In spite of this apparently flawless definition which more than justified the presence of Syrians in Egypt in national terms, Zaidān felt a certain uneasiness about his own position:

> In modern times there are some people who consider immigrants Egyptians if they belong to the state religion, but not Christians or Jews. This conclusion is strange and does not fit the principles of civilization, since it is clear that nationality, *waṭanīya*, and religion are two different things.[30]

---

27. XII 14; *Ta'rīḫ tamaddun* III 14.
28. XXI 273.
29. XIII 349; XVI 15.
30. XIII 351.

The notion that the Syrian immigrants (and most of them were Christians) were actually a detrimental force in the Egyptian nation had been made popular especially by Muṣṭafā Kāmil who coined for them the derogative term *duḫalā'*, intruders. The pro-British position taken by many Syrians who preferred a British occupation to the Ottoman regime was suspect to the Egyptian nationalist, Muṣṭafā Kāmil. Perhaps also his professional ambitions, which brought him into direct competition with the Syrian journalism in Egypt, made him antagonistic to the Syrians.[31]

Once Zaidān took the trouble to answer the accusations made against the "intruders" from Syria. He argued that (a) Egypt had always been a melting pot for various ethnic groups: (b) Syria and Egypt are really one country, *balad wāḥid,* since no natural boundaries such as mountains, deserts or seas separate them (!); (c) the Europeans consider them one nation calling them Arabs or Easterners; (d) economically politically and culturally they more often than not constituted one unit in the course of history and they were closely interrelated at all times. Zaidān strongly idealized here the relations between Egypt and Syria in order to create an image of unity. It says something about the general impact of European thinking in Zaidān's time that he would use as proof for the unity between the two countries also the argument that the Europeans tended to see them as one country. However forced the argument of unity and close co-operation between the two countries may be, it proved to Zaidān's own satisfaction that their welfare was closely connected and that, therefore, every Syrian was by necessity also interested in the welfare of Egypt.

Insisting upon the near unity between Syria and Egypt, Zaidān did not restrict himself to Islamic history in looking for proofs. Pharaonic expansionist politics, Phoenician trade relations, all helped his argument. More so than with Syria, Zaidān conceived of Egypt as a historical entity reaching back in its history far beyond the Islamic conquest. Speaking about learning and education, he observed that Egypt was the source of learning until the Roman conquest[32] and indeed the cradle of all civilization. The usual apologetic argument is that the Europeans

31. Steppat 358.

32. I 123.

learned everything from the Islamic World and that all knowledge was already existent in its original form in the Near East. Zaidān made use of the same argument, eliminating, however, its Islamic-religious connotation, yet adding historical weight to it by taking his example from the time of the Pharaohs, when "scholars from contemporary nations in Phoenicia, Greece and Rome came (to Egypt) to obtain knowledge".[33]

Zaidān was aware of the pre-Islamic history of Egypt and Syria. He recognized the historical continuity between the Islamic and pre-Islamic history of these countries, but he never used pre-Islamic history to argue that either possessed independent cultural and political identity. Having left Syria, his horizon had grown beyond a local identification with Syria, but being an immigrant in Egypt he could not identify himself with a specific Egyptian entity, as did many Egyptian contemporaries of his. Neither "Pharaonism" nor "Phoenicianism" could appeal to him. He searched for an identity that would include the two countries in one entity. It is with the Arab-Muslim conquest that the history of these countries becomes relevant to him. He explains,

> In view of the fact that Egypt's history after the Muslim conquest is of closer connection with its present state than its history before that, it is more profitable and more necessary to record it. This is what we call the modern history of Egypt.[34]

It is the Arab people whom he is interested in and whom he considers the historical entity with which he can most successfully identify. This entity includes both Syria and Egypt; if Zaidān mentioned other Arab areas only *en passant*, he did so mainly because either they were not confronted yet with modern civilization so intensely as Syria and Egypt or such confrontation had not yet led to an awareness of a general intellectual development beyond local boundaries. In Zaidān's consciousness the other countries remained, therefore, rather marginal. In theory they would all be included in his concept of the Arab entity. Occasionally he would enumerate some of them, usually adding Iraq and the Arab Peninsula to Egypt and Syria. Trying to define the Arabs of today he spoke of "the inhabitants, *sukkān*, of the Arab Peninsula, Iraq, Syria,

33. XV 131.

34. *Ta'rīḫ miṣr* 4.

Egypt, the Sudan and the Maghreb".[35] It remains remarkable that for Zaidān Egypt and, marginally, the Maghreb constitute definitely integral parts of the Arab entity and Arab identity, when even for the Pan-Arabists of one generation later it was by no means taken for granted that Egypt was part of the Arab nation.[36]

Yet the fatherland had no strong attraction, at least not in the narrow sense of Egypt and Syria, for the immigrant who could not claim an innate identity with the fatherland. The one force that could create a solidarity between Muslims and Christians, Syrians and Egyptians, was the Arabic language which as we will see was closely tied to a common Arab history. There is hardly an opportunity Zaidān missed to point out the importance of language as the most important criterion to define a society and the most decisive factor for a common identity.[37]

> The Arabs introduced Arabic in Iraq, Syria and Egypt with the result that all feel today as Arabs. It is the greatest mistake of the Turks not to have done this with their own language. It is, therefore, the greatest weakness of the Ottoman Empire today.[38]

That is to say that sharing a common language overrules all other forces of identification, be they ethnic, religious or of any other kind. He who speaks Arabic considers himself Arab. The Persians clung to their own language in spite of the Arab-Muslim conquest and regained, therefore, their own identity and nationality.[39] On the other hand, the national element would be weakened and eventually would perish if one's own language was not guarded and used. Therefore, it was so important for Zaidān to prove that Arabic was a living language, capable of being adapted to modern needs.[40]

Zaidān provided the proof for the vitality of the Arab language in a modern surrounding with the help of the theory of evolution. Changes and innovations in the Arab language were for him not symptoms of decadence and deviation from one obligatory classical standard of

---

35. *Al-ʿArab qabla 'l-islām* 38.
36. Haim 45-47.
37. XV 393; XXI 454.
38. XXI 451.
39. XV 396.
40. *Al-Luġa al-ʿarabīya kā'in ḥaii* 23; *Ta'rīḫ ādāb* II 6.

language, but evidence for a language that is alive and responds to the intellectual needs of a changing society. His repeated demand for the re-introduction of Arabic as a teaching language was not only based on the desire to spread education to those layers of society which did not master any other language but Arabic, but also on the fear that the Arabic language and literature if not used would decline and that with this the Arab national community, *al-ǧinsīya al-ʿarabīya*, would be weakened.[41] National identity and the existence of a living language became almost synonymous for Zaidān. Whatever other factors might influence the shaping of a nation — and he did admit a certain role of the fatherland — the language remained the most essential factor. In 1913 Zaidān travelled through Palestine and visited the Hebrew secondary school in Tel Aviv. He was deeply impressed by the fact that the teaching language was Hebrew and came to the conclusion that Zionism constituted a genuine national movement.[42]

This emphasis upon language as a different source of national consciousness Zaidān shares with many other Arab nationalists. Its importance resulted from the threefold function it could fulfil: (a) it constituted that aspect of Arab culture that was most easily secularized and adapted to the dynamism of change; (b) it was the instrument of education and, therefore, decisive for the emancipation and modernization of the Arab society; (c) it served as a symbol as well as the means for Arab solidarity and identity.

---

41. XV 405. Discussing the importance of foreign languages in contemporary Egypt, Zaidān declared: « ... and if the Egyptians want to disregard the national entity, *al-ǧāmiʿa al-qaumīya*, then there is no need for them to demand the revivification of Arabic. But people are keen for their national identity, *dānin al-ǧinsīya*, and desirous of their nationality, *ḥarīṣ al-qaumīya*, however weak and feeble its state of affairs. How much more the Arabs, whose history is so glorious and demands pride from everyone who is related to its founders. The disappearance of the language means indisputably the disappearance of the national identity, *al-ǧinsīya*. If the Egyptian nation, *al-umma al-miṣrīya*, would continue and [make], for instance, English its language, its consequences would be of no harm after many generations because they [the Egyptians] would have forgotten their old national identity and not know anything but the new one. But for the immediately following generations the loss of what they possessed would be unbearable: the symbol of their independence. Even if they do not see any path open towards their independence [now], they hope, nevertheless, that they will be granted what [those] nations, *umam*, were granted that guarded their language in spite of their subjection to other nations and succeeded in [attaining] their full or spiritual independence ».

42. XXII 603.

Participating in the general discussion concerning the feasability and desirability of converting various local Arabic dialects into literary language Zaidān had always demanded adherence to the literary Arabic because only the literary and not the spoken language was developed enough to cope with the problem of incorporating modern sciences and knowledge into it. Perhaps even more important for him was that only the literary Arabic constituted the link between all Arab regions and provided a shared cultural historical background. The language is the only factor that still unites "the Easterners", *ahl aš-šarq*,[43] "and by God, are you not going to keep it alive?" Upon the fate of the literary language depends the fate of the Arab national entity:

> Whosoever says that each of these nations, *umam*, should acquire its own language — the Syrians writing the dialect of Syria and the Egyptians the Egyptian dialect, ... — believes in the dissolution of the Arab world, *al-ʿālam al-ʿarabī*, and the dispersion of the union, *šaml*, of those who speak Arabic, since the exclusive use by each nation *umma*, of its dialect would sever what literary and religious relations there exist between it and the other nations... The literary language is the only guardian of the Arab union, *rābiṭa*, between those who speak this language. The merit for guarding it goes to the sublime Koran.[44]

Zaidān's remark that the Koran guarded the literary language and other remarks about *al-Azhar* having kept the Arabic language alive during the centuries of decay,[45] or even his observation that with the prevalence of local dialects the reading of the Koran would become difficult,[46] should not be understood as an attempt on the part of Zaidān to promote Islam by reviving the Arabic language. He explicitly defended himself against any such suggestion:

> Some might think that the purpose of the Arab union, *ǧāmiʿa*, is an Islamic union, parallel to what existed during the apex of Islamic civilization and that the aim of reviving the language is the strengthening of the Islamic element and the re-establishment of the

43. This is a good example of Zaidān's use of the term *ahl aš-šarq* meaning essentially the Arabs.

44. X 279.

45. XV 131.

46. I 77; X 279.

> Islamic Empire. Perhaps some believe this, relying upon the statements of some extremists in the political newspapers, but this is sheer fantasy. The Arabic union has become something different from what it used to be. It comprises today all those who speak Arabic, regardless of their different denominations and religions. The Christians, for instance, occupy themselves more with the spreading of this language than the Muslims. It was the Syrian Christians who translated the sciences into this language at the time of the Abbasids, and they are spreading it today to the farthest corner of the World by founding newspapers and schools, especially in the New World ... Consider how many Syrians work for its revival in Egypt and in Syria... Add to this the fact that the work for the revival of Arabic as a service for the Islamic element, *'unṣur*, would not agree with the purpose of our *Nahḍa* and not befit the spirit of the present civilization, which is the foundation of this *Nahḍa*. The goal at which we are aiming must be limited to the revival of the language disregarding denominations. If anything else is intended, we will regress to the darkness of the Middle Ages....[47]

Zaidān's Arabism is defined first and foremost by language, vaguely and without theoretical implications by territory, but never by religion. His concept of an Arab identity is totally secular. It seems surprising, therefore, and even contradictory that he should have dedicated so much of his efforts to write about the history of *Islamic* civilization and to writing novels dealing with *Islamic* history. The surprise seems twofold: first, that in spite of his dedicated secularism he should conceive of historical periods according to their religious circumstances and, secondly, that in spite of his Christian background, he should be interested in Muslim history in particular. W.C. Smith explains his phenomenon as the result of an identification between Arabism and Islam:

> An Arab need not be pious or spiritually concerned in order to be proud of Islam's historical achievements. Indeed he need not even be a Muslim. Christian Arabs have taken a share in that pride.

For the same reason he argues Arab Islam "is uninterested in and virtually unaware of Islamic greatness after the Arab downfall".[48]

---

47. XV 405-406.
48. Smith 99.

Indeed the most cursory glance at Zaidān's works tells us that his interest was restricted to only that period of Islamic civilization in which the Arabs constituted the main historical force. The "sharing in the pride" of Arab-Muslim history might have been a sufficient explanation for a precursor of Zaidān in this field, the Christian Lebanese Ǧamīl Mudawwar[49] and his work about the Abbasid court in Baghdad. For Zaidān more was involved. He, too, certainly was proud of this period of Arabic history, but it was his main purpose to make this history a common property of all Arabs, regardless of their religion, a shared experience which would strengthen the cohesion of the Arab entity, by assuring also the non-Muslim Arab a place and role in it. This he could achieve only by a secular approach to the history of this period. He was not interested in the religious history of Islam, its tenets and theology, but in the cultural achievements of the Arabs unified by a common national identity and culture which, admittedly, was based at that time on a religious experience. The Koran, for instance, is not important to Zaidān for its revelations but for its role in shaping and guarding the literary Arabic language. He used the term "Islamic civilization" and meant in reality a secular civilization created by the Arabs who at that time were guided by the religious experience of Islam.

Zaidān made every effort to approach the history of this period in a scientific, analytical way in which he was strongly influenced by the results of early European research and study of the Near East. He emphasized often that he was writing about the history of Islamic *civilization*, i.e. about the social structure, administrative hierarchy, economy and literary production. He was not interested in a history of Islam and certainly not in a paradigmatic religious history of Islam. Even though Zaidān was careful to avoid any outright attack on the tenets of the religion of Islam, it could not escape the intelligent Muslim reader that Zaidān's secular historical approach to the phenomenon of Islam was an assault on the foundations of this religion; he did not take the authority of the *ḥadīṯ* for granted, he did not ascribe to the Koran any ultimate position as far as its historical information was concerned, and he used

49. Ǧamīl Mudawwar (1862-1907) born in Lebanon, went later to Egypt where he worked as a historian, writer and journalist and worked eventually as an editor for al-Mu'ayyad; DĀǦIR III 1170; KÖCHER.

sources other than the traditional Muslim sources. Ultimately he regarded the development of religion, of any religion, as being embedded in and dependent upon the general evolution of man's history on earth. This secularism provoked sharp criticism and attacks from Muslim as well as Christian religious quarters.

Even the accusation of anti-Arab feelings had carried at Zaidān's own time very strong religious overtones. Today we find an occasional writer who will accuse Zaidān of lacking pro-Arab sentiments on more nationalistic ground. Ṭāhā Badr, for instance, tries to prove an anti-Arab attitude of Zaidān by claiming that all the heroes in Zaidān's novels are members of other nationalities or — and here the religious aspect of the criticism against Zaidān surges up again — members of denominations other than Sunni Islam.[50] It is true that Zaidān did not hesitate to be critical of the Arabs in his works. He was able to do this because his secular attitudes and belief in rationality did not permit him to substitute chauvinism for absolute religious values which had just been overcome; second, he did not feel himself so alienated and threatened in his own independent identity by the West as to seek refuge in preaching national supremacy. The success of his novels with other Muslim readers bears witness that he never did display an offensive Arab chauvinism. It would be utterly wrong to deduce from his criticisms of the Arabs that his attitudes were guided by anti-Arab sentiments. His life-long pre-occupation with Arab history and culture prove the opposite, and his frequent statements about the heights Arab culture attained during its history leave no doubt about his positive identification with the Arabs.

Originally he focused his interest upon the Islamic part of Arab history. He wanted to show that the Islamic experience in the beginning was an exclusive Arab experience uniting all the Arabs.[51] At the same time he repeatedly made the point that Christian and Muslim Arabs fought together against the Persians and Byzantines because the "Arabic element", *al-'unṣur al-'arabī*, was stronger than religion[52] and that in general the symbiosis between Christian and Muslim Arabs was, with a few regrettable exceptions, most harmonious. This leaves us with a

---

50. Badr 102.

51. *Ta'rīḫ at-tamaddun* II 37, IV 39.

52. *ibid.* IV 31.

contradiction: either it was religion that unified all the Arabs, or it was an "Arabic element" which apparently superseded religious cohesion. This confusion is augmented when Zaidān speaks of the Arabs as having been unified only in small kinship group during the *Ǧāhilīya*; then being united by religion and eventually inclining, with the establishment of the Arab Empire, towards a division according to geographical solidarities. This description is very much in accord with Zaidān's concept of the relativity and interchangeability of the values and means of cohesiveness in a society. But if the Arabs were once organized in small separate kinship groups, then unified (and that, too, with obvious exceptions) by religion, then divided again by geographical identity and still are recognizable in all of these stages as Arabs, the question arises as to what was the distinguishing "Arab element" that identified them throughout all the historical periods as Arabs. The answer is clear for Zaidān: the factor that creates a common identity and cohesiveness beyond these particular solidarities is the language. Does this imply, then, that Zaidān did construe after all an absolute value that could serve as an object of secularized belief and would limit the concept of the relativity of all values? Zaidān certainly claimed that language in general is the strongest factor of cohesion for any society. This, however, does not imply that any particular language has a special value. Languages can be more or less developed, and Zaidān did not stop repeating that Arabic is one of the most developed languages, but they all may under certain circumstances disappear without constituting and irreplaceable loss. He could even imagine the disappearance of Arabic and its replacement by Turkish which would strengthen the Ottoman Empire, or by English which would be, in his opinion, of no harm for later generations, except, of course, the loss of their Arabic cultural identity.[53]

In practice, however, the Arabic language was of greatest importance to Zaidān because Christian and Muslim Arabs shared it in common and both could benefit from or participate in the creation of its literary products. It is with this motivation that Zaidān wrote his *Ta'rīḫ ādāb al-luġa al-ʿarabīya*, and it is for this reason that Zaidān was particularly interested in the secular, cultural and civilizing aspects of Arab history

53. cf. footnote 41.

during its manifestation in Islam because these aspects could easily be shared by all Arabs, regardless of their religion.

If, however, one takes language as the main factor for social cohesion and national identity, there seems to be no inherent reason why one should restrict one's interest exclusively to the history of the Arabs after the appearance of Islam. Indeed we find that Zaidān's interest shifted slowly to the pre-Islamic history of the Arabs. It is significant that after having dealt with that part of Islamic civilization which is characterized by the predominance of the Arabs, he concentrated his research not upon the other periods of Islamic history but upon (a) literary and scholarly products in the Arabic language, and (b) the history of the Arabs before Islam. Both subjects were suitable to prove the cultural-historical unity of the Arab people beyond the boundaries of religion.

It seems that initially Zaidān did not have a very high opinion of pre-Islamic Arabic civilization.[54] But already in 1902 we read that even though the climate did not permit a development of civilization in the Arab Peninsula, the Arabs were "prepared" for culture and higher civilization. Four years later he wrote a lengthy article criticizing severely W. Robertson Smith's *Kinship and Marriage in Early Arabia* in which the author attempted to prove the existence of totemism in pre-Islamic Arab society. Disregarding here the merits of Smith's theory, it seems that Zaidān's main irritation with such a theory was that in his eyes totemism was a phenomen connected only with extremely primitive societies such as the Australian aborigines and the Indians of North America. It is the implication of the primitiveness of the Arab society which motivated his attempt to disprove Smith's theory:

> One should not close one's eyes to the fact that it is incorrect to compare the Arabs with respect to their conditions and relations with those primitive people who believe in totemism such as the Indians [sic] of Australia and North America and the Negroes in Africa, because the Arabs belong to the most advanced peoples as far as their intelligence and their spirit are concerned. They are the bearers of an ancient civilization similar to the civilization of the most developed ancient people... Some scholars who did research on the ancient sites in Yemen and the Hadramaut claim that the

54. I 310; VII 591.

> ancient Arab civilization was the source of the ancient Egyptian civilization, i.e. that the Pharaohs took their civilization from the Yemen. Whatever the degree of truth in this claim may be, it proves that the Arabs were steeped in civilization for their language, its syntax and idioms, bears witness to the development of the intelligence of its speakers from earliest historical time and even before that. Would it be reasonable to expect that they would take plants and animals for their forefathers as do the oldest primitive people today?[55]

Two years later when Zaidān published *al-'Arab qabla 'l-islām*, he was even more self-assured about the age and range of the Arab civilization. He emphasized strongly the history of the South Arabic civilization in Yemen and dealt in great detail with it. But he went far beyond that when he tried to prove that Hammurabi and the Babylonians were Arabs. The proof, Zaidān believed, was to be found in a similarity of structure in the language and in etymological connections with the Arabic of today. Making allowances for differences that developed during twenty-four centuries, Zaidān nevertheless believed that the Babylonians were not just a Semitic nation but that they were the "Arabs of their time".[56] On a similarly shaky basis he identified the Hyksos in Egypt as Arabs.[57] The meaning he attributed to the establishment of such historical continuity became evident when he commented on his claim that Hammurabi was an Arab:

> It is obvious what honour, *faḫr*, the establishment of this fact would mean for the Arabs because if it is correct, the Arabs were the first of all people to have established laws and enacted an order and promoted the affairs of society.[58]

Zaidān created an Arabic past which could give a common identity to the Arab people of his day. This past was characterized by a common language, culture(s) and history. It transcended the Islamic experience by being extended not only to the time which is usually called the *Ǧahilīya* or pre-Islamic period, but also to Babylonian and ancient Egyptian

55. XIV 400-401; XIX 227.

56. *al-'Arab qabla 'l-islām* 64.

57. On another occasion he even claims the Book of Job as a piece of Arabic literature; XIX 227.

58. V 527; *Ta'rīḫ ādāb* IV 14-15.

history. By incorporating the Babylonians and the Hyksos into an Arab identity, Zaidān created a national history, the aim of which was to show that the Arabs were the first to build a civilization and that in fact they built several civilizations, implying that the Islamic civilization is not the only, indeed not even necessarily the best, manifestation of Arab civilizing powers and that the Arabs in modern times are again capable of building a civilization, different from the last one they constructed.

To our knowledge Zaidān was the first to project a national identity of all Arabs into the distant past — somewhat comparable to the attempts of Pharaonism and Phoenicianism with regard to an Egyptian and Lebanese identity respectively.

After having ascertained the identity of the Arabs throughout history and their capability to develop various civilizations to high cultural levels, Zaidān could admit without hesitation that the modern civilization differed profoundly from Islamic civilization and that the Arab *Nahḍa* had been influenced and stimulated by the modern European civilization. The historically proven identity of the Arabs was not threatened by a changing content of civilization. Zaidān's commitment to an Arab national identity was deep. But his own position was a more complex one. His own identification with the Arab nation was not quite as assured as one might believe. An indication for this remaining ambiguity is his enthusiastic support of the Young Turks and their regime after the revolution of 1908. This turn seems surprising in the light of Zaidān's continuing scholarly and literary preoccupation with the Arab cultural and national identity. Indeed it was only after the Young Turk Revolution that he wrote his major work about Arab language and culture, the four volumes of *Ta'rīḫ al-luġa al-'arabīya.* Yet his positive interest in the Revolution is undeniable. What great importance Zaidān attributed to the event can be easily seen from the sheer amount of articles in "al-Hilāl" supporting the Young Turks in particular and the constitutional system in general. Zaidān deemed it even necessary to interrupt his continuous series of novels about Islamic history in order to write a novel about the Young Turkish Revolution.

Even now, Zaidān did not overcome his personal shyness and his social inhibitions as a Christian Syrian in Muslim Egypt and refused to participate actively in politics. He declined the proposition of friends to run as a candidate in the elections for the new Ottoman Constituent Assembly in 1908 and remained also otherwise withdrawn from public political life.

A marked change occurred, though, in his attitude as a writer. Until 1908 he had made it the policy of "al-Hilāl" to stay aloof from any explicit participation in politics. But after the Young Turks ascendancy to power, he became a politically *engagé* who staunchly supported the cause of the Young Turks. From Zaidān's articles the following picture of his position towards the Ottoman Empire under Young Turkish rule emerges.[59]

The tyrannical rule of Abdülhamid had forced the various nations of the Ottoman Empire to seek independence. This played into the hands of the European who, under the pretext of demanding constitutional rights for the subjects of the Sultan, enlarged their own sphere of influence in the Ottoman Empire. Once a constitution was established, this pretext for European designs was eliminated. Those nations that had earlier demanded their independence, in order to free themselves from despotic rule, could and would now remain part of the Ottoman Empire and participate in its government economy and military, thanks to the constitutional rule. Zaidān believed that only political mismanagement was responsible for driving the Balkan nations, for instance, towards political independence, a trend that could be reversed with the introduction of constitutional rule in the Empire. In the same manner he tried to explain all mistrust and tension between the Arabs and the Turks as the result of the activities of the Abdülhamidian regime. Zaidān dismissed the claim that the Arabs wanted to return the Caliphate to themselves as an "old hoax", *uḏḥūka qadīma*, invented by the Abdülhamidian secret police in order to spread discord between the Turks and Arabs.[60] In his effort to create harmonious relations between the Arabs and the Turks, the two main elements of the Ottoman Empire, he seemed to be prepared to make

59. See, for instance: *al-Inqilāb as-siyāsī al-'uṯmānī*, XVII 13 ff; *al-'Arab wa 'l-turk*, XVII 408 ff; *al-Ustāna al-'ulyā* XVIII 131 ff; *al-Mas'ala aš-šarqīya* XX 105 ff. Mention should also be made of Zaidān's historical novel *al-Inqilāb al-'uṯmānī*, which he uses as a vehicle to vent the same ideas; cf. in particular the "letter" of Midḥat *Pāšā* addressed to the following generation of revolutionaries, *ibid.* 248-253.

60. XVIII 156.

light of any serious differences in aspirations as inventions of the former regime.

The Young Turk Revolution had been successful because it was based, as Zaidān believed in the beginning, on a wider participation of the masses. Yet the counter-revolution in 1909 showed that the new regime was still weak and relied only on the educated and the army. But there could be no doubt for Zaidān that constitutional rule was the only possible basis upon which the Ottoman Empire could continue to exist. In his concern for the safeguarding of the constitution against the reactionaries and its misuse by the as yet uneducated masses, he went so far as to demand the application of martial law and the temporary establishment of an extra-constitutional regime until society was prepared for constitutional rule.[61] The irony of this demand escaped him in his urgent desire to see the unity of the Ottoman Empire preserved.

Zaidān assumed that the Young Turks were most keenly interested in the preservation of the Empire and that they believed, as Zaidān believed, that constitutional rule was the only way to achieve this goal. He was, therefore, not worried by the fact that the Turkish element continued to dominate all government agencies and all official positions in spite of the fact that constitutional rule should actually give more room to the participation of the other religious and national elements of the Ottoman Empire. He denied that there existed any international policy of the Committee of Union and Progress to "Turkify" the political and administrative organization of the Empire. He went to great lengths to justify the rule of the Young Turks and their dominance over the other elements in the Ottoman Empire. Zaidān was in particular concerned with the relation between Arabs and Turks. He made every attempt to discourage the Arabs from demanding more political rights. Zaidān opposed the Decentralization Party and any Arab attempt to form independent organizations.

It is interesting to compare the development of positions that Zaidān and Rašīd Riḍā took respectively towards the Ottoman Empire. Rašīd Riḍā had conceived of a certain superiority of the Arabs over the Turks in terms of religion, but he felt nevertheless a strong loyalty towards the

61. XVII 408; XVIII 131.

Caliph, even though the latter was a Turk. After the Young Turk's secularism became more and more evident Riḍā felt fewer ties binding him to the Empire. He helped to found the Decentralization Party in Cairo.[62]

Zaidān, on the other hand, had never felt a strong loyalty towards the Abdülhamidian regime, but when the Young Turks gained control and introduced a secular constitution, he became one of the staunchest supporters of the idea of an Ottoman union; so much so that Rašīd Riḍā observed about him bitingly that he granted the Turks rights that he refused to the Arabs.[63] The reaction among at least part of Zaidān's readers must have been negative. He was accused of helping the "Turks and the despots" and of betraying his own kin.[64] Zaidān carried on with his support for the centralistic rule even after the short outburst of brotherly feelings between Turks and Arabs had withered away with the increasing realization that the Turks were not willing to share in the rule of the Empire. In the summer of 1909 Zaidān visited Istanbul and reported about his journey later in "al-Hilāl".[65] He obviously had many personal talks with Young Turks and more than ever was willing to defend their political programme.

The intensity of Zaidān's political support for the Young Turks seems somewhat surprising and contradicts his professed concern and interest for things Arabic. The thought might occur whether he did not receive some kind of financial reward from the Young Turks for lending them political support in his magazine. We have no evidence that would point in this direction. This in itself is, of course, no proof since our general knowledge about Zaidān's financial situation is almost nil. Yet the notion of material benefits for adopting a favourable position towards the Young Turks must be discarded when one reads Zaidān's personal letters to his son, which were written after the occurrence of the Young Turk Revolution. He suggested there to his son to learn Turkish — as he himself was doing at the time — since "it is the language of

62. Haim 25.

63. Al-Manār IV (1914) 636.

64. *Letters*, anonymous to Zaidān, no date, no place.

65. XVIII 131 ff.

the government and it will become of great importance for all subjects".[66] He emphasized that Emile was foremost an Ottoman: "You are an Ottoman by nature, *bi-'ṭ-ṭab'*, because your parents are Ottomans and because all Egyptians are Ottomans. Even if not all Ottomans are Egyptians, you are also a Syrian Ottoman".[67] It is unlikely that Zaidān would have displayed in his private letters to Emile such pro-Ottoman loyalty, if the latter had not sprung from his own conviction.

Why, then, did Zaidān demand a political loyalty to the constitutional government of the Ottoman Empire when, at the same time, he insisted on an Arab historical and cultural identity? With the knowledge of hindsight, we can say that these two concepts were bound to clash with each other. But even Zaidān, when scolding his compatriots for anti-Ottoman aspirations, must have already been aware of the possible conflict between the two trends. That he, nevertheless, tried to combine them shows the complexity of his own position.

Zaidān's life's work had been dedicated to establishing the achievements of the Arabs throughout history, which he himself had extended far beyond the Islamic period. He never ceased to emphasize their cultural and historical identity. Yet, he still questioned the ability of the Arabs of his day to rule themselves. He doubted their "preparedness" for political independence. He had denied that the time had come to demand Egyptian national independence. For Syria he saw the advent even of "administrative independence" a necessity only "at the time suitable for it, i.e. after the Ottoman people have progressed and have learned what their rights and duties are".[68] Once he even went so far as to participate actively in the collection of signatures protesting against the statements of a certain Syrian by the name of Rašīd Muṭrān who had demanded political independence for Syria.[69]

Behind this denial of political maturity to the Arabs linger, we believe, his own feelings of marginality as a Christian Arab and his doubts whether an independent Arab state with a large Muslim majority

66. *Letters*, Zaidān to Emile, Cairo, Nov. 3, 1908. One should take note though that at the same time Zaidān took great pains in his letters to correct Emile's Arabic.

67. *Letters*, Zaidān to Emile, Cairo, Nov. 10 1908.

68. *Letters*, Zaidān to Emile, Cairo, Jan. 7, 1909.

69. XV 131, see 209 n. 5.

would be secular enough to guarantee to its minority members equal rights and status.

These doubts, however, did not lead Zaidān to consider it a desirable solution for the Christian minorities to hope for the collapse of the Ottoman Empire and to seek outright European protection. Many of his Syrian contemporaries wished for exactly such a development. In the highly readable memoirs of the Protestant Syrian Edward Atiyah one finds the following comment on the war of Italy against the Ottoman Empire over Tripoli and Cyrenaica in 1911/12: "The sympathies of the Christian Syrians were entirely on the Italian side. I was then just old enough to take notice of such an event, and from what I heard came to take a keen interest in it. Our detested sovereign Turkey was at war with a Christian power and, naturally, I wanted the Christian power to win. I would sit and listen to the war news being discussed in privacy (for no one dared to discuss in public) by my grandfather and his friends, and exult over the defeats of the Turks".[70] Zaidān's feelings at the time were of quite a different kind. In a letter to Emile he described the impression the war made upon him and the family: "If you could only see how your brother Šukrī is a loyal supporter of the Ottoman cause... If he reads any news of Ottoman victories he will sing for joy. He begins to praise the courage of the Arabs and to proclaim that the Europeans, *al-ifranǧ*, despise the Arabs, but that they should come and see the Arabs or read about their history and contributions to civilization etc. Frequently meetings are organized in school to discuss which side is victorious: The Arabs or the Italians. I am truly happy about his support of the Ottomans. This is what his patriotic duties demand. I wish to God that the Ottoman government emerges triumphant from this war..."[71] On the occasion of the outbreak of World War One Atiyah writes: "For us Syrian Christians, the victory of England and her allies would realize a dream we had dreamt for many long years, the dream of a Syria free from the Turkish yoke and from the fear of the Muslims and placed directly under the protection of a European power".[72]

70. Atiyah 19.

71. *Letters*, Zaidān to Emile, Cairo, Nov. 11 1911. Without wanting to over-interpret the source, it seems to us that a certain difference of identity can be observed: the father speaks about the Ottomans, the son praises the Arabs.

72. Atiyah 40.

Zaidān had his own hesitations about the Muslims' willingness to accept their Christian compatriots as equals. But he deplored the distrust between the two sides and wanted to overcome this situation. This he thought was possible within the framework of the Ottoman state. He denounced Ottoman Christians who had put their hope in the protection by the European powers and who did not believe that the Muslims "have torn out of their hearts the hatred against them..."[73] The direct protection of the Christian minorities by European powers would only have deepened the differences between the Christian and Muslim Arabs; it would have eternalized and strengthened the traditional religious forces in the life of the minorities and prevented the emancipation of their members towards a new and more inclusive secular identification with the Arab nation. Zaidān certainly was not anti-Western and had often said that the East had to learn and accept the features of modern civilization from the West. But he saw that direct political interference by the Europeans would only further the traditional forces in the Middle East. The Ottoman state seemed to be the only force able to resist such direct political interference.

Yet, Zaidān resented the Abdülhamidian regime, the unenlightened despotism of which he blamed for the backwardness and disintegration of the Ottoman Empire. The constitutional revolution of the Young Turks promised, in Zaidān's opinion, a viable way out of the dilemma: the constitution would guarantee justice and equal rights to all people of the Empire. This would eliminate their dissatisfaction with the central government and their leaning towards the various European powers. Through the constitution the unity of the Empire would be preserved. Zaidān was foremost concerned with this unity, because he foresaw that the collapse of the Empire would not bring about the political independence of the Arab people — as many of his Muslim Arab contemporaries assumed — but the intensification of European control over the area.[74] The secular character of the constitution would also give protection and rights to the members of the minority religions. The Muslim Arabs would not be able to dominate the Christian Arabs, because all would be subject to the rule of the central government.

73. I 123.

74. XIII 131.

Neither, of course, would the Christian Arabs be able to obtain a position of control through European support. The constitutional government of the unified Ottoman Empire would be able to prevent such outside interference.

In the light of all these considerations Zaidān's strong support for the Young Turks becomes more understandable. But at the same time we feel that it demonstrates some serious shortcomings in Zaidān's own perception and analysis of the situation. One weakness is a certain *naïveté* in his expectations from the powers of the constitutional system and the immediacy of its efficacy. He assumed, that once a constitutional government had been proclaimed, every individual subject and national or religious grouping within the Empire would accept the constitutional principle and discard its own political ambitions. But perhaps this *naïveté* was quite a forgivable weakness. It was the hope and enlightened belief, which was shared by many contemporaries and which was not yet seriously questioned by actual experience.

More serious seems to us the fact that, in spite of his own work and lifelong preoccupation, Zaidān apparently had not yet grasped the full force of nationalism. It surprises us to read that the centrifugal developments on the Balkan were only the result of Abdülhamidian misgovernment exploited by European power interests; a development that could, Zaidān believed, be reverted by a just, i.e. constitutional rule. Certainly, misgovernment had been abundant and without doubt did various European powers exploit the situation to enhance their own position on the Balkan. But did Zaidān not realize that the Balkan nations had also become conscious of their own language, their own cultural identity in the past — issues that were of such utter importance for him with regard to the Arabs? Did he believe that the insistence of these nations to safeguard their identity was exclusively a Machiavellian device of European power politics?

The question must be repeated with even greater emphasis when we look at Zaidān's relation to his own nation. His preoccupation with Arab history and culture and his largely successful attempt to establish an Arab cultural identity in the past, which included Arabs of different religious and geographic regions, is beyond doubt. And yet, Zaidān's labour to establish the existence throughout history of an Arab entity defined by a common language and culture never lead him to the formulation of a political programme for this nation. We can understand from Zaidān's own psychological structure and from his socio-political position why he never became himself active in politics. This certainly goes a long way to explain also his lack of interest in the political aspects of nationalism. But it remains remarkable that in all his writings he did not even theoretically came to terms with the political implications of nationalism.

It seems not possible to deny a certain lack of creative intellectual imagination or at least consistency of thinking on the part of Zaidān, which would have enabled him to envision a political future for the Arabs as an independent nation.

This absence of any political nationalism in Zaidān is probably the reason why later generations of Arab nationalists easily overlooked the actual merits Zaidān had for Arab nationalism. He had succeeded in his work to establish a secular Arab identity in the past. Through his novels, magazine and even his more scholarly works, he had made a large part of his contemporaries aware of this identity, which they, too, could share. With that Zaidān had contributed considerably to establishing the intellectual and emotional basis for all later political Arab nationalism.

CONCLUSIONS

Zaidān was a self-made man in two meanings of the word: socially he had risen from lower class origin to a well-established bourgeoisie; intellectually he had attained most of his knowledge and education by his own reading and effort without much systematic guidance. He not only fitted the description of a self-made man, but he knew that he was one ever since he had read Ṣarrūf's translation of *Self-Help*. The mid-century liberalism and an anticipation of social Darwinism which find their expression in this book made an everlasting impression on Zaidān. This is not to say that his intellectual development can be reduced to and exclusively explained by an indebtedness to European liberalism and social Darwinism. In an electic manner typical of his period and circumstances, his thinking was influenced and formed by fragments from various systems of thought. Zaidān shared fully the intellectual confusion and vagueness of his contemporaries. We saw, for instance, how sometimes concepts of mediaeval Muslim philosophy, of 18th century enlightenment and, again, of social Darwinism prevailed in his approach to politics and religion in society.

Two concepts clash basically in his thought, and their conflict is never resolved. In his demand for the spread of education, its improvement and modernization, in his insistence on abstaining from all political action until a sufficiently high level of learning and knowledge had been achieved, and his belief that the foreign ruler would relinquish voluntarily his control over the nation once this nation had matured in character and education, Zaidān showed great reliance upon the powers of the rationality of the human mind when supplied with adequate learning and knowledge. Rationality, learning and knowledge are universal qualities and not inherently restricted to any class or section of society. Zaidān, therefore, at least in theory made the whole society the object of his educational efforts. This egalitarian notion was counterbalanced in his social and political thought by a strong inclination towards elitist concepts often couched in Darwinism terminology, yet as often seemingly based on mediaeval philosophical thought.

It was Zaidān's conviction that the Arab *Nahḍa* was inspired by Western civilization and that if the *Nahḍa* was to be successful it was imperative to familiarize the Arab with European civilization and to educate him towards participation in it. "Al-Hilāl" bears witness to his indefatigable efforts to introduce the Arab readers to every aspect of modern civilization. It is perhaps his greatest merit — a merit he shares with the editors of "al-Muqtaṭaf", Fāris Nimr and Ya'qūb Ṣarrūf — to have popularized knowledge about the West and about the learning and scientific achievements that were the product of this modern civilization. "Al-Hilāl" constituted an almost encyclopaedic source of information about Western civilization. From constitutionalism to street cars and the discoveries of Pasteur, everything was significant enough to be reported about and explained to the reader.

Zaidān's conviction about the importance of Western civilization should not lead us to put him into the cliché category of the "Eastern Christian who identifies totally with Europe". Quite to the contrary, he felt a strong identity as a non-European in general and an Arab in particular. As much as he deemed necessary the adoption of modern Western civilization, so he sincerely believed an Arab cultural entity could be and should be the mould into which this civilization was to be cast.

If Zaidān had made it his task to introduce the reader to modern civilization, he thought it at least as important to demonstrate to him that Arab society was a viable cultural entity. Zaidān made use of two approaches in order to provide the proof: he investigated the history of the Arabs in order to show that in the past they had been able to build great civilizations. Initially, he followed the traditional Muslim view of history, even though his analysis was different, locating the height of Arab history in the early stages of Islam and disregarding to a large degree the history of the Arabs before Islam. Zaidān's perspective widened as his research progressed. He came to conceive not only of the Arabs of the *Ǧāhilīya* as carriers of culture and civilization, but incorporated the history of the Babylonians and the Hyksos as part of Arab history, thus creating an Arab history that consisted of a sequence of civilizations. Zaidān did more than create an awareness of the Arab past and imbue in the reader the pride of a glorious history; he was not even interested in relating solely the glory of the past. Zaidān intended to describe the dynamic movement in Arab history to give his readers the confidence that a new dynamic upsurge was possible.

The second approach he used to prove the viability of an Arab cultural entity was the linguistic one. We saw that language played an extremely important role in Zaidān's thinking. Its importance resulted from the threefold function it could fulfil: (a) it constituted that aspect of Arab culture that was most easily secularized and adapted to the dynamism of change: (b) it was the instrument of education and therefore decisive for the modernization of Arab society; (c) it served as a symbol, as well as a means, to establish Arab solidarity and identity.

Zaidān conceived of his own role as that of the educator of society towards a modern way of life and thought. In his opinion effective change could only be achieved in a gradual process through education and excluded any radical revolutionary notion.

Zaidān was a man of the pen. Hardworking, he spent his time either at his desk studying and writing or in the *Dār al-hilāl* taking care of the technical aspects of printing and publishing. He did not have too much time left for social life and shied away from any participation in organizations or political activities. Conscious of his marginal position as a Christian and Syrian in Muslim Egypt, but also following his own taste temperament, Zaidān refrained from any public political activity, so much so that he avoided mentioning daily political news in his magazine.

His was a glamourless life compared with that of contemporary political and social activists. In the political correspondence of the British authorities in Egypt, Zaidān was not mentioned — he was not a public figure in the political sense.

His success with the Arab reader, however, became established beyond any doubt. His conscious effort to appeal to as wide an audience as possible, his desire to inform and teach through his writings soon yielded fruits. Until today some of his works enjoy great popularity. But in spite of the popularity of his writings, he never achieved final recognition as a scholar. He stood too much under the influence of European scholarship yet made use of its methods only in an elective manner which suited his didactic purposes. Addressing specifically the Arab reader of his time his works did not contribute to European scholarship. European orientalists related to him in a kind but slightly patronizing fashion showing "more interest in procuring books from Zaydān than offering real constructive criticism of his work".[1] While Western scholars withheld recognition of Zaidān's academic merits on the ground of his questionable scholarly qualifications — and perhaps also out of a certain feeling of superiority vis à vis the "native" student of Arab history, Zaidān's educated compatriots frequently disqualified him as a scholar of the Arab Muslim past on religious grounds. As a Christian, they claimed, he lacked the necessary training in religious matters to write about Islamic history. The lack of recognition as a scholar, especially by his learned Muslim contemporaries, embittered him towards the end of his life to the point where he seriously considered to turn away from the study of the Arab Muslim past.

It would indeed be difficult to claim much scholarly merit for Zaidān's work. His works — in particular those dealing with the history of the Arab *Nahḍa* — provide valuable factual information about the time, but in thoroughness and analysis they rarely reached and never excelled the level of European scholarship of his own age. Even though he liked to think of himself as a scholar, it is not in scholarship that we should look for his achievments. Zaidān's decisive role was that of a vulgarizer of knowledge and a popularizer of new methods and trends of thought. He wrote in a didactic manner successfully attempting to familiarize the Arab reader with everything worth knowing about the Western civilization, and to make him at the same time aware of his own national past from a secular point of view.

Of greater importance than the lack of scholarly recognition is the fact that the Arab nationalist movement has ignored by and large Zaidān's role and contribution to the development of an Arab national consciousness. The reasons for this lie partially in the history of this movement itself and partially in the contradictions and also limitations of Zaidān's own thought.

---

1. Ware 205.

As has been pointed out, Zaidān lived in Egypt a life withdrawn from active politics. He could not readily be identified with any of the political groups and he was even somewhat critical of people like Muṣṭafā Kāmil and Aḥmad 'Urābī whose nationalist activism seemed too radical for Zaidān's taste. After having abstained from politics for most of his life he eventually supported the Young Turk Revolution and its political programme of increasingly centralized Ottoman Rule. He went as far as to actually deny the Arabs the right to their own political expressions and action or at least postponing such rights into a vague future. The reasons that led him to take this position were twofold. Firstly, he foresaw that the collapse of the Ottoman Empire would lead to greater European penetration of the Middle East rather than to the independence of the Arab territories — a prediction that was to be proven correct only too soon. Secondly, he was convinced of the forces of rationality, politically expressed in the constitution, which would make everyone, regardless of his ethnic, religious or lingual background, a fully participating citizen in this political entity. Not only did he believe that a rational constitution would provide the legal framework for equal participation, but he also assumed that all people would be equally motivated by their own rational thinking to participate actively in such a constitutional framework. He did not perceive that people who were just then preoccupied with forging their own national identity would resent any multinational political structure, regardless of what enlightened rational constitution it called its own. In other words, Zaidān never realized the link between a national cultural identity, which he himself had helped to develop and the resulting national political ambitions. He lacked the imagination to translate his concern with the national cultural identity of the Arabs into a nationalist political programme. However, he should not be judged too harshly because here, too, he was rather typical for the intellectual and political mood of his time. Even the most pronounced political activists amongst the Arabs spoke at the eve of World War I only of a constitutional decentralization of the Ottoman Empire and denied explicitly any ambition for political independence — as is made evident in the proceedings of the First Arab Congress in Paris in 1913. Zaidān did not live to witness the collapse of the Ottoman Empire and the resulting rise of the political ambitions of the Arab countries who in the post-war period were increasingly frustrated by the new role of European political domination. Since that time the Arab national movement has been preoccupied with the formulation and execution of a political programme for national independence, to which Zaidān's writing could contribute very little in explicit form.

But one would not do justice to Zaidān's work in dismissing it only because it did not yet provide a political programme for Arab nationalism. His work helped to provide the intellectual tools and framework which were the pre-requisites for political-national consciousness and action. His investigation into the Arab language and history, which found expression in his scholarly works and perhaps more importantly in his magazine and his historical novels, made the Arab reader intensely aware of his own history and heritage. Zaidān was the first who defined the Arab entity not only by the language, but also by a historical perspective that was apt to demonstrate the vitality of this entity which would prove itself again in a new symbiosis with Western civilization.

With his definition of the Arab entity by a common language and a common history reaching far beyond the Islamic period, Zaidān laid the secular foundation for a specific brand of Arab nationalism, that Pan-Arabism which would reach its full development one generation after his death.

PART II

THE AUTOBIOGRAPHY OF ǦURǦĪ ZAIDĀN

INTRODUCTION TO THE AUTOBIOGRAPHY

This autobiography is remarkable for various reasons. First of all it is one of the best independent sources for the history of the Syrian Protestant College, especially regarding the crisis of 1882. Secondly, the autobiography contains a wealth of information about contemporary Beirut and the life of its inhabitants. Social structure, traditional mores, the beginning of Westernization, the economic impact of Europe and the development of a westernized social class — all these are topics about which information can be gathered from the autobiography. Thirdly, the autobiography gives us insight into the private life of Zaidān's family and, perhaps most important, into the psychological and intellectual development of the young Zaidān. In other words it is a genuine autobiography in which the development of the personality of the author provides the centrepiece of the narration. It is not a *vita* in which particular stations in the life of the subject are described in an exemplary or almost symbolistic fashion and it is not a form of memoirs, in which the person of the author serves only to connect between various political events or to introduce the description of important contemporaries of the author. Zaidān's autobiography was unique at his time and it was only a generation later when the first autobiographies were published in Arabic literature.[1]

Twenty years before Zaidān's autobiography was written 'Alī

1. It is noteworthy that until today no technical term has itself been firmly established in Arabic for the literary genre of the autobiography. Zaidan himself referred to his autobiography as *sīrat ḥayātī*; *Letters*, Zaidān to Emile, Cairo Oct. 24, 1908. Ṣ. Munağğid added to his edition of the autobiography the title *muḏakkirāt* which is frequently used today but usually means memoirs, for which genre it is indeed an appropriate term. None of the older dictionaries gives a technical term for autobiography and even the recent SCHREGLE gives for "Autobiographie" only an explanation rather than a specific term: *tarğamat* (*sīrat*) *kātibin linafsihī*. It seems, however, that in most recent usage the term *sīra ḏātīya* is becoming accepted as the technical term for autobiography in Arabic.

Mubārak wrote a summary of his own life, *tarǧama* as he called it.[2] 'Alī Mubārak was a man of the new age, a man with a Western technological education who himself helped to introduce the modern times to his society. But his *tarǧama* does not yet reflect this modernity. It is a very detailed report which begins with the historical background of his family and then records 'Alī Mubārak's education from the age of six onwards. The first half of the narration is focussed upon the person of the author himself. The second half of the *tarǧama* becomes increasingly a general report about reforms and educational innovations in Sa'īd *Pāšā's* (1856-1863) and *Ḫidīw* Ismā'īl's (1883-1879) Egypt, though 'Alī Mubārak does not fail to note carefully all official functions he occupied and — somewhat pedantically — all the orders and medals he was awarded. But in spite of the large amount of information about the reformer and author 'Alī Mubārak we learn very little about the person 'Alī Mubārak, his private life and his feelings. About his (second) wife we only hear in connection with some unpleasant struggle over inheritance and property. We never read, for instance, what made the author write *al-Ḫiṭaṭ at-taufīqīya al-ǧadīda*, the encyclopaedical work about Egypt which contains this *tarǧama*. When all is said and done 'Alī Mubārak's *tarǧama* remains a traditional *curriculum vitae* providing information about the formal education and professional career of the author. *Al-Ḫiṭaṭ at-taufīqīya al-ǧadīda* are organized alphabetically — with the exception of Cairo and Alexandria — according to names of places. Under each entry 'Alī Mubārak reports about history and landmarks of the place and records the biographies of famous people born there. It is typical for the traditional concept of the *tarǧama* that the author's own *tarǧama* should appear under the entry of "*Birinbāl*", his own place of birth. 'Alī Mubārak did not intend to write an autobiography but wanted only to supply all the information relevant to the place of his birth. His *tarǧama* still belongs to that category which F. Rosenthal describes as follows: "Keine der Autobiographien ist aus dem Bewußtsein eines Eigenwertes des einmalig Persönlichen entstanden, sondern alle... verfolgen sachliche

---

2. 'Alī *Pāšā* Mubārak (1823-1892) was born and lived in Egypt, where he as a trained doctor and engineer became deeply involved in modernization programmes. His special attention was drawn to education reform. For his *vita* see his famous work on Egypt, *al-Ḫiṭaṭ* IX 37-61.

Zwecke, die dem gesamten übrigen Schaffen des Verfassers weitestgehend kongruent sind".[3]

Of greater autobiographical character are Muḥammad 'Abduh's autobiographical fragments.[4] In them some mention is made — even though marginal — of the author's relationship to his family and parents. But again the only personal narration relates to his education. Here, too, the description of his early dislike for reading and studying and his sudden conversion to education and learning is close to a cliché-like symbol rather than a personal record.

Modern Arab literature abounds with political or other memoirs. The genuine autobiography in which the development of the personality is the continuing subject of the narration is rarer. The first autobiographical work to be published was Ṭāhā Ḥusain's autobiographical novel *Ayyām*. It is a work of great literary quality, which displays a profound understanding of and psychological insight into the growing-up of the boy *Ṭāhā* in his rural and traditional environment. His emotional and intellectual development is complicated by the fact that he lost his eyesight early in life. The result is a very tender and intimate record of Ṭāhā Ḥusain's own childhood.

When twenty years later Salāma Mūsā publishes his autobiography,[5] he is already fully aware of the problems that the writing of an autobiography pose, the subjectivity of the author, his inhibitions and prejudices, his own understanding of his time and society, etc. Salāmā Mūsā delineates his task in the following way: "Thus, my first aim is to give my life story, while to history proper I give a second place".[6] Clearly, Salāma Mūsā is aware of the "Eigenwert des einmalig Persönlichen". Since his and Ṭāhā Ḥusain's autobiography before him have been

3. F. Rosenthal "Die Arabische Autobiographie" 40. To this category would also belong Rustum Bāz' (d. 1902) *Muḏakkirāt rustum bāz*. Here we really have to do with a political history of Lebanon in the first half of the 19th century. At the most we can speak here of political memoirs but not of an autobiography.

4. Riḍā *passim* in the first part of the book.

5. Salāma Mūsā (1888-1858) born in Egypt of Coptic origin, studied before World War I in Paris and London. In his articles and books he insisted on reform and modernization of Egypt. Close to the European liberal tradition he inclined towards moderate Fabian socialism. His autobiography *Tarbiyat salāma mūsā* was first published in 1947; Gibb & Landau 219-221.

6. Schuman transl. 4.

published, the number of autobiographies in Arab literature has increased considerably. One of the recent and outstanding examples of the autobiography proper is Miḫā'īl Nu'aima's *Sab'ūn.*[7]

To this category of the autobiography proper belongs also the autobiography of Ǧurǧī Zaidān. Parts of it were published in 1952 in *al-Hilāl* and in 1967 by Nabīh A. Fāris in *al-Abḥāṯ*. In 1968 all of the autobiography was published by Ṣalāḥ ad-Dīn al-Munaǧǧid.[8] Thus the autobiography, which was probably the very first to be written in modern Arabic was published only some sixty years later. Like Ṭāhā Ḥusain, Salāma Mūsā and others after them Zaidān, too, made the emotional intellectual development of the author the centrepiece of the narration. But the historical and social setting (Beirut 1860-1883) belongs to a period considerably earlier — and geographically different — from that of the above-mentioned autobiographies.

Zaidān began to write the autobiography in October 1908 apparently fulfilling a promise to his son, Emile.[9] Obviously he was stimulated to write it by his son's departure for Beirut, where Emile like his father before him was to study at the American University. The autobiography is broken off in the middle, covering only the period from 1861 to 1883, when Zaidān left Beirut for Cairo. Quite clearly he had intended to complete the autobiography. We do not know what kept him from continuing to write it, whether more urgent work had to be attended to or whether he lost interest in it.

The translation is based on the manuscript of Zaidān's autobiography and has been closely compared with the edition of Ṣalāḥ ad-Dīn al-Munaǧǧid and the partial edition by Nabīh Amīn Fāris. The title "The Autobiography of Ǧurǧī Zaidān" is our addition. The manuscript itself is not titled at all. The division of the autobiography into two parts, the second part being sub-titled "The College" follows Zaidān's own arrangement of the manuscript.

---

7. Miḫā'īl Nu'aima born 1889 in Lebanon, received his first education in Nazereth in the seminary of the Russian Orthodox Mission. From there he was sent to Russia for further education. 1911 he went to Paris from where he emigrated to the U.S. He began there his literary career. Social criticism and social reform and literary criticism were the main themes of his work; GIBB & LANDAU 279-282. His autobiography was published in Beirut 1962-1966. See also GABRIELI.

8. See XXXIII 271-275, 373-376, 516-520, 637-640.

9. *Letters*, Zaidān to Emile, Cairo, Oct. 24 and Nov. 3, 1908.

In the translation ( ) has been used to indicate Zaidān's own use of parenthesis. Square brackets [ ] have been used for additions made by us.

A general comment seems to be necessary for the various currencies and denominations that are mentioned in the autobiography. After the monetary reform of Sultan Abdülmeğīd in 1844 the smallest monetary unit in the Ottoman Empire was the *pāra*, a copper coin. 40 *pāra* equalled one *ġirš* (pl. *ġurūš*), a silver coin of 1.2 gram silver content. This coin was also known, especially amongst the Europeans, as *piaster*. 20 *ġurūš* or *piaster* equalled one *meğīdī*, a silver coin. 100 *ġurūš* equalled one *līrā*, a gold coin. In 1885 a *ginī miṣrī*, an Egyptian guinea was introduced in Egypt, equalling one Ottoman *līrā*. Zaidān probably meant the latter when he referred, anachronistically, to the former.[10] The *riyāl* was an Ottoman silver coin with a 3.097 gram silver content, but was in the 19th century also a common name for the Maria Theresia Taler. After the establishment of Lebanon as an autonomous province of the Ottoman Empire apparently also the French currency began to play a role in Beirut. Approximately five *ġurūš* equalled one *franc*. Occasionally Zaidān also used the term *dirhem*, a silver coin which disappeared from circulation in the 15th century and is used in this context as a general term for money.[11]

10. See 154 ff.

11. See EI[1] *Dirham*, *Ghrūsh*, *Pāra*, *Riyāl* and SCHAENDLINGER, 55, 56, 65 and *infra*.

THE AUTOBIOGRAPHY OF ǦURǦĪ ZAIDĀN

When I was a boy my father told me about the origins of our family: our grandfather was called Zaidān Maṭar (or Zaidān Yūsuf Maṭar), he was a supervisor for the Lady Ḥubūs, the mother of *Amīr* Muṣṭafā Arslān.[12] She ruled over 'Ain 'Anūb and the areas attached to it at the beginning of the century. My grandfather worked as an overseer for her, i.e. he was an inspector over her possessions and business enterprises. When Ibrāhīm *Pāšā* attacked Syria, conquered Acre and planned to take possession of Mount Lebanon, Lady Ḥubūs was one of those who opposed him and feared his power. Her feelings told her that she should flee from him. Once she had made up her mind she demanded that my grandfather accompany her on her flight. He refused to do so, since he saw clearly the inevitable superiority of the Egyptian power. Besides, he had children and a family and he did not have the heart to abandon them or to take them along as refugees. She implored him to accompany her, but he excused himself with the above-mentioned reasons until she was infuriated with him and departed. Ibrāhīm occupied Mount Lebanon with the help of the *Amīr* Bašīr in 1832. The Lady Ḥubūs remained in hiding until Ibrāhīm's cause lost out.

The aforementioned Lady returned to her town 'Ain 'Anūb. Full of resentment against Zaidān she confiscated his possessions and money: in other words she intended his humiliation. This grieved him and affected his health so that he died prematurely leaving behind him his wife, two daughters and two sons. The eldest son was my father, who was not yet ten and already the head of the family. His mother did not cherish the idea of staying in 'Ain 'Anūb and moved down to Beirut

---

12. Lady Ḥubūs al-Arslānī (1768-1826) was married to the *Amīr* 'Abbās Ibn Faḫr ad-Dīn al-Arslānī (d. 1809). They had four sons: Manṣūr, Ḥaidar, Aḥmad and Amīn. Zaidān must mean here either Amīn or the son of Amīn, Muṣṭafā; F.A. AL-BUSTĀNĪ, I 163.

with her children, my father being their sole support. In those days Beirut was small. The only way of making a living was by trade or production of the necessities of daily life such as food, cloth and the like, or government services in an office or the military.[13]

But my father was illiterate. The Latin[14] missionary schools were still few and he did not have the luck to be taken to them by somebody. Even if he had been given this opportunity he could not have taken it because he was needed to support his mother, his brother and his sisters. He did not have any skills and his will to work was his only capital. His mother found a way in which she could help him: she began to bake bread and he would carry it on a flat board, making the rounds amongst the people in the markets to sell it at five or ten *pāra* per loaf. In this way he earned enough to still the hunger of the family.

My father continued, "I kept doing this for a time until I grew somewhat older. Then, however, I found out that there was a bakery or something of that sort in the city which baked the bread for the army. I entered this service, since I knew very well how to knead; that is to say they would put a hundred or two hundred *oqqa*[15] at one time into the kneading through — I was then in the bloom of my youth — and then I would knead it very well in spite of the size of the lump of dough. I took home a handsome salary and would boast in front of my fellow dough kneaders."

His two sisters were older than he, and when they grew up they married. He remained with his brother Miḫā'īl but the main burden of work was on him, since his brother was inclined towards amusement

---

13. Zaidān is mistaken here. The Arslans and other Druze feudal families had supported the *Amir* Bašīr II aš-Šihābī (1788-1840) for a long time in action and with money. When the *Amīr* succeeded in establishing his exclusive power in Lebanon they turned against him. Lady Ḥubūs, too, became his active enemy. Lady Ḥubūs died in 1826 or, more likely, was killed in connection with the rebellion of Bašīr Ǧanbalāṭ against the *Amīr* Bašīr II. She had left her estates and fled to Bešāmūn where she found her end long before Ibrāhīm *Pāšā* invaded Syria. According to Zaidān (see p. 130) his father was born in 1833, left 'Ain 'Anūb around 1843 and married at the age of 27. It appears, therefore, that the Zaidāns had fled to Beirut as a result of the crisis between the Druze and the Christian communities in Lebanon in the early forties and not under the pressure of the Lady Ḥubūs who had died before Zaidān's father was born. F.A. AL-BUSTĀNĪ, I 163 ff, K. AL-BUSTĀNĪ, 106-117, SALIBI 9 ff.

14. I.e. Roman Catholic.

15. Ottoman weight. According to HINZ one *oqqa* is equivalent to 1.2828 kilo. It would seem that Zaidān's father was exaggerating considerably.

and distraction. Eventually my father advanced from the baker's trade to that of a restaurateur. At that time trade had been attracted to Beirut and the number of foreigners coming there had increased. It occurred to him to open a restaurant and so he did. He made a profit on it and his general circumstances improved. He then considered marriage — at that time he was twenty seven — and proposed to my mother. She came from the family al-Hā'ik whose origin is.....[16]. My mother had a number of sisters, but no brothers. They married in 1860.

During that year the well-known disturbances occurred and the people of Beirut feared a general upheaval like that which had taken place in Lebanon and Damascus.[17] They began to make preparations for flight. Grandmother said to my father, "We find ourselves in great distress and the city is in danger. So, either you marry the girl and take care of her or you dissolve the engagement and we take her with us". He preferred marriage and they were wed in the same year.

The disturbances ceased and Beirut did not suffer any damage worth mentioning. People returned to their work. My father worked his little inn close to *al-Burǧ al-kaššāf*, and his profits grew. Children were born to him. I, being the first, was born at the end of 1861, but I did not know the exact date of my birth since neither my father nor my mother knew how to write. I was told, though, that I was born during *at-tišrīn*,[18] that is to say in the autumn, and perhaps people mentioned a specifically known feast in this connection, but I do not remember it.

After I grew up I wanted to find out the date of my birth. I was already living in Egypt when I decided that on my visit to Beirut the first thing would be to check the date of my baptism in the church register,

16. Sic in ms. Family originated most likely from Bišmizzine.

17. Since the early forties of the 19th century, the Lebanon was shaken by inter-confessional strife. In 1858, the Maronite peasants of the North revolted against their Maronite feudal lords. In the South Lebanon, where the feudal lords and part of the peasantry were Druze, this revolt attained immediately the character of religious rather than social strife. The Druze made a last attempt to assert their vanishing ascendency in the Lebanon. The disturbances came to a peak in 1860. For a while, the safety of the Christian population of Beirut seemed to be in question. Many of the Christians left for the Maronite North or overseas for Egypt and Greece. When the Muslims of Damascus committed in July 1860 a massacre amongst their Christian neighbours, killing about 5,500 of them, the French government decided to send a French military contingent to Beirut and the Lebanon. SALIBI 53-110.

18. See also BARTHELEMY 85.

assuming that the church would register by date the baptism of its members. Once I found the record of my baptism perhaps I would see entered with it the date of my birth. When I travelled to Beirut in 1891, the year I married, I asked our old priest al-Ḫūrī Mūsā —a simple man, living out a long life. His flock loved him for his sincerity. When he came to greet me I enquired about the book in which the above-mentioned records are kept. He answered me: "We do not have any records and registry, my son, because we used not to baptize". I was disappointed and showed my astonishment. My father, who was present, asked me what I wanted and I told him. "I enquired with the Father about the baptism registry and he tells me that they do not have any". My father wanted to know what I needed them for and I explained that I intended to find out the date of my birth. He laughed: "Ask me and I will tell you because nobody could miss your birthday. You were born on the day the King of England (he meant the husband of the Queen, Prince Albert) died." "And how did you know this?" I enquired. "I knew it because I remember very well that during the night you were born — and we both were awake — we heard a gun shot from the sea from the British cruisers anchored off shore. We asked the reason for this and were told that the King of England had died." So I learned that, assuming those were the circumstances, I was born on December 14, 1861, which is the day Prince Albert (the husband of the Queen of England) died.

As far as the origin of our family is concerned, there are no records. My father left his father's house with the rest of the family like a refugee. He was an ignorant child, and we are not aware of any family records in 'Ain 'Anūb. He himself grew up in Beirut, a poor illiterate fellow, preoccupied with the support of his family and not interested in searching for the roots of our family tree. When I became a youth I wanted to enquire about it and wrote to several people 'Ain 'Anūb asking them if they knew of the family Maṭar there and its origin. I received an answer from an old man of the people there who remembered that some of the family Maṭar came to 'Ain 'Anūb — strange and stern people, and that one of them, Zaidān, advanced in the services of the Lady Ḥubūs. I heard from another man, through my brother Yūsuf, that from the family of my father from 'Ain 'Anūb some successive offspring followed, the last of which was my father. Concerning the first who settled here, some of the family Maṭar claim that the ʿAin ʿAnūb or Šūf branch is one of three branches which originate from Tripolis or Ihdin and that there were three brothers who fled the oppression of the local ruler almost two hundred years ago: one of them reached the Šūf, one went to Ḥāṣbayyā and the last to Maṭan. But all claims of this kind are conjectures upon which one cannot rely.

I think it likely that the origin of our family is the same as that of the majority of the Greek Orthodox families in the Šūf, namely Ḥaurān. In view of the wretchedness and poverty by which they were stricken, the Arabs of this country settled in the mountain as is the habit with Bedouins who settle in cities and villages in order to ....[19] Often the Christian Arabs from Ḥaurān took refuge in the Lebanon fleeing from the Muslim oppression there. The most famous of these repressions and riots occurred in the Ḥaurān four hundred years ago, and similar ones followed it. I am inclined to believe that most of the Greek Orthodox people in South Lebanon are Arabs from the Ḥaurān. Perhaps they are Ghassanids. It could be that amongst the Arabs in Ḥaurān there was a clan or portion called Banū Maṭar. Amongst the Ḥāṣbānīya family of Maṭar there was a group that was called the Banū Maṭar al-Ḥāwārina. Perhaps our grandfather was one of them. But all this is guesswork and surmise and, as far as I am concerned, nothing has been substantiated except what my father told me as I have related above.

My father told me one day after he had settled in Beirut and had become a young man, the revenue officer for the *ḫarāǧ*[20] in the mountain came to him and asked him to claim his title to some land that belonged to him in ʿAin ʿAnūb. But he, [my father,] did not take care of this and did not pay the *ḫarāǧ*, and when he repeatedly refused to do so, his title to the land lapsed. This stuck in my mind and I took the first opportunity during my summer vacation in Lebanon in 1896 to tell some of the government people from ʿAin ʿAnūb about what was known in this matter. They promised me to examine the government records. Eventually they came back to me and informed me that in the mentioned village there still was some land which appeared under the name "Maṭar

19. Illegible in manuscript.

20. In classical Islamic times, *ḫarāǧ* was the land tax. The correct technical term in the Ottoman Empire was, however, *mīrī*, which Zaidān must have had in mind here.

Cliff" meaning the foot of a mountain that was now government land. I knew then that this was the plot for which my father abandoned payment of the *ḫarāğ* and the title to it reverted to the government.

I was born in Beirut in a house belonging to Ilyās aš-Šuwairī. On its location stands today the school of the Jesuit Fathers.[21] It had two floors. The lower consisted of three large rooms and a hall. Then we moved to a second house, then to another one. In twenty-two years we moved to about sixteen houses. They were in the following order 1) Bait aš-Šūbī, 2) al-Fairnainī, 3) 'Aramān in the Jewish Quarter, 4) next to the workshop of Daḥdāḥ, 5) Bait aš-Šawābī (second time), 6) 'Īsā Surūr, 7) al-Ḫūrī Mūsā, 8) Karkar, 9) al-Qassīs, 10) aš-Šuwairī (third time),[22] Ra'd, 15) Bait at-Tayyān, 16) Bait al-Ḥāyik.

This list of names shows that we were not house owners. The tenant carries his house on his back. Most of these houses were in the East[23] and the North of the city and most of them consisted of two rooms: one bedroom, a salon to receive people, and a hall to sit and to eat in. Some houses had three rooms. There was no urgent need for many rooms since people did not use any beds. In the same room one could receive guests in the daytime and sleep at night. When getting up one would fold the bed rolls and pile them one on top of the other on a chest on the ground, which was used for utensils. One would arrange the bedding on top of it and fit in front of it a curtain. This place was called a niche, *al-yūk*. Thus, the bedding was not visible to anybody. There was usually a beautifully arranged and very clean place to sit in the room. The people of Beirut are famous for their cleanliness, especially those of the Greek Orthodox community. Some of them exaggerated it to the point where cleanliness became an *idée fixe*. Most famous for that was the Bait Fayyād and the Bait Trād; some would soap the clothesline, some would soap the marble of the house and the doors every day. If they saw a visitor touch any utensil, they would soap it; some would wash the firewood when they carried it into the house. Nothing was left but to soap the soap.

The dwelling of a family, consisting of a man, a woman and several children, had two rooms. This would indicate average circumstances —

21. Not clear which one is meant.
22. The spelling varies in the ms., aš-Šuwairī is most likely the correct one.
23. I.e. in the Christian quarter of the town.

not poverty. This family might even live in one room; yet they would not appear to live in misery and ignominy. Because whenever you would enter that room you would find it clean. White curtains of calico cleanly washed would drop over the bedding (*al-yūk*). On the chair you would find a similar cover clean and proper. The mats would be wiped clean and everything in that room would be put into best order. You would smell the smell of cleanliness from everything. I do not mean a smell of delicate fragrance or perfume. It is a smell for which there is no other description but the smell of cleanliness, which one can smell if one sniffs a cloth that comes from the hands of an experienced washerwoman. Perhaps the smell of soap prevails in it. Once you enter this room — and you would enter it only after taking off your shoes — you would long to sit on the bench or on a mat and drink the coffee which the lady of the house serves you herself, since those people rarely hire servants. You would observe the housewife, when she cooks, cleans or washes; with rolled up sleeves does she sweep or rinse something, launder and spread things, cook and knead; and health and liveliness is visible in each of her movements. When she finishes her work she arranges her things in the most simple manner, and puts on an unpretentious clean dress. She starts to receive her guests or visitors, prepares coffee for them and serves it. If she has a daughter able to serve it, she will do it instead of her mother.

In spite of all this she does not neglect for a moment the education of her children. She instructs them as to what to wear and to eat, she teaches them cleanliness and accustoms them to activeness. The majority of women at the time could neither write nor read, and had not been to school. Nevertheless, they possessed with their acumen and their willpower the best means to educate their children to activeness, work and punctuality, *muḥāfaẓa ʿalā ʾl-waqt*; they made them hate cowardice and laziness; they made them eager and aroused courage and initiative in them. My mother was one of them. She had a strong constitution, a sound mind and fine feelings. She was discreet, taciturn and hard working; neither day nor night would she cease to supply the necessities for the house — especially since my father did not return home and see his children before they were asleep. His work kept him in the restaurant every day from very early in the morning till almost midnight. For him there was no Sunday, no holiday. He could, therefore, not help my mother with the raising of the children. Perhaps most people of average means, *mutawassiṭū 'l-ḥāl*, in those times lived under similar circumstances. If I used to find my mother to be the most active and hardest working of them all, the reason was that her family consisted of seven or eight people and she alone provided everything that the family would need in terms of food, clothing, protection and education. Yet, my mother still found time to conduct some business at home: she saw for instance that my father bought the bread for his restaurant from the bakers. She knew, of course, that they were making a profit on their work. So she suggested to him that she would bake the bread and sell it to him at the rate of these two bakers. This she did for several years and saved in this way some money with which she paid for necessities. In her free time she would occasionally busy herself with embroidering skull caps, cleansing silk or similar activities, without finding it tiresome or disgraceful.

So I grew up seeing my father leaving for his restaurant in the morning and returning only about midnight, and observing my mother never standing still from dawn to dusk. She herself ignored visits, festivities, social and even religious gatherings. Only rarely did she go to church to pray. She was more interested in conducting her household and educating her children. Thus, I grew up and became accustomed to this way of life. It ingrained itself on my mind, that, in contrast to those youngsters who looked wide-eyed at their parents spending most of their days amusing themselves and strolling around, man was created to work and that sitting around without work was a great disgrace. Their only concern is their food and their drinks. Once they have finished their meals they proceed to gamble or do similar things. They kill time this way. They venture to work only when forced and consider work a disgrace and drudgery. If they should decide to work, some illness or weakness would provide timely protection from it. No wonder that youngsters who grow up with such parents become indolent young people and tend towards distractions and vices.

My father was illiterate but he felt the need of writing and reading when he opened his eating place. He had patrons who would settle their accounts with him on a monthly or weekly basis. The number of his current accounts increased. In the beginning, he would put them down in his own hand with numerals that he had learned, leaving the name of the debtor to memory. Later he entrusted with the bookkeeping whomsoever he employed in his restaurant. Writing became a necessity for him and it caused him to initiate my learning to read at an early age. When I was four years old he sent me to school to a teacher with the name Ilyās (or Ǧirǧis), a brother of our family's priest al-Ḫūrī Mūsā. At that time, knowledge was still the monopoly of the clergy and people associated with them. The thought would not have occurred to anybody that the teacher Ilyās was a learned philosopher: even the gospel he could hardly read properly. His school consisted of a wide vaulted cellar room in the building of Ya'qūb Ṯābit in the neighbourhood of the Jesuit school of today. Later on this vaulted cellar was converted into a baking oven. It resembled more a cattle pen than a school. There the children of the neighbourhood between the ages of four to ten — boys and girls — would convene and sit on the mat or mats unrolled on the ground. The teacher would sit in front of the room on a hassock, in front of him a small box, *baštaḫteh*[24] upon which he put his book, his inkwell and his pens. At his right he had assembled a number of sticks varying in length and thickness. He would use each of them appropriately, according to age and sex of the child and according to his closeness or distance to him. I remember that I learned from him the reading of the psalms, which served as the first reader in those days after learning the alphabet. We used to memorize a psalm, because we repeated reading it — but we never understood it. The principle was, that we would declaim it to him in a loud voice. This is what is called "reciting", *tasmī'*. We would declaim it, perhaps two or three together, while the teacher was sitting crosslegged behind his box, his head sinking on his chest in sleep. His snoring would blend with our voices and the louder the noise became the deeper he sank into his sleep. When his neck got tired from bending down he would lean his head against the wall and put his feet on the box, so that his soles would face us. We did not pay any attention to him. When he was about to take a nap or if something happened that woke him up, he would open his eyes and shout coldly, "Shut up kids!" If they did not do so he would go into motion and reach for one of the sticks and hit the boy closest to

24. From Persian *pīštaḫteh*, WAHRMUND.

him, even if he was not guilty of anything. He would scream and the rest laughed about him. Then he would grab a longer stick and beat somebody else. He might even rise when absolutely necessary, seize the rebel amongst the children and throw him to be ground. He would call the servant for help, or a strong boy in order to put the *falaq* on the rebellious child's feet or the feet into the *falaq*. Then he would hit him on his feet ten or twenty times; more or less according to what he thought appropriate. The *falaq* is an instrument for punishment which we have to describe nowadays because it has vanished from the civilized cities: it consists of a thick stick to which a rope is fastened. Its ends are connected with the ends of the stick, while its middle remains loose. The feet of the boy are put between the rope and the stick. Two persons rotate the stick and whatever remains of the rope is wound around it. The legs are confined and the two lift them up and the boy comes to lie on his back. One of those present seizes the ends of the *falaq* and the teacher begins to beat the soles of the feet with his stick.

I do not remember that I sampled a taste of this instrument in school, not because of any innate virtue but because of my great timidity and strong fear of punishment. I like to avoid the causes of enmity — from my childhood I noticed this natural disposition in me — therefore, I avoided anything that would infuriate the teacher or would cause him to rebuke me or beat me.

I spent, I believe, two years in this school until the teacher told my father, "Ǧurǧī has finished his studies. He has begun to spell words!" My father was extremely happy. Concluding the reading exercises meant I could read the psalms well, and it is true that I read them well, but I did not understand a word I read.

This did not satisfy the ambitions of my father for my education since I had not yet learned writing and arithmetic and I was not able to make a note of a name and put next to it what was owed. He transferred me from this so splendid a school to a school that had been newly opened in Beirut known by the name of *Madrasat aš-šuwām*, referring to the people of Damascus. Those who had established the school were a group of educated people from Damascus, from where they had emigrated to Beirut after the massacre of 1860. In this school I learned some principles of arithmetic, grammar and penmanship. I began to gain understanding and insight and my eyes were opened. Our teachers had a great interest in teaching. The school was known for its education, especially because of the strictness of its rules. There was no law but the will of the supervisor or principal. In those days the principal was Ẓāhir Ḫairallāh aš-Šuwairī.[25] He used violent language and commanded great respect. Originally he was a mason. He possessed intelligence and taught and educated himself until he became a teacher of high rank. The students used to be scared of him and fear his voice. He used to teach arithmetic and grammar, fields in which he was a great expert. There was another grammar teacher with the name Ilyās al-Ḫūrī who later on became judge in al-Kūra. Then there was a teacher from the family Naufal who was called Ğurğ Rağīḥa, and another one from the family 'Āsī, whose name I don't remember. The school had a good name, but did not continue for very long. I do not know the reason, but I remember that it was closed, when I was about nine years old (1870). The people regretted its closure since its educational system was good.

When I left this school I had a basic knowledge of grammar inflection, penmanship, arithmetic and some very scanty knowledge of French. The teachers of the school advised the fathers at the time to send their children to the Greek Orthodox school, "The Three Doctors".[26] Ẓāhir had been appointed there as principal or as a teacher. His fame helped to transfer most students of the *Madrasat aš-šuwām* there. It was not long before he founded a private school of his own to which I transferred. Ẓāhir was extremely interested in teaching the students, maintaining the fame of his school and striving for its good progress. Language, arithmetic and French were taught there. I spent about two years in this school and had begun to take great pleasure in knowledge and its understanding. Nothing but learning interested me. I differed from the other students with regard to playing, because I had absolutely no inclination towards

25. Ilyās Ẓāhir Ḫairallāh aš-Šuwairī (1834-1916) born in Šuwair. Greek Orthodox. Taught in various schools in Beirut and Damascus; wrote for al-Muqtaṭaf, al-Āṯār, etc. DĀĠIR III 406.

26. In Arabic: *al-Aqmār aṯ-ṯalāṯa*, the three moons. Meant are the three Churchfathers Basil and Gregory of Nazianzus and John Chrysostomos. The school was founded in 1833 by the Greek Orthodox community in Sūq al-Ġarb. 1866 it was transferred to Beirut, became one of the major schools of the Greek Orthodox community. It exists until today as the College de Trois Docteurs. HANF 71, ZAIDĀN *Ta'rīḫ ādāb* IV 38.

amusement and distraction. I used to consider this a defect in myself: only rarely I flew kites, played ball (*al-kūra*) and with marbles (*ballieh*). I might stand and watch or accompany the pupils when they went out to fly a huge kite around which the children of the neighbourhood would gather and I would follow them marvelling at their courage and expertise in constructing a kite and flying it.

At the end of the two years, when I was eleven years old and my knowledge still faulty, my father needed me in his restaurant to render him temporary help in writing down the names and payments of customers until he would succeed in substituting another waiter for the one who had just left him. He had had this servant for the tables — from Bait Šabāb but raised in our house — whom he entrusted with bookkeeping and cooking, etc. He was fed up with him for I don't know what reason. The boy left for his village and did not return. My father did not insist on his coming back because he thought that his son Ǧurǧī had come to know bookkeeping and could give him a hand with the cooking and other work even if it was only temporary until this boy would return in spite of his anger. He told me, "Ǧurǧī, come assist me for seven or eight days until I find someone to replace you!" I went there full of disgust because I enjoyed my studies very much. I obeyed him, but still cherished the hope of returning to the school. These seven days stretched into seven or eight years. I spent them in the markets of Beirut amongst their crowds and was forced to associate with the lowliest groups amongst them, because our eating place — or restaurant — was in the areas of the *al-Burǧ* square. It was moved from one location to another but never was far off this square. The *al-Burǧ* square was in those days the meeting point for the crooks. the rowdies and the idle — amongst them drunkards, gamblers, pimps and quarrelsome people. I used to keep away from their company for I had no free time for idle amusements. Most of the regular customers whom I was obliged to associate with were strangers coming to Beirut for trade or other purposes. If there was one of the townspeople amongst them, it was likely that he avoided his father's house in order to execute some mischief which he had planned for that night. The people of Beirut would eat only during the day in a restaurant, and only if somebody was in his store and his home was far away. But in the evening everybody would repair to his house to take his dinner together with his children and wife and parents. Most of our customers came at night for dinner. From the townspeople only the vagrants and their like would come. Thus, most of our clientele consisted of drunks, vagrants or strangers.

After one and more years had passed by, while I was working in the restaurant, my mother feared that my situation would protract itself and my future would be ruined. She hated restaurants. Ever since my father had demanded that I help him she had beseeched him not to extend my job there and he had given her his word. When the first year had thus passed, she insisted that he take me out from there and return me to school. But he told her, "He has already finished his studies and there is no use in too much study — be it then that you want to make him into a scribe or a teacher. It is better not to exaggerate with education which would only make him into some westernized dandy, *mutafarniǧ*, who eats only with fork and knife — and perhaps it will occur to him to wear Frankish clothes". (Those clothes were rare at the time and no Syrian would wear them with the exception of high officials in consulates and similar places. To eat with fork and knife was still counted as one of the elegant habits of westernization, *tafarnuǧ*.) My father did not say this because of his distaste for civilization but because he liked to guard the Eastern habits and hated the artificiality or pretention of Europeanized appearance. My mother was convinced by his answers, but she still disliked me remaining in this trade, and asked him, "Let him enter another trade than this one. I dislike this work, the smell of greasy food and his sticking around the eating place day and night without a holiday or Sunday." He yielded to her objection. After contemplating the matter, they decided that I should learn the trade of European shoemaker, which was still a novelty in Beirut. The argument for their choice was that Ǧirǧis aš-Šuwairī and his brother Naḫleh, the sons of ....[27] had taken up this craft and succeeded in it until they had opened a shop for selling hides. They had already bought some real estate and built a house. Thus, they made up their minds that I should learn this trade. They arranged a place for me with the Mssr. Šuwairī. I was then twelve years old. I spent there a year as an apprentice, then transferred to another place that belonged to two brothers from Damascus of the family aḍ-Ḍuḥayyik

27. Illegible in ms.

or aḍ-Ḍāḥḥāk. Their shop was on the *Baihum* market. With them I spent another half year. At aš-Šuwairī my salary had been half a Franc per week; at the two aḍ-Ḍāḥḥāk brothers I was promoted to one Franc, because I was still counted amongst the apprentices in the trade, even though I had learnt most of it. I spent about two years in the shoemaker trade before I was obliged to quit because sitting all day on a chair to work was not agreeable to my health. Having been stout and energetic in the restaurant, my health began to fail after a year in the shoemaker's trade. Such weakness struck my stomach that they worried about me and decided on my giving up this trade and returning temporarily to the restaurant until they would think of another craft. I myself did not yet at that time understand the meaning of future, selfreliance, *al-i'timād 'alā 'n-nafs*, and quest for higher levels, *ṭalab al-'ulā*.

I said, I was struck by weakness during my work as a shoemaker, and they attributed this to the long hours of sitting and the lack of movement. I do not deny the impact of these two factors on health. But there was another important reason, a secret one, which every boy or youngster encounters. I got into this habit before I worked in the shoemaker's trade. I did not take any particular pleasure in it because I was too young. My desire for it was increased by my association with the other working children, as well as by my long hours sitting quiet.

All these factors together weakened me. I remember, however, one benefit that my working in the shop aḍ-Ḍuḥayyik had, a benefit that had a great influence on my future, because through it I understood the extent of damage resulting from this habit. I understood it by incident, and it made a deep impression upon me: a son of one of the dignitaries of Beirut came frequently to the shop of the aḍ-Ḍuḥayyik. He was a friend of the two brothers, joked with them a lot and discussed many questions sincerely with them. He was not cautious lest the little artisans should hear him, because he was a frivolous person. Once he came and complained of exhaustion and weakness. When he left the shop one brother said to the other, "poor chap, our friend. Do you know the reason for his weakness?" He replied in the negative. "The reason is," the other continued, "that he plays with his hand." It was the first time I had heard this expression for this harmful habit, but I understood it. I decided then to suppress it, and so I did. I felt a general improvement in my health.

I had gone back to the restaurant and this change, too, helped the progress of my health.

During the first years of this period ignominiousness took hold of me. I played what my peers played, not knowing the meaning of initiative and of taking care of my leisure time or of enterprise. However, I did not have much leisure time that would permit me to play, since the restaurant was usually open from the morning till the third or fourth hour of the Arabic evening, that is till ten or eleven o'clock.[28] But I used to seize the opportunity and enjoy some of the entertainment that took place close to our place when it was situated on the street of the Damascus coaches. Next to it there was a cafe in the fashion of the Beiruti cafes of those days; a big courtyard covered with rooftiles in which coffee would be served and a waterpipe to those who desired it. During the day its customers would play checkers, backgammon, cards or knuckle bones. When the sun had set, plays and shows would be staged. The most important were sword games and the performances of *Karagöz* (the shadow play), jugglery and storytelling. These entertainments would alternate and change according to the seasons or other circumstances. Our restaurant looked upon the cafe from the rear door, from where one could observe everything. I would sit on a chair there and with all this entertainment it was my greatest passion to listen to stories. When I saw the storyteller walking up and down reciting the story of 'Antar[29] or az-Zīr[30] or the like of it, while the people sat bent forward listening to him, and enacting the scenes of the tale with his gestures and voice — then I would forget my circumstances and would be totally absorbed in listening. The narrator related, usually during the course of the year, the four stories that were in those days the most famous ones: Fīrūz Šāh,[31] 'Antar, az-Zīr and 'Alī Zaibaq.[32] When the year came to

28. The hours of the day are counted from sunset in Arabic.

29. *Sīrat 'antar*, popular romantic epic, which centres around the idealized person of the pre-Islamic poet 'Antar(a), author of a *qaṣīda* dealing with Arab tribal warfare. EI[1], NICHOLSON.

30. *Sīrat az-zīr*, popular epic of the exploits of al-Muhalhil Ibn ar-Rabī'a, a pre-Islamic poet and warrior. See *Sīrat az-zīr abī lailā al-muhalhil*, Beirut, 1866, and NICHOLSON.

31. *Sīrat fīrūz šāh*, popular epic based on the historical figure of Fīrūz Šāh (1307-1388) who ruled as Sultan over the Panjab, Dehli, etc., since 1351. EI[2].

32. *Sīrat 'alī zaibaq* BURTON VII 172-209.

its end, he came back to the first one again. I heard them many times. I had no objection to listening to them and I do not complain about the time that I wasted doing so.

Karagöz — that is what the Egyptians called "shadow play" — was very much in demand during that time. Today I wonder how people, would be prepared to attend this performance, since it was obscene, thoroughly loathsome, and indecent. No wonder, though, since it reflected the mores of the lowest classes in Beirut, and of those who were known in the usage of the townspeople as the "crooks of '*Aṣṣūr*" (*'alā'ṣ-ṣūr*) square — and spread to *al-Burǧ* square — whose only occupation was pimping, stealing and provoking the passers-by; they would run around almost naked, and would sleep on the streets; perhaps they were the rest of the *'Ayyārūn*[33] of the Islamic empires. In any case, they were the lowest stage mankind could reach in terms of appearance and speech. Most of the spectators of the *Karagöz* were from their ranks. But I also used to see elegantly dressed people willing to attend this performance; I was not obliged to sit with all these people on the wooden benches of the cafe in order to see the performance, it was enough that I would look from the door of our restaurant and see most confortably everything they saw. I found the obscene words that I heard and the shameless acting that I witnessed repulsive; I felt embarrassed about it, regarding this feeling, however, as weakness in myself. I would see the rest of those present delighted, clapping ther hands and asking for more; their speech contained not less baseness and obscenity than what they heard. This is not surprising since they were all of one kind.

The sword game, or the *ḥakm* (a game with sticks instead of swords), dominated the stage only during the *Ramaḍān* nights in this cafe or in the one opposite to it. Both I could observe from one of the doors of our restaurant. I used to love to watch the sword game because it ignited and stirred up action and enthusiasm. Because of my young age, I felt shy sitting with the spectators and contented myself with surreptitious watching. At that time, the sword dancers constituted a troupe, the head

33. *'ayyār*, lit. vagabond, rascal, tramp. In the 9th-12th century with decreasing central authority groups of *'ayyārūn* developed, whose role was partially religious as fighters for Islam, partially social by terrorizing rich people and re-distributing their wealth to the poor, and partially simply criminal. EI [2].

of which was known as Qaddūr Dūġān, a Muslim. The rest of the dancers were also Muslims. But all the communities would watch the game. Prestige and rule belonged to the Muslims. Martial law prevailed in those days and, therefore, the military commander, *ḍābiṭ*, of the city did what pleased him. There occurred an accident which almost led to his [Qaddūr Dūġān's] killing and caused the government to abolish the sword games. This came about in the following fashion: there was a young Christian boy by the name of Yūsuf Ṣa'b in the crowd which observed the game. He was muscular and agile in spite of his corpulence, and expert in the sword game. While the Dūġān troupe was performing and the sword passed from one to the other the eyes of the spectators were glazed, trying to spot the winner in order to praise him and applaud him. It so happened during this night that Qaddūr approached Yūsuf Ṣa'b and passed him the sword and the shield, inviting him to fence. Yūsuf excused himself, realizing the friction between the communities that might result from this. But they were very civil and polite in inviting him, so he stood up and played one round, which filled the onlookers with awe. I was in their midst and my heart beat every time I saw him leaping from one position into another, taking the strokes with agility and expertise. I saw sparks flying between the swords and the shields. Eventually, people feared that the issue would turn from a conciliatory gesture or a joke into a disaster. The game was stopped, but people had the impression that Yūsuf was the winner. This aroused bitter feelings in some of the Muslim spectators and they planned to take vengeance the next day. When the news about their decision against him reached Yūsuf the next morning he preferred to remove the cause of friction. He did not agree to come down until *al-Ḥāǧǧ* Qaddūr Dūġān alluded to those who made light of Yūsuf; he said that in his own opinion Yūsuf surpassed even himself, [Dūġān], and that he, [Yūsuf], should present himself to the challenge. In spite of his being a Muslim, he thus proclaimed that victory belonged to Yūsuf. Perhaps he did this only to induce the people to attend (*reklām*). Yūsuf, for one, could not remain silent any more. He got up, reached for a sword and stepped forward to fight with somebody who was one of the relatives of the military commander of the city during this time (Sa'īd Āġā). The game between the two became heated until their eyes were red with anger, and a serious feud was on the verge of breaking out, at which point the police intervened. The government, fearing the consequences, forbade the sword game in popular cafes from this time on.

Such were the amusements in the milieu I lived in. My companions, however, were not less of a danger to decency and propriety. Most of them — for reasons that I mentioned already — were idle people. With those customers who had work to do or belonged to respectable families, my contact was restricted to business dealings and the accounts. They would eat, pay their due and leave again. There remained for company only the idle people who had no work that they enjoyed. These people would gather in my place; some would spend their leisure time during work between morning and evening here. Their talk differed from the talk of the crooks only in form and expression: one would boast how he committed adultery taking possession of so-and-so, the wife of the honourable such-and-such, and the next would pride himself in a trick he played on the wife or the mother, or in his expertise as a swindler. Another would show off with his abilities in fornication. Amongst them was a young hunchback whom I heard saying that his hunch was the result of immoderation.

Listening to their talk I felt sad deep inside that I was not able to understand a thing of what they were bragging about. I told myself time and again that I was going to do just like them. I felt my own inhibition and I regretted my weakness. Occasionally, I would cover up my shame with a story which I decided happened to me and which contained the things they were boasting about. Such were the mores of the masses of Beirut.

During this period of my life, I was enraptured by stories that made the rounds in another circle of bums. Their gatherings were restricted to boasting about their prowess. One would claim that he faced a whole group and defeated them, or how he entered a dark place and saw there demons which he chased away with a "*basmala*"[34] and other fairy tales and curiosities of the like. These stories gave me great pleasure and awakened in me the zeal to imitate the heroes and courageous men. In Beirut there was a number of youths who were famous for their courage and who were the talk of boys whenever they gathered. Amongst the

34. Utterance of *bismi' llāhi 'r-raḥmāni 'r-raḥīm*, "In the name of God the Beneficent, the Merciful".

Christians there was Naḫle Baulī and his brothers — they worked in European tailoring, their family being Greek; their youngest was Qusṭā Baulī,[35] who was killed through treachery. They were all brave and generous. Al-Ḥāǧǧ Fāris was agile in defending himself with the knife. As'ad Baideh, from the inhabitants of Mazrā'a, was deadly, quick in his movements, an expert in striking with a rod and in the stick game. His is a long story and he had some encounters with me. Maybe they will be mentioned later on. Amongst the Christians there was also a Maronite youth with the name Iskandar al-Abras. He slaughtered pigs and sold their meat; he had extremely strong forearms. From among the Muslim youth there were Ibrāhīm 'Abd al-'Āl and his brother 'Uṯmān and the children of as-Sardūk and al-Ġazzāwī and others, who distinguished themselves by their courage. Each community used to exaggerate in the proofs of bravery and strength that were told about its heroes.

There were still other social gatherings which brought together the young toughs and libertines, *riǧāl al-futūwa wa-'abnā' al-hawā*;[36] I mean the drinking bouts. They occurred very frequently and would be attended by the wise man and the ignorant, because the Beirutis have for a long time believed Araq to be of benefit before the meal and wine with the meal. Rare the person who did not drink on one or both of the two occasions. These drinking rounds are only important in our context insofar as their participants were decent people who — once the alcohol went to their heads — became boisterous, shouted and boasted. Amongst all the

35. About him Edward Attiyah had the following to say in his own reminiscences about Beirut: "In the days just before I was born, the leader of the Christians' champions was a man called Osta Bawli — a corruption of his original Greek name, Costi Paoli. He was a redoubtable champion, loved and admired by the Christians, dreaded by the Moslems. Every Christian in difficulty with the Moslems or with the Turkish government was his protégé; every Christian murdered was sure to be avenged by him or by his lieutenants; Christians in danger of being arrested sought refuge with him. He concealed them, gave them money, helped them to flee to America... At last the Moslems got him. He was stabbed in the back one night and died. By the next morning the staggering news had spread throughout the Christian community of the town. Osta Bawli dead! Osta Bawli murdered! His funeral was the occasion of a fervent demonstration by the Christians; it might have been that of a great captain or statesman. For once the Greek Orthodox and Protestant, Maronite and Roman Catholic forgot their differences — forgot even their fear of the Moslems and Abdulhamid, and turned out to a man, to pay their last tribute, in warlike fashion, to a fallen hero." ATTIYAH 11 ff.

36. It is not exactly clear whom Zaidān meant with these terms.

people I associated with during this period, there was also a group of those. I used not to sit down with them to drink, but I would observe them while they were drinking in the taverns; one of them would pretend friendship and I would respect him for his sagacity or his courage or his distinction in one thing or the other, and I would enjoy sitting with them. But I was not able to drink. If I was made to drink a glass, I did not see myself reaching their high spirits full of pride and conceit. Usually three or four would sit together to get drunk. One of them would order a *ḫamsīnīya*[37] and it would be served to him. It would be poured for him and his friends until it was empty. Then another one would order a second, and so on until none owed the others anything. Sometimes one of them would insist on paying everything if he was a man of eminence or merit. But rarely would they acknowledge the right of someone to do so. Sometimes hell would break loose against whoever acted as the first in this. When the wine went to their heads, one would start singing a Baġdadi *mawwāl.*[38] They would listen well to his song and would interpret from it something that he wanted from them, be it by way of praise and laudation or criticism and negative comments. It would then behove him or one of his friends or his companions to answer to the *mawwāl.* Provided the singing was done with good humour, the party would take a turn for the better. But if it consisted of criticism and insinuations, it would lead to quarrelling and eventually to the drawing of knives and unsheathing of sticks.

I used to envy these young people for their quickmindedness in their answers when I was present at their parties, and I used to feel unable to keep up with their enthusiasm and clamour when singing; since I had experienced only this milieu, I believed it to be a virtue to triumph over people in things like this.

Those were the mores of the Beirut lower class, *'āmma,* which was uneducated because of the few schools available for it. Obscene expressions and indecent talk prevailed in their speech. But obscene language was not restricted to the poor and the masses, *'āmma,* but was used also

37. A fiftieth of a bottle of wine or oil. Exact measurement not clear. BARTHELEMY: *ḫamsīn.*

38. *Mawwāl* or *mawālīyā* is a kind of popular song making use of alliterations and being composed in the vernacular. EI[1].

by the rich people. At that time the people of Beirut consisted of two classes, *ṭabaqatān*: the lower class, *al-ʿāmma*, which means the riff-raff, the artisans, all the other people with menial occupations, and the small merchants. The people of the government and the rich constituted the upper class, *al-ḫāṣṣa*. But the social norms were basically one and the same as far as family life, manners of speech, eating and drinking were concerned. Food and living style differed only very little. Obscene expressions were predominant in the speech of the rich as well as in that of the poor. Regard in the same way the consumption of alcoholic beverages and the like, keeping in mind, however, the difference in means and resources.

During that period, i.e. after the unrest of the sixties, there developed a third class amongst the people of Beirut educated in the Christian missionary schools, especially the American, English, and German ones. Following the French occupation of Beirut, a result of the clashes of the year sixty, missions flocked to the city. They founded schools in order to spread the knowledge and culture of modern civilized Europe.[39] Out of this grew a group of educated girls who graduated from the school of the English Lady, Mrs. Mott[40] of the English School, and a group of young men, consisting of graduates of the Syrian Evening School,[41] the School of the Jesuits,[42] or the Patriarchal School,[43] etc. This third social group was determined to change the social norms from what they were to what they became, so that the contemporary morals of Beirut became

39. Zaidān is not quite correct here. Educational efforts of local communities began in the second half of the 18th century. In the twenties and thirties of the 19th century, Jesuits, Lazarists, British and American missionaries had started and intensive drive for education in Lebanon. The civil war of the early sixties only saw a temporary reduction of these activities. HANF 62.

40. MUNAǦǦID 28 has here erroneously Mrs. Sut. Mrs. Mott was the wife of an English missionary who had come to Beirut in 1861. She took over the English missionary girls' schools in Lebanon after the death of the founder, Mrs. Thompson, her sister-in-law, in 1870. RICHTER 203.

41. Could not be identified.

42. Jesuits returned to Lebanon in 1831 and established a first day school in Beirut in 1842. TIBAWI 182. The College de Jamhour was founded in Beirut in 1874. Since that year there existed also the Université de St. Joseph which developed out of the Jesuit School in Gazir, transferred to Beirut in 1874. HANF 164. Not evident which school Zaidān meant.

43. Founded 1864 as a secondary school by the Greek Catholic Patriarch. Today it is the College Patriarcal.

comparable with the most advanced habits and customs of the Europeans, as far as good manners in talking or sitting, etc., were concerned.

Yet this group grew gradually. When it first appeared, the common people of Beirut considered it a sinful breach with tradition, manifesting effeminateness and licentiousness. Especially after these students began to dress in Western clothes, they faced the contempt of many. I myself regarded these students with contempt because they did not quarrel or beat each other and did not drink.

This opinion, however, did not prevail for very long in my mind, as I did not see myself capable of keeping up with the young toughs and since I never made any real friends amongst those who condemned these Westernizing movements. Eventually, I had occasion to keep company with an educated young fellow, who had an impact upon the course of my future life, even though this had not been his intention. I will come to speak of him shortly.

I realized how incapable I was of comparing myself with these youngsters in boasting about beating, killing and drinking, while at the same time I was a boy like any other boy in his early youth who loves high distinction and seeks fame. I regarded my place amongst these people as that of a strange bird. I spent about three or four years in this situation, during which time I did not read a book nor learn a word, until I forgot what I had learned in the school. I forgot even my desire to learn and my love for knowledge. It so happened that I met, as I have already hinted, this young man with the name Ḫalīl Šāwūl. He was originally from Dair al-Qamar. He was a year older than I and he worked repairing watches in the *al-ʿAǧūrī* store in *Sūq aṭ-ṭawīla*. I became acquainted with him by accident, meeting him at one of our neighbours from the Maronite community who ironed tarbushes. When we met we liked each other very much. I was very fond of him and regarded him with respect for the sagacity, pride and gentleness that I perceived in him, and he made me his friend.

He had a number of friends who revered him and respected him. Most felt that he was intellectually their superior. When we got acquainted, we began to arrange walks outside every Sunday sometime in the afternoon. We went out to the *al-Ašrafīya* Heights or the *Karantīnā* or other places for promenades. We took none of the devices of pleasure with us. Some of us would bring a small flask with Araq, but nobody would touch a sip of it. Amongst the group was a boy by the name of As'ad Mus'ad whose soft voice delighted all of us when he sang. We had not been acquainted with each other for long before I felt a special effection for Ḫalīl and he felt the same for me. When we went out for a walk — fifteen or twenty of us — we began, he and I, to separate ourselves most often from the rest and immerse ourselves in deep conversation. It was of great benefit to me that he used to memorize much poetry and assumed that I knew some myself. He would recite one of the verses of al-Mutanabbī[44] or of [Ibn] al-Fāriḍ.[45] He admired it and imagined that I understood its meaning. For me, all this was new. It was enjoyable to contemplate the meaning of the poems. I began to read them and to interpret them. My desire to read poems grew daily. The understanding of their meanings increased my wish to exchange opinions about them. But none of our companions took pleasure in such an exchange. They would more likely dismiss us and keep busy with drinking and singing while we would investigate the meaning of a verse and carry on a dispute about the purpose of the poet.

Initially, he stirred up my interest in reading poetry. I purchased the books of al-Mutanabbī and [Ibn] al-Fāriḍ, who.... in Beirut.[46] I began to read those two and to study closely the meaning of what I was reading. It pleased me when I succeeded in understanding one of the obscure verses, just as if I had conquered a country or hit upon a treasure. This encouraged me in my reading, and strengthened my affection for Ḫalīl. Eventually, our group broke up and our friends scattered; only Ḫalīl and I remained as if we were one. To him goes the credit of having awakened my interest in reading which meant the opening of a new future for me.

Ḫalīl had friends amongst the students. Some of them, whom I met through him, were from the College.[47] From them I heard, for the first

44. Al-Mutanabbī (905-965). His *Dīwān* first time printed in Beirut in 1860 before that several prints in India since 1814; GAL I 86 ff. Suppl. I 138 ff.

45. 'Umar Ibn al-Fāriḍ (1182-1235). His *Dīwān* lithographed 1872 in Aleppo, first printed in Beirut 1882; GAL Suppl. I 463.

46. Illegible in ms.

47. Here and in the following College refers to the Syrian Protestant College.

time, a rebuke of the ability to shout, drink, and draw knives, things to which I had lent myself; so much so that I wanted to get used to drinks, as other people did. I suggested to a neighbour of ours, by the name of Isṭifān al-Ğammāl, who used to buy tobacco and Araq from us, that he should cool a *ḫamsīnīya* for me — hidden from my father — so I could drink it slowly during my work from around sunset to the time of the evening prayer. He cooled it for me and I went out the first time and took a glass of it. Soon I went and had a second glass. I had hardly taken a third drink when I threw up everything in my stomach. Dizziness overcame me. But I suffered through it quietly so that my father would not sense what I had done. In my innermost self I was sad, that I was indeed not one of these manly young people. You should have seen how much I was relieved when I heard these friends denouncing the habit of drinking and other deeds of those youngsters. They made wisdom, calmness, and conciliation desirable and I felt as if a veil had been pulled away from my eyes. I realized that I was on the right path, but had tried to delude myself. I continued to hold on to those friends and I began to make my own mind judge each issue, even though I had little knowledge and experience.

During this period of friendship with Ḫalīl and my newly developed desire to learn it happened once that the teacher Su'ūd aṭ-Ṭawīl from aš-Šiyāh in the neighbourhood of Beirut, one of our customers, sat in our restaurant — just being sociable in an hour of leisure. He mentioned that he had opened a school to teach boys English during the evening hours. The term "English language" was strange for the Beirutis to hear because the only characteristic of the English they knew was contained in the expression "English drunkenness". Frequently they used to observe drunken members of the English navy in the streets of the city. Some of the English cruisers, which used to patrol in the Mediterranean, would from time to time anchor in the port of Beirut and their crews would come ashore on leave after being for weeks and months isolated on their tours. They would roam around the city, eat, drink and most would be overpowered by drunkenness. When they were drunk they would quarrel boisterously in a language nobody understood. So the expression "English drunkenness" was on everybody's lips in Beirut, implying excessive drinking. Few understood, indeed, the English language, amongst them dragomans who made friends with the sailors while those were roaming through the markets. They would mediate between the sailors and the merchants — dividing the profits or receiving a commission for whatever was sold.

I don't know what aroused my interest to learn this language, when the teacher Su'ūd mentioned the school. I don't remember that I did this out of ambition for the future or desire to translate for whoever of the English navy came to us to eat. I was far too timid to do something like that. But I know that I asked Su'ūd how much the fee was. He told me thirty Beiruti *ġirš* (i.e. less than six francs) per month. The teacher Su'ūd used to eat in our place and I told him that he ate for much more money than this and that we should cut the fee off his food bill and I would not notice the payments at all. I informed my father that I wanted to learn the English language. He did not object, but wondered how I would be able to do this, when I was busy all day and part of the night in the restaurant. I was then fifteen years old. I began to visit the teacher frequently at home. There were about fifteen students who learned together, both young and old. Some were dragomans for tourists, and their language was poor; some were servants who wanted to advance to the class of dragomans. But very soon they found the learning of this language difficult and began to leave the teacher. Before two months had passed, only I and one friend by the name of Darwīš Ṣufair remained together. He is today an expert accountant in Egypt. Only he and I remained, and the teacher used to prefer to turn us away, since taking sixty *ġirš* from us per hour each night [sic] was not sufficient for him. When we finished the fourth month and began the fifth the teacher told me: "You know now as much English as I do". I believed him because man is misled in his youth and in his mature age as well by the praise of people attributing to him an achievement which he did not accomplish or in which he has no merit, especially at the age of immaturity. I was reaffirmed in my misbelief because I began to translate easily from the book the *Third Reader*. The teacher confirmed that I had got to know the English language very well. I ceased to go to him and tried my hand at reading a book of Captain Cook's voyages to the ocean islands. I realized that I was much weaker than I had thought myself to be and I began to study on my own.

What helped me to accomplish in reading and the like by myself as much as I did was my strong determination, *qawīy al-'azīma*, my sturdy physique and my perserverance in work, *ṣabūr 'alā 'l-'amal*. Take for instance the learning of English. I have told you already that I was busy in our restaurant all day and some hours of the night. My father needed me every moment because the accounts and the dealings were in my hands. Only at night after returning home did I have time for myself. I would light a lamp which I had put on the window sill next to my bed and spend the hours in learning and reading. Once my father knocked at the door of my room while I was sitting on my bed reading and writing. I rose and opened the door to him assuming that he was still awake and had come to admonish me to sleep, as was his habit. But when I opened the door I saw that the dawn had already begun to show. He asked me, "How come that I see you got up early this morning?" I answered him, "I haven't slept yet!" He got angry and advised me to take care of my health and asked how did I stay awake until the rise of the day? I apologized but I reverted to similar sessions quite unintentionally.

My effort to learn this language affected my work. I usually cooked in the morning. Cooking for us meant to put ten pots on the stoves all at once: one for the rice, one for beans and so on — I would take care of all of them. Then I would open my English book to study and to translate. When I was needed during my readings for moving a pot or cutting meat, I would put the book face down on the writing table, *baštaḥteh*, and do the work; then I would return to it.

During this time I had the idea of compiling an English-Arabic dictionary. The dictionary of Abkāriyūs[48] had not yet appeared. I acquired the Douglas dictionary, which was only in English. The Jesuits had a French-Arabic dictionary. I used these two dictionaries and linguistic connections and whatever expressions I knew to compile my English-Arabic dictionary. I reached he letter E before I became weary of it. No wonder I gave up, since I had very little language knowledge. I was extremely sad when I discontinued this work, since it spontaneously came to my mind that I was by nature weak-willed and of little ambition.

---

48. Yūḥanā Abkāriyūs (d. 1889) brother of the poet Iskandar A. Born in Beirut of Armenian origin. Besides some other books by him he wrote and published in Beirut an English-Arabic dictionary; ZAIDĀN *Ta'rīḫ ādāb* IV 260.

I regarded it as an evil omen that I did not do the work and did not persevere in it to the end. I was then sixteen years old.

But this did not dissuade me from studying. I began to read Arabic books of poetry and literature, and the *Kitāb maǧmaʿ al-baḥrain.*[49] The latter had a great impact upon me since it helped me to learn linguistic terms with the knowledge of which I boasted in front of my companions. The reading of poetry led me to try composition myself. I would compose a verse or two without knowing their meter or desinential inflection.

The story of the acquisition of the *maǧmaʿ al-baḥrain* is not without interest and is worth mentioning for its humour. When my inquisitiveness began to grow, I had heard about *Kitāb maǧmaʿ al-baḥrain* and I wanted to buy it. But I found it to be too expensive because its price was, I believe, four or five francs. When I was sitting one day in the restaurant a boy passed by with a used copy in his hand, which he offered to sell. I bought it from him for nine Beiruti *ġirš*, i.e. less than half the price. I was very happy with it. But when my father came back from his promenade towards evening — he went out every afternoon to relax together with a friend by the name of Ḥannā az-Zailāʿ who originally had been his partner — when he came back towards evening he saw the book and asked me about it. I told him, "I bought it for nine *ġirš*." He, however had no idea of its worth, since he could not read. He thought somebody had cheated me and he, therefore, was annoyed. He took it in his hand and enquired, "Did you pay nine *ġirš* for this book and exchange money just for paper?" I in turn got angry, which was visible on my face, and preferred not to answer him. He remained convinced that I had made a mistake. When we returned home in the evening my mother had already prepared dinner, but I pretended not to feel like eating and went to the bedroom, expecting that they would call me and would not let me go to sleep hungry. I heard my mother scolding my father for having irritated me to the point that I would go to sleep without eating. But he insisted on his opinion. It so happened that one of our neighbours, Amīn Fayyāḍ, one of the dignitaries of Beirut, came over to see us that night for an evening visit. He used to show some affection for me. Asking about me he was answered that I had gone to sleep. My mother seized this oppor-

49. Nāṣīf al-Yāziǧī, *Kitāb maǧmaʿ al-baḥrain*, Beirut 1856. Collection of essays written in the style of the *maqāmāt* of al-Ḥarīrī in rhymed prose; GAL Suppl. I 765.

tunity and complained to him about the obstinacy of my father. Asked about the reason for his anger, he replied, "He spends money to buy useless paper!" Amīn Fayyāḍ answered, "Thank God, Abū Ğurğī, that your son uses the money for buying books and not for drinking and the like — indeed this is a blessing for which you ought to thank God". I had heard his words very well, even though I pretended to be asleep. Immediately, my mother gained the upper hand, she woke me up, sat me at the table and put my mind at rest, so did my father. This story is still before my eyes and it was of benefit to me.

During this time "al-Muqtaṭaf"[50] appeared. It was, I believe, in its second year of publication when some of the school teachers, who came often to us, pointed out to me an article about the lunar eclipse in one of its issues. I read it and when I understood it I felt a great joy because I knew the reason for the eclipse and how the earth turns and stands in the middle between the moon and the sun and the eclipse comes about. In some other issues I read about the clouds and the cause of rain. My inquisitiveness about the laws of nature grew and I desired to obtain a book, the only one there was about the philosophy of nature in Arabic — I mean the *Kitāb al-ʿarūs al-badīʿa* by aš-Šudūdī,[51] which was very popular. It so happened that some of the students of the Imperial Medical School returned from Istanbul in order to conclude their studies in the College. I got acquainted with one of them, Samʿān al-Ḫūrī,[52] sone of one of the notables of al-Kūra (today Dr. Samʿān al-Ḫūrī). He came frequently to our restaurant to eat since he was a stranger in Beirut. I was delighted to get to know him since, in general, I had a strong inclination to associate and to converse with the students of the colleges. I was convinced of their superiority to all other human beings. When I sat together with one of them, I looked up to him as a teacher. After Samʿān had visited me often and I had become friends with him — he was an amiable companion —

50. See 12, n. 2.

51. Munağğid 36 reads here Qašdūdī, but clearly meant is Asʿad Ibrāhīm aš-Šudūdī (1826-1906). He was a teacher at various schools, since 1866 at the Syrian Protestant College. His *Kitāb al-ʿarūs al-badīʿa fī ʿilm aṭ-ṭabīʿa* appeared in Beirut in 1873; GAL III 339, Dāğir III 616, Zaidān *Taʾrīḫ ādāb* IV 200. Tibawi 181 has Asʿad Šadūdī.

52. Samʿān al-Ḫūrī (d. 1921) born in Lebanon, obtained M.D. degree from the SPC in 1882, worked as a physician in Beirut; *Alumni* 11.

he felt my congenial reception and felt like disclosing to me his circumstances. He told me about his determination to enter the College to learn medicine. But he had no knowledge of the sciences which were required prior to entering the field of medicine. He consulted me about the way to study these fields and I explained to him that the best book was *kitāb al-ʿarūs al-badīʿa*. He bought it and brought it to me, complaining, "I do not understand what I read. It is necessary that I learn again what I learned in Istanbul in Turkish". So I began to read with him together and to explain to him what he did not comprehend. In this way, I was compelled to understand the topics very well myself. After a short while he managed to study on his own — or perhaps he took a teacher to help him. But I remember very clearly that I drew some benefit from reading this book.

From that time on I began to question myself whether it was necessary for me to remain stuck with this job I had. I would not have minded staying with it had it been conducive to my obtaining knowledge. I felt my passing from one stage into another. I had reached the age of sixteen. Until then I had considered myself weak and incapable, existing only to emulate others, assuming that what occurred around me was proper and I could only imitate it; and when I did not succeed in doing so, I regretted my weakness. Now, however, I felt that I was an individual with my own will, believing that most of what happened around me was mostly wrong and that I was on the right and proper way. I felt myself inadequate. This coincided with my entering the age of self-deceptions and illusions. It is the age in which a youngster is overcome by conceit thinking himself the smartest of all people and assuming for himself an outstanding future. He blames the people for failing to appreciate him according to his true ability. But the cowardice for which I had a natural disposition usually mitigated my delusions.

During the first part of the time I spent at the restaurant I was convinced that the people who wore *bantalūnāt*[53] were of higher intelligence, wider knowledge and better judgment than those wearing the *sirwāl,*[54] because most of them belonged to the educated people. But

53. The French word *pantalon* is recognizable. What is meant by this term are Western-styled pants.

54. *Sirwāl* pl. *sarāwīl* or *širwāl* pl. *šarāwīl* are the traditional Ottoman baggy trousers.

when I began to open my eyes and read a little of the scientific principles, this opinion of mine was somewhat weakened. I stopped being surprised any more when people wearing the *sirwāl* and the *qunbāz*[55] kept up with those wearing pants and hats.

When my mother noticed my progress she helped me and reiterated the attack against my father, demanding that he should take me out of the restaurant. He did not oppose her. But the idea was that one had to deliberate about the occupation which it was desirable to take up after leaving. He believed that being a cook was the most profitable vocation, if one's cooking became popular. He contradicted my mother very much on this point since she vehemently criticized this vocation because of the filth and work day and night.

Through Šāwūl, I had already made the acquaintance of many of his friends among the commercial clerks in *Sūq aṭ-ṭawīla*. I felt myself strange and sordid amongst them, in spite of my delight about their kind praise for me. Whenever I saw one of them in front of his desk, the account book open before him, with the pen stuck behind his ear his clothes and desk clean, then my heart started to beat with desire for a similar position. Therefore, I mentioned to my parents when they were deliberating what to do with me that I should work as a clerk in some store in *Sūq aṭ-ṭawīla*. They agreed with me. It required, however, the study of double-entry bookkeeping, *ḥisāb ad-dūbiyā*, to keep the books. I told them that I would learn it. There lived at the time a famous teacher of this art, by the name of *al-Ḫawāǧa* Ḥabīb Saʿd. He gave private lessons in his house to those wanting to learn double-entry bookkeeping. I knew this and arranged to study with him. We agreed upon 250 *ġirš* for teaching me this art, without, however, setting a time limit. I payed the money and began to come frequently to the house of the teacher. Several well-educated people also studied this subject with him and I considered them to be better in studying because they came from the schools. Not two months passed before I mastered the double entry bookkeeping. I noticed that my teacher was very astonished about this; I, in turn, was bewildered by his astonishment until I learned that my colleagues who learned together with me had spent a month on it already when I came and stayed for another month after I had left. I

55. A sleeved garment worn by men, open in front and held together by a belt.

maintain that I had no merit beyond theirs other than endeavour, because I acquired this knowledge out of my own desire, while they were urged on to it by the wish of their fathers.

After I completed the studies, it only remained that I should join one of the warehouses. One of the friends introduced me to the store of *al-Ḫawāǧa* Ġarzūzī on *Sūq aṭ-ṭawīla.* I agreed to come down to work for him. I put on clean clothes as the clerks and accountants did and went down to the store. My first task was the dusting of all the shelves. When a customer came I was to help *al-Ḫawāǧa* Ġarzūzī to fetch the silk cloths or other things for inspection by the customer. It happened that I spent the first half day without anybody coming. I felt lonely being a confined employee, while in the restaurant I had been my own master in full command of affairs. I was dispirited and I could hardly wait for it to be lunchtime so that I could ask permission to go to eat. I did not return but went back to the restaurant.

However, I had acquired some independence of mind. I left the sphere of blind submission and began to rely upon what appeared to me to be contradictory to my common surrounding. Gradually, I dared to criticize the talks and acts of others. I started to respect myself and my opinion, the more so as the pride of the young man grew in me. I created an attitude around which revolved my endeavours to raise my worthiness: guarding over my conduct by avoiding obscene expressions and the company of uneducated people and ceasing completely to make jokes. Soberness dominated my talk and my deeds. So exaggerated was my attempt to keep above any suspicion of adultery that I would not look at a woman any more. I would not pass a street where people were gossiping about one of the women residing there. My friend Šāwūl and I had agreed together on this conduct. We became famous for this amongst the Beirutis and they cited us as examples; parents would mention it to their children so that they would imitate us. The more praise I heard for this attitude, the more I clung to it. I am not ashamed to declare frankly that I spent eight years in this dangerous environment as I described it, but I emerged from it unblemished and clean — though I do not deny that more than once I was close to faltering because of so many temptations. In the beginning I had to control myself, then it became an inner conviction with me.

I wanted to read as much as my time permitted me. I courted the educated people and when somebody famous in scholarship or journalism came to me I would outdo myself in showing my respect. I would watch every word he said and quote from him. If indeed one of them spoke to me or was friendly with me, I considered this a great condescension on his part; after all, he was a scholar or a writer and yet addressed one of the common people, *aḥad as-sūqa*. Amongst those educated people who frequently visited the restaurant was the *Šaiḫ* Ibrāhīm al-Yāziǧī.[56] He wore the Arab *sarāwil* and a North African fez. He impressed me very much with the neatness of his clothes and the arrangement of his outfit. *Šaiḫ* Ibrāhīm had attained great fame in the world of scholarship and had many admirers. Occasionally he would come to take his lunch at my place. It was his habit to come shortly after noon when I was alone. I wondered how I could serve him best. By nature he was courteous and agreeable. When he addressed me or joked with me I would remember every one of his words and repeat them. I still remember how he once had his lunch and left but had forgotten his glasses on the table. I followed him, holding them in my hands and gave them to him, He smiled and said, "I left my eyes with you, but no need to be worried about them; I left my heart with you a long time ago and nothing has happened to it." Another time he rose from the table giving me a big coin, I believe it was a *riyāl* in order that I should give him back the change after subtracting the price of the lunch. I reached for the drawer of the little cash box to give him back the change and said, "In the name of Allāh, the Beneficent, the Merciful, Owner of the Day of Judgment." I pulled out the drawer and pointing with his finger to the money he addressed it, "Thee we worship, Thee we call for help!" I was delighted with this pun and related it to many.[57] I was happy that *Šaiḫ* al-Yāziǧī was so kind to me.

Amongst those was also 'Abdallāh al-Bustānī,[58] the teacher. I

56. See 6, n. 7.

57. Zaidān quotes here the first and the third verse of the first Sura, *al-Fātiḥa*. Al-Yāziǧī answers with the fourth verse. Assumedly he changed the gender of "thee" in Arabic from male to female, *īyāki*, instead of *īyāka*, thus making it clear that he is referring to the money.

58. 'Abdallāh al-Bustānī (1854-1930), member of an illustrous Lebanese family. Several generations of it were involved in the intellectual and literary revival of the

benefited much from his talks about poetry and language. I once showed him some verses that I had composed and he encouraged me even though I knew that they were no good. He recited often to me from his *ǧāhilī* poetry, much of which I memorized. During that time the people of Dair al-Qamar happened to oppose Rustum *Pāšā*[59] and to write against him. 'Abdallāh, the teacher, published in the *Lisān al-ḥāl*[60] a dream in which he alluded to the *Pāšā* and his actions and in which he included many names of the Iblis and the devils. I used to discuss this with him when we met.

Amongst them was also the teacher Ibrāhīm al-Kafrūnī,[61] and.....[62] I had subscribed to "al-Muqtaṭaf" to read it. I boasted about the fact that I was a subscriber to it and liked other people to know that I read it. I wanted to embark on writing for it. I wrote an article, doing my utmost correcting and embellishing it according to my abilities. I did not know grammatical endings and forms but I wrote it from the heart, its topic being a criticism of fathers who neglect the education of their young children, because once they are grown up the opportunity for education is lost. This was at the time my situation. I sent the essay to "al-Muqtaṭaf" in care of its director, Šāhīn Makāriyūs,[63] and I waited patiently for the forthcoming issue. It appeared — and then another one and a third one, but the essay was not published. I was amazed that it had not been published since I believed it to be useful. After some months the director of "al-Muqtaṭaf" happened to come to me with some friends for

---

Arab world. 'Abdallāh himself was interested in literature and was one of the first to write a piece for the theatre in Arabic. He worked as a teacher of Arabic in various missionary and government schools; DĀĠIR II 193.

59. Rustum *Pāšā* (1806-1895) Italian by origin he entered the service of the Ottoman Empire. After serving as the Ottoman Ambassador to Italy he was appointed in 1873 *Mutaṣṣarif* of the Lebanon in which function he served for ten years. The position of *Mutaṣṣarif* or plenipotentiary, had been established for the Lebanon together with *Règlement Organique* after the disturbances of 1858-1860. The *Mutaṣṣarif* had to be a Catholic Christian and was directly responsible to the government in Istanbul; ZAIDĀN *Tarāǧim* I 202 ff.

60. *Lisān al-Ḥāl*, a semi-weekly journal founded in 1877 by Ḫalīl Sarkīs in Beirut. It eventually became a daily paper offering a melange of topics ranging from politics over literature to agriculture; DI ṬARRĀZĪ II 27-33.

61. Ibrāhīm al-Kafrūnī (d. 1896) obtained a B.A. from the SPC in 1873, taught as an instructor in the preparatory school of the Medical School, 1880-1885, later went to Egypt where he worked as a translator; *Alumni* 4, *Catalogue* 80/81-84/85.

62. sic in ms.

63. See 23, n. 37.

lunch. We knew each other already from before. He greeted me and I admired him for his modesty and friendliness. I ventured to find out from him about my article and asked whether it had reached him. He answered that it had reached him and that perhaps the next one would be better than this one. So I understood that he did not publish it because of its weakness. I took this as a lesson and my self-confidence regressed to what it had been ten years ago. It did not at all enter my mind that the manager of the newspaper treated me unfairly, as is the case with most who write for a newspaper and their articles are not published. But I was convinced after this that I would not insist on anybody publishing my articles. I did not again write for any newspaper from that time on until after I had studied sciences, entered the medical school and had understood some of the subjects of medicine. Even then my writings remained controversial, as will be mentioned below.

I began to think about ways that could help me to acquire knowledge. My father had cast upon me the most important tasks of his restaurant and its bookkeeping. I cooked, I shopped, I collected the money, gave credit and settled the accounts. I became indispensible to this place in order to keep it from falling apart, since my father did not know how to write and had got used to depending on me and not trusting anybody else.

All this I realized and waited patiently for an opportunity. My desire to study had been augmented through my association with students from the College. A large group of the medical students studied there but lived outside. Most of them were strangers and came to eat in the restaurant. My friend Sam'ān al-Ḫūrī had entered this school, but he kept coming back to us to eat and even brought some other students to us. They used to socialize with me a lot. After the meal they would sit when we finished serving food to the people, and we would talk and discuss and they would discern in me an inclination for learning, or sometimes I would embark upon a scientific discussion and they would hear talk from me that would show my inquiry into this science the like of which they were not accustomed to from cooks or other lower artisans or vendors in those times. The number of students that came back to us increased and I was delighted with them, not because of the gains I hoped to make from their meals but because I enjoyed their conversation.

Amongst those who visited my place frequently during that time were Ḫalīl Ḫairallāh,[64] As'ad Raḫḫāl,[65] Ḥasan Naṣṣār,[66] Bāḫūs Ḥakīm,[67] Sam'ān al-Ḫūrī and others. They used to invite me to their festivities which took place in the school after the exams and the distribution of the diplomas. I listened to the public addresses and observed the successful students, and I felt depressed because I was excluded from this. I would not leave such a festivity without feeling low. I was rarely present at such occasions without my friend Ḫalīl Šāwūl. He possessed a similar inclination towards study and used to complain about his being tied down as a watchmaker, just as I would complain about my confinement to the restaurant. My companions would often notice my depressed mood and ask me the reason. I would excuse myself and deny it. Only to Ḫalīl I once said, "Shall there not come a day when I stand where these speakers stand?"

I also attended the festivities of the *Šams al-birr* association, which was a chapter of the English Y.M.C.A.[68] It was a club filled with educated people, most of its members consisting of students at the College. Speeches and conferences were given there. I was, of course, friends with some of its members from amongst the students of the College. They encouraged me to join this association and I considered their encouragement a great favour. I became a member of its organization and believed it to be a great honour, since I did not deem anything more valuable in this world than knowledge.

One of the marks the friendship with Šāwūl made upon my future was the fact that he introduced me to Doctor Iskandar al-Bārūdī[69] who was then a student at the School of Medicine. I am greatly indebted to al-Bārūdī because it was he who placed me at the gates of knowledge and prepared me for the world of culture. I met him through Šāwūl who

64. Ḫalīl Ḫairallāh (1860-1899), born in Lebanon, obtained M.D. degree from SPC in 1883, served as a medical officer with the Egyptian army in Sudan; *Alumni* 13.

65. As'ad Raḫḫāl (1959-1927) born in Lebanon, obtained M.D. degree from SPC in 1883; *Alumni* 13.

66. Ḥasan Naṣṣār studied medicine at the SPC but did not graduate. No further information.

67. Bāḫūs Ḥakīm (1857-1897) born in Lebanon, obtained M.D. degree from SPC in 1883, worked in Lebanon; *Alumni* 13.

68. See 22, n. 28.

69. See 20, n. 25.

was his friend. Iskandar was a member of the *Šams al-birr* association. His was a lofty position because of his learning; he was popular and his opinion was relied upon. In those days he was known as "Iskandar the Teacher" because before entering the medical school he used to teach in some schools. When he took up medicine the name stuck with him. The students and teachers used to love him: they esteemed him highly and tried to emulate his activeness and intelligence — and Iskandar the Teacher, too, of course, took an exalted position in my own heart. He became for me the example of what an educated, diligent young man ought to be.

With all this I still increased my desire to study until I finally told my father of my thoughts. He answered me, "Do what you think behoves you!" But when my mother heard of my decision she almost lost her senses out of happiness, and she encouraged me very much. However, I did not find any way to leave the restaurant. My father believed that my leaving would lead to closing the avenue to a livelihood for my family. I considered what benefits I hoped for from the study of sciences. I realized that the only profession I could take up was teaching. When I graduated from College I would be able to teach at a salary of 200 to 300 *ġirš*, which at that time were worth quite a lot. But I reconsidered this and began to think of a better way. It occurred to me that most of my knowledge came from the medical students, and I said to myself, "Why don't I study medicine? Once I have passed the period of my studies I will graduate as a physician. From this profession I as well as my family can make a living. I did not know what I needed to know before I entered the study of medicine, other than the difficulties preventing me from leaving my job. But with regard to this I was lucky enough to find a good way out, namely during that year my father went into partnership with his friend. Ḥannā az-Zailāʿ, a colleague of his. They joined in opening an over-night hotel close to the theatre "Syria" and, together, bought the necessary beds. This work was neither fatiguing nor did it demand any knowledge of reading. They made me and the son of my father's associate partners. His name was Ǧurǧī, like mine. We knew each other and had been companions since childhood. His father was more convinced of my sedateness, my diligence in work and my considerate conduct than of that of his son. Therefore, he wanted to attach him to me so that he might perhaps improve.

We became partners for the restaurant underneath the hotel, which our fathers had opened. This was a big cellar. In its place today is a plant for chick peas, pistacio and assorted nuts, owned by ʻUmar al-Maḥmaṣānī. About this noble man praiseworthy recollections will be mentioned later in my story.

When I became independent in my work from my father and when I had assured myself that I need not be concerned about his income if I left him, I began to think about a way to realize my plans. I already had many friends among the medical students. Very frequently they came to me, and the desire to become one of their group had grown, even though the work in our new restaurant meant a lot of profit. By way of illustration I shall only mention that our neighbours would never sell anything before we had sold out. We had a neighbour, Qaiṣar Ǧāwīš, who owned a restaurant close to ours. He used to come to me towards evening, look into the pots and if he found something in them he would exclaim, "We would like to finish and get rid of our stuff; when are we going to make a living for ourselves?" Nevertheless, my mind was overcome by the quest for knowledge through the study of medicine.

I had read parts of the book *The Secret of Success* which Dr. Ṣarrūf had translated into Arabic.[70] Vigor and zeal sprang up in me. I read, as I said, some of it but was unable to finish the rest. Too great was the enthusiastic impact it had upon me to read about the lives of men who reached highest achievements by their own diligence and efforts and self-reliance. Amongst them, barbers and shoemakers, servants, artisans and maids who rose through their eagerness and vigilance to the station of great people. If I read a few pages I would be so agitated that I could not sleep any longer or be calm, and, finding myself tied down, pity would overcome me and I would get depressed. So I would put the book aside and till today I have not finished reading it.

When it occurred to me to attain knowledge by way of medicine, for the sake of its material in addition to its ethical benefits, I related my thoughts to my friend Šāwūl, who suggested, "Let's ask our friend al-Bārūdī." So we joined him once in the *Šams al-birr* association and presented my idea to him: "If I wanted to study medicine, how much time and

70. See 12.

money would be necessary for it?" He deliberated and looked at me, finding my venturing upon such a ponderous issue unusual, and answered me that the medical student has to learn the preparatory sciences and that their study takes several years — not considering the English and Arabic languages. I asked him about these preparatory sciences and he explained, "They are natural philosophy, algebra, geometry, arithmetic, lexicography, grammer and English. In these subjects the student takes an examination on the day he applies for entering the first year. If he passes he enters medicine. This takes four years if he passes all the exams, and the orals. He then receives the diploma of the school." I found the number of subjects distressing, of some I understood only a very few bits and pieces. My *élan* to study, however, eased every difficulty for me. So I asked him, "If somebody like me wants to study the preparatory sciences, how much time would that take for him?" He answered, "If they are taught at the College, it takes two years for a hardworking person. After these two years many spend additional time studying and perhaps even then do not pass the exams."

When he told me this I almost reversed my decision. But I had great self-confidence, *ṯiqa binafsī*, with regard to the required steadfastness and effort. So I enquired, "Is there not any way to study these subjects outside the school in a condensed form?" "That is possible", he said, "but you will need books, reports, practical exercises and no doubt the necessary time for learning it will have to be spent. At home some have recourse to teachers from outside to help them in their studies".

We were, at the time, just in the last days of the school year and the school was about to be let out for summer vacations. So I said, "Don't you think that if somebody made an effort he could learn these subjects during the summer intercession and take the exams at the beginning of the next school year?" He looked at me and laughed, scorning this idea, "That is impossible. I know three students who spent two years learning these subjects in the preparatory school and do not consider themselves competent to take the exams, so they also study during this summer to complete the requirements. So how would you manage not having learned in a school and without any knowledge?!" "Let us try it", I said. "Try it!" "On the condition", I added, "that Iskandar the Teacher shall be my guide in pursuing these subjects", since I had observed him to be intelligent and having an efficient way of instruction. He answered, "I believe I will not be in Beirut this summer. If I would stay here I would give you as good lessons as possible". He said that in order to encourage me even though he was not convinced of my ability.

Then I enquired about the necessary expenses for the school year, and he told me that the fee was ten Ottoman *līrā* for instruction only, without meals and not considering books and other expenses. Even though I knew that I did not possess a penny of this money, I was determined to carry out my plan. I disclosed my idea to my father's partner and he disapproved of it...[71] about the confession as to what were his intentions and, shedding two tears, he complained, "You know that you are like my son to me, nay, dearer to me than he is. It did not excape you how I tried hard to establish a companionship between you and my son, because I know your diligence to work. But now any hope for the betterment of my son is lost!" What I heard from this old man grieved me and I expressed my regrets to him. But I did not see myself able to go back on my decision, even though I ventured upon an onerous and serious task. I consulted with my father and he did not discuss it again. You should have seen my mother's happiness when I came that evening and announced my decision to her. She was exuberant and encouraged me strongly. She knew that I did not own a penny to pay for the school and that I would not ask for it from my father and that I was determined to pay myself for the school by taking up some job, not knowing yet what it would be. She asked me therefore, "How much is the fee for the first time, that is, the first instalment?" When I explained to her that it was seven Ottoman *līrā*, she told me, "I possess this amount, having collected here a penny there a penny. I'll give it to you. Don't worry about it. Be diligent and rely upon God!" The words of my mother moved me very much.

I began to consider what I should do for the future. One of my ideas was to open an eating place in the neighbourhood of the school, since I knew that many of the day students ate there in some restaurants. If they would eat in my place, I would earn enough to pay for the school. I agreed with my brother Mitrī,[72] who was then still young, that he

71. Illegible in ms.

72. See 29, n. 57.

should take over the management of the place, and we both were content with this arrangement.

But first of all I began to study the preparatory subjects under the guidance of Iskandar the Teacher. During the first two weeks, I encountered such difficulty that it almost dissuaded me from my decision, since I did not understand completely the terminology of these sciences. After this initial period, I came to consider this as easy. I would go every day from our house in Ašrafīya to al-Bārūdī's dwelling in Ra's Beirut to take a lesson — this was during the days of the summer in the afternoon heat around three o'clock. Yet, I did not mind the discomfort and did not know fatigue. I took many lessons in a short time. Somewhat more than a month had passed when we had covered already the mentioned subjects to the extent that they were required. My teacher wanted to continue teaching me when he recognized my assiduity. After we had finished with the requirements, he advanced with me beyond that. Once he praised me for my efforts, and I did not comprehend that they should be called "efforts".

So he told me about the students whom he had mentioned before, who had studied for two years and were now repeating the same subjects with the help of a teacher during the vacations: in spite of this one of them had not even accomplished half of what I had. I thanked him for his praise, which gave me confidence. He named the students for me and pointed me out to his professors, one of them being Ya'qūb Ṣarrūf.[73] "I told my professor Ya'qūb about you", he said, "and I would like you to meet him." Until that day I had never met the teacher Ya'qūb. We once encountered him in the pharmacy of Murād al-Bārūdī and he introduced me to the teacher Ya'qūb. I regarded him with great respect because of what I had heard about his knowledge and virtue. When professor Ya'qūb addressed me with "Bravo, I heard about your hard work from Iskandar the Teacher, and I am very pleased", his words touched my ears like a tune of lovely music and encouraged me very much.

When the first month of instruction had passed, I went to Iskandar the Teacher to enquire about the fee, in order to pay him. He told me, 'The fee is due at the end of the period". When the time was over and

---

73. See 12, n. 2.

the date of the exams arrived, I asked him again about the fee, but he said, "Let us see about it after you take the exams." I understood from this that he intended to take a fee only if I passed the examination and entered the School of Medicine. When the day of the exams had come and I took them and the professors had given me permission to enroll in the Medical School. I hastened to the house of Iskandar the Teacher. He was already on the look-out for me form the window, in order to see me before I entered. When he spotted me, he waved to me with a questioning gesture. I told him that I had passed the exam with success and he was very glad. Entering his house I saw his delight, which was not less than my own. Then I asked him about his fee, but he began to put me off and declared, "My delight with your success is more than my pleasure for money", and refused to take a fee. I decided, of course, to present it to him anyway and perhaps compensate him later. But I will not forget his merit and his affection nor that he helped me to take a great step forward in my success. I confess that the greatest credit for my success with so many lessons in such a short time goes to his excellent explanations. When I did not understand a geometrical, algebraic or natural science problem, he would change the approach of explanation continuously, until I understood it.

I also had drawn moral benefits from the association with Iskandar the Teacher which were of great help for my future life. I learned from him to be conscientious about time, *muḥāfaẓa ʿalā ʾl-waqt*. I observed that he was most conscienctious in putting his time to good use. The high esteem in which I held him made him an example for me. Especially his economizing attitude towards time amazed me. We would study some lesson, and if he left me to do some experimental work by myself, which would take two minutes, he used to turn to a book which he was in the process of translating and would occupy himself with it. He would translate two lines, or three, or a page, rather than sit idly while I was finishing my work. I acquired this virtue from him and it was of great use to me.

After I had studied natural sciences and mathematics I became aware of myself and understood as if a veil was drawn from my eyes that I had entered a new phase. I perceived in myself a faculty of deduction and judgment. After I had imitated others in my movements and thoughts, venting statements and opinions only after I had heard somebody else doing so and thus imitating him, I now became master of my own views on each issue. I began to form my own opinions and to express independent views. The credit for this goes to the natural and mathematical sciences: they condition the mind to correct judgment based on coherent reasons.

It was my good fortune that during the phase of imitation I did not succeed in emulating my first friends in their vices. I spent a long time amongst them, saddened by my incapability to emulate them. When I met Šāwūl and his friends I found myself able to follow them, and I imitated them successfully in their virtuous ways. Perhaps this is the root of the saying, "Send your son to the market and see with whom he associates". This contradicts the other saying, "Wicked company corrupts good character". In my opinion, man is born with certain tendencies and he will only be at ease in the company of those who are agreeable to his tendencies. A youth who is corrupted in the company of educated people has an innate inclination to corruption. He will associate with virtuous men and not benefit from them, but when he meets evil people he will turn to them and keep their company. Though I do not deny the impact education has upon the rectification and improvement of character, I do not believe that it changes the essence.

At the root of my success were my consciousness of time and perseverance.

I woke up on Wednesday in..... [74] the year 1881 and I was one of the students of medicine at the College, I could hardly believe that indeed I had achieved this aspiration. I opened a shop near the gate of the College to sell food stuff, and entrusted my brother Mitrī with it. I also rented a room to live close to it. I operated the eating place for some months, then I discovered that it did not fulfil my expectations and abandoned it. So I devoted myself exclusively to studying. But it did not take long before I took care of the second instalment of the fee: I came across a boy to whom I taught Arabic. He was 'Abduh, the nephew of Iyās al-Ġanī — a man famous in Beirut — and he lived in his house close to the College. I also did other odd jobs, using them to pay for the second instalment and books.

74. Sic in ms.

But for all my happiness about entering the College I kept seeing myself as a stranger in it, as if I wore clothes cut for someone else. I still was convinced that I was less intelligent and weaker in my appearance than my companions, since most had spent years studying science and had become familiar with it. They had fathers or guardians who carried the burden of payments and other expenses for them, while I was the only one who had to work to raise these funds. My class was that of the freshmen, *mubtadi'*, in medicine and consisted of nine students whom I regarded with the same respect as all other students. My uneasiness about this big leap from behind food dishes to the College prevented me from associating with them. They, on the other hand, believed this to be arrogance on my side. But only a few months passed before I mixed with them and some of my bashfulness disappeared because I saw them approaching me. I realized that with regard to our studies I was not less intelligent then they. In spite of my preoccupation with many jobs, seeking an income, I found myself equal to most. Indeed, when I came to the College to enter a class in chemistry, or botany, or anatomy, or Latin — those were the subjects in the first year of medicine — it came to the point that I would see them gather around me, be very friendly to me and request that we should go over the lesson together. They would listen intently to what I read to them from what I had understood of the lesson. Some would ask me about things that had been difficult for them and I would explain them. I noticed in the course of time I was no different from them as far as intellectual abilities or anything else was concerned. The poor opinion I had about my own intelligence vanished from my mind. I began to notice congeniality on the side of professors and students. They were amazed at my entering medicine and at my ability to keep up with them in the studies in spite of my many jobs. Iskandar the Teacher remained for a while there, and whenever he would meet me he would exclaim jokingly, "You are now in the Medical School, Ǧurǧī!" as if he was astonished about this accomplishment. This made me happy and I considered it as congratulation and praise.

My class consisted of Ǧurǧī Kafrūnī (died),[75] Ilyās Sābā (died),[76]

75. Ǧurǧī Kafrūnī (d. 1896) born in Lebanon, obtained M.D. degree from SPC in 1885, was an instructor there 1880/81; *Alumni* 16.

76. Ilyās Sābā (d. 1888) born in Beirut, obtained M.D. degree from SPC 1885, worked in as-Salṭ, *Alumni* 16.

Ḫalīl Birbārī (died),[77] and the *Amīr* Salīm Šihāb (?),[78] Atanāsiyūs Saiqalī,[79] As'ad Rašīd,[80] Salīm Zaidān,[81] and......[82] I also became friends with the students of the advanced medical classes: Sam'ān al-Ḫūrī, Niqūlā Nimr,[83] and As'ad Raḥḥāl from the senior year, *ṣaff al-muntahī*; also Iskandar Bārūdī, the Teacher, Ḫalīl Ḫairallāh, Ibrāhīm Maṭar[84], Ibrāhīm Ṯābit,[85] Ibrāhīm Ṣalībī,[86] Anṭūn Naufal,[87] and Bāḫūs Ḥakīm from the junior year, *ṣaff al-mudrikīn*, and Ḥasan Naṣṣār and Amīn Fulaiḥān[88] from the sophomore year, *ṣaff al-muḥawwalīn*. I also knew of the science students Na'ūm Šuqair,[89] Iskandar Šāhīn,[90]

---

77. Ḫalīl Birbāri (d. 1899) born in Lebanon, obtained M.D. degree from SPC 1885, worked later in Muscat; *Alumni* 15.

78. *Amīr* Salīm Šihāb, born in Lebanon. According to *Catalogue* 81/82 18 he was a class ahead of Zaidān. He obtained his M.D. degree from SPC in 1884 and worked later in Ba'abda; *Alumni* 15.

79. Aṯanāsiyūs Saiqalī studied at the SPC but did not graduate; *Catalogue* 81/82 19.

80. As'ad Rašīd (d. 1933) born in Lebanon, obtained M.D. degree from SPC in 1885. 1907-1920 served in medical corps of Egyptian army in Dongola, Sudan; *Alumni* 16.

81. Salīm Zaidān originated from Tyre, apparently no family relation of Ǧurǧī Zaidān. He studied at the SPC but did not graduate; *Catalogue* 81/82 19.

82. Sic in ms.

83. Niqūlā Nimr (1859-1906) born in Lebanon, obtained M.D. degree from SPC 1883. 1886-1893 served as surgeon in the Egyptian army; *Alumni* 13.

84. Ibrāhīm Maṭar (1863-1913) born in Beirut, obtained M.D. degree from SPC 1883, worked as physician in Beirut; *Alumni* 13.

85. Ibrāhīm Ṯābit obtained M.D. degree from SPC in 1883 lived in Beirut; *Alumni* 14.

86. Ibrāhīm Ṣalībī (born 1852) obtained M.D. degree from SPC 1883, worked in Lebanon as a physician and writer. His articles appeared in al-Hilāl and al-Muqtaṭaf; *Alumni* 14.

87. Anṭūn Naufal born in Tripolis, obtained M.D. degree in 1883 from SPC, went later to Egypt where he edited amongst other newspapers al-Fallāḥ; *Alumni* 13, DĪ ṬARRĀZĪ III 26.

88. Amīn Fulaiḥān (d. 1929) born in Lebanon, obtained M.D. degree from SPC in 1886, worked as a physician at the English Missionary Hospital in Jaffa and later Lebanon; *Alumni* 17.

89. Na'ūm Šuqair (1863-1922) born in Lebanon. B.A. from SPC in 1883. He went to Egypt in 1884, joined the Wolseley expedition of the British to Sudan, and later he worked as a historian for the Sudanese Government. Author of various books; *Alumni* 14; DĀǦIR III 644.

90. Iskandar Šāhīn (d. 1921) born in Beirut, obtained B.A. degree from SPC in 1883, worked as an editor and emigrated later to Sao Paolo; *Alumni* 14.

Ǧibrā'īl Ḥaddād[91] and others; from the teachers of the School I also knew Anṭūn Ḥaddād.[92] I experienced more and more friendliness and kindness from my companions in the course of the weeks and months and in particular towards the end of the school year, when the exams drew closer and the talent of the students came to the fore. I used to hear praise from them, which I took as a way of encouragement since I knew that I did not have the leisure time to penetrate the lessons thoroughly. I had no intention of being first. My interest was to acquire knowledge and not to fall short of my peers. Then I realized that they esteemed me higher than that, until some even insinuated once to me that I would obtain the honours that year. I did not believe this, knowing there were intelligent ones amongst my classmates. Some had studied most subjects of the freshman class in the school of science before they embarked upon the study of medicine. The most outstanding of them in intelligence, as well as diligence, was Ǧūrǧī Kafrūnī. He had friendly relations with the chemistry teacher. He taught him Arabic. The said chemistry teacher, Dr. Lewis, by name, was very precise in his teaching. In the beginning of the year this exercised us very much, but then I soon understood his style of instruction and comprehended the basic principles of chemistry until I thought his method to be easy. I enjoyed chemistry immensely. When I got to chemical analysis during the last half of the year I was greatly amazed at it. When we would come to the laboratory and each would stand before his shelf upon which there were tubes and burners and glasses with material for examination, the professor would give each of us some of the stuff he wanted analyzed. I used to be the first to analyze it and he would smile at me and give me other special materials which I would set out to analyze until my classmates finished analyzing the first stuff. I would enjoy this greatly and till today I still am convinced that chemistry is the most enjoyable and pleasant of all sciences.

Ever since I began to study the preparatory subjects I used to think, every time I studied one subject, that this was the most enjoyable of all;

91. Ǧibrā'īl Ḥaddād (d. 1923) obtained B.A. degree from SPC in 1883, worked for the Ministry of Interior in Egypt as Director of Public Security; *Alumni* 14.

92. Anṭūn Ḥaddād (1861-1924) obtained B.A. degree from SPC in 1882. He is nowhere mentioned as a faculty member or instructor; cf. *Catalogue* 81/82 20, *Alumni* 12. Perhaps Zaidān confused him with somebody else.

such was my relation to natural and mathematical sciences. When I learned about chemistry, botany and anatomy I came to the conclusion that these were better than the former sciences. Then, after I studied physiology and pharmacology, I changed my mind, and considered them the most gratifying ones — with the exception of chemistry. Till today I am convinced that this is the most delightful of all sciences, because through it man sees the world as he has not done before.

Anatomy, too, is very gratifying, because one learns how the human body is composed. For these studies it was necessary to purchase the bones of a human skeleton. Bones were rare because of the difficulties in getting hold of corpses, since people refused an autopsy on the corpses of their dead. Usually the College would procure corpses furtively, paying high prices for them. The students would pass on the bones by purchase, and it rarely happened that one had a whole skeleton with all its small and big parts. I told myself that I would get a complete body. One day I was informed that a man from the people in Ra's Beirut, had died and been buried in a grave in the sand. I arranged with a friend that we would go and steal him. We took along a man with his hoe to unearth and carry the corpse. We went on the third or fourth day after the death had occurred, assuming that the corpse would be in a coffin and it would be easy to carry it away as it was. We went there after midnight like frightened thieves. We dug out several graves because we were mistaken about the place of the grave we wanted — even though we had gone there during day time to identify its place. Finally, we found him not buried in a coffin. We carried away as many parts as we could, because the dawn apprised us and we retreated in fear. Nobody from the College knew of this except my friend. On the next morning the people noticed the opened graves and accused the students of the College for this, but did not know who did it.

I shall never forget a scene from the first year when they brought in one day the corpse of nine year old boy, who had been buried the preceding evening in the cemetery of Saint Mitrius in Ašrafīya. I did not know that he was from there even though most of the inhabitants of that quarter are our people and friends, because our house was there. When the corps arrived in the College it was hoisted up secretly to a shelter between the ceiling of the Medical School and the roof. We were summoned to attend the dissecting and I was sent up with the others. This was the first time that I witnessed this procedure. I will always remember the moment that the coffin was opened: the body was covered with flowers and a smell of amber emanated because of the many leaves and flowers. My look fell upon the body of this boy, and its sight made an everlasting impression upon my soul. Till today, whan I smell the smell of an amber leaf or its flower, the sight of this corpse appears before me.

Dr. Wortabet,[93] the professor of anatomy, began to dissect the corpse and divide it amongst the students of all classes. After two days came the time for me to go home to see my folks — I used to go home every Saturday staying until Sunday. When I arrived and greetings were exchanged, my mother surprised me by saying, "Poor chap, the son of so-and-so. He died and his body has been stolen. People say that the College stole it." I pretended to know nothing of this, but I felt sorry because this boy was a relation of ours.

The professor of Latin was Mr. Porter,[94] but during this year he was preoccupied with something else, and the teacher Fāris Nimr was commissioned to teach it. I had met him once in his house before I entered the College; some of my friends had introduced me to him. When I entered the College, my only contact with him was during the lessons. The medical students hated studying Latin because they did not find any pleasure in it, and did not deem it valuable enough to justify the drudgery. At first sight, I found its study difficult because my knowledge of the basic principles of Arabic and English was not sufficient to be of help in understanding the basics of Latin. Mastery of the basic principles of one language helps to comprehend another one. But before some months had passed I enjoyed studying it; I loved it and I perceived the satisfaction of the teacher with regard to my progress.

---

93. Yūḥanā Wortabet (1827-1908) born in Beirut of Armenian origin, educated by American missionaries. After 1860 he went to Edinburgh for medical studies. He became a faculty member of the SPC Medical School in 1866. After English became the teaching language at the SPC, his services were no longer required. He resigned in 1890. TIBAWI *passim*, ZAIDĀN *Tarāǧim* II 232-237; *Bibliography of AUB* 338.

94. Harry Porter (d. 1923) came 1870 to Beirut as a professor of history at SPC. He wrote various books on history, especially a history of Beirut; *Bibliography of AUB* 123.

Our professor in botany was Dr. Post,[95] a scholar in this field. I enjoyed the study of botany, especially physiology and dissection, on account of its inner order and underlying reason. In spite of his expertness, activeness, and knowledge, Dr. Post was hot-headed and quick-tempered, with an inclination towards vengeance. Therefore, the students thought ill of him and he of them. What added to his distrust towards the students was the fact that he was hard of hearing. When he saw a student move his lips without being able to hear what he said, he assumed that he talked badly about him. Therefore, his judgement about the knowledge of this students in botany was not always objective. But I studied for the pleasure I found in science, not because of obedience to the order of my father or my two guardians, and I understood very well what I studied. If somebody finds himself in such a situation, he has no fear of failing.

When the time of the annual exams came nearer, the students began to prepare for them. Especially for those who have no experience with it, it is like the Day of Judgement. Most of my classmates had got used to them in the school of science, but for me it was the first time that I took exams in a big school. I could tell from the faces of some of my student friends that they concealed something from me. Later I found out that they were discussing in my absence as to who was going to obtain the honorary degrees. They were divided into two groups: one believed that I would get it, the other claimed [Ğurğī] Kafrūnī would be the one. The School of Science students entered the discussion. They took my side, following the lead of the teacher Anṭūn Ḥaddad, since he was entrusted with registering the students' grades. Usually he would extract their average and he was the one to know best what the case would be. All this happened without my knowledge, although later I remembered that I was befriended by the teacher Anṭūn and some companions, a point that they found worth mentioning.

We took the written examination, each subject separately — with the exception of anatomy. They would come back to it in the following year, that is to say, they studied for two years and then would take an exam in it in the alternating year. We were first examined in chemistry.

95. George Post (1838-1909) came to Beirut as a missionary-physician in 1863, was since 1867 professor at the Medical School of SPC, wrote various textbooks of medicine in Arabic; TIBAWI *passim*, TANIM 303, ZAIDĀN *Tarāğim* II 238-242.

The procedure of the exams in the College was that the students would sit in a great hall on chairs with tables in front. The professor would sit on a bench observing all from there. The students would come in, carrying only white paper and pens with them and sit down. The professor would write the required questions on the big blackboard in front of the room. He would request the students to write each question separately in his notebook and write down the answer below it. Usually the questions consisted of two sets: one obligatory part and a second part which the student chose to answer or not. I used to answer all questions. Most often I had finished my work before the others, because I wrote fast. I must admit here to transgressions during these exams, which were caused by my concern for some of my companions who, I feared, would fail in chemistry or botany. I would write the answers down for them and throw them from under the seat. I believe it helped them, especially in botany, where the Doctor claimed that we had misunderstood the intention of several questions and did not answer what was asked. Strangely enough, we all had understood the intention of the question in the same way! He insisted that he meant something else. He held us responsible for this question and the grade average dropped so that the weak ones failed; in such actions the students were united against Dr. Post. In chemistry nobody failed as far as I remember. In spite of his exactitude in teaching, Dr. Lewis did not rely upon wording and formulation. He usually knew the abilities of each student even if the appearance was to the contrary.

In Latin, however, there was no chance of helping friends because Professor Fāris Nimr was very vigilant. No secret dealing of the students in this respect would escape him, He seated us in a room where there was for each of us a table and a chair along the walls, while he would stand in the middle at a spot where he could observe each student. He wrote the questions on the blackboard and we answered all of them. I finished writing when the time was not yet over. I was embarrassed at being the first to get up. I showed the exam paper over to Nimr and left quickly in order to check in a book an expression which I believed I had put down incorrectly and then changed it. I realized now that I had first written it correctly and then changed it into a mistake. I was sorry, because it was the only mistake in the test. On the other hand, I thanked God that indeed it was the only one.

I began to walk up and down in the school hall expecting my classmates. I was concerned about some of them because I knew their weakness. Soon they came down together with the teacher Fāris Nimr. Outside the classroom no conversation had ever taken place between us, but this time I saw him turning towards me and stretching out his hand greeting me and shaking hands with me cordially exclaiming, "Congratulations, Zaidān, bravo! Your exam is outstanding!" This laudation embarrassed me; I changed the subject and remarked, "I hope that none of my classmates failed." He did not answer to this and left. Later I found out that my grade was ten out of ten, which is a rare achievement, especially in Latin.

The time of the commencement festivities on the last day of the school year arrived. They make the distribution of the diplomas a ceremony which the notables and educated people attend by special invitation. Speeches are given, while the dignitaries of the College sit in their official robes on a bench in the front of the great hall of the church. After the speeches are ended, the president stands up and calls the students who earned their medical diploma or the B.A. — one after the other. He hands it over to them and the people applaud. Then the professors stand up and distribute the distinctions to those who scored great success in the subjects they studied. I sat in the rear of the hall and, when the distribution began, I noticed the School of Science students and some of my classmates turn their faces towards me and laugh, until Dr. Lewis stood up with a certificate in his hand calling my name, because I had won a distinction in analytical chemistry. I did not see any other way out but to come forward and receive it. I was overcome with embararssment while the people were applauding — especially the students, as if they were happy about their victory. I approached the bench, accepted the distinction and returned, while the applause persisted. I looked on the ground out of embarrassment. I heard some saying, "Don't go back, wait for the second distinction!" but I did not take any notice of it. I had not yet reached my seat when I heard Porter call my name: I had won the distinction in Latin. I returned under continuous applause and received it. I went back to my seat and almost vanished for embarrassment, but my heart jumped with delight.

My friend Ğurğī Kafrūnī won the distinction in descriptive

chemistry, which he deserved, since he was intelligent and diligent. In botany nobody distinguished himself because the error upon which Dr. Post insisted lowered the grades altogether, and one would only win a distinction if one's grades were eight out of ten.

When the session was concluded, the students revealed to me what they had been discussing in my absence, and I saw their happiness for my sake upon their faces. I will not forget the happiness that I felt in this meeting. It increased my application and perseverance in studying. When the school openened in the following year, I transferred to the sophomore class. Dr. Wortabet taught anatomy and physiology. Dr. Post pharmaceutics, and Dr. William van Dyck,[96] the son of our professor Dr. Cornelius van Dyck, had been appointed to teach *tarābiyūtiyā*,[97] or characteristics of drugs. This was a new science, introduced that very year. I took a particular fancy to physiology, because it points out to man the function of his vital parts such as digestion, respiration, circulation, etc., even though the above-mentioned science was still imperfect. Our class distinguished itself from all preceding classes by the instruction in *tarābiyūtiyā*. This is a beautiful science, the subject of which is the study of the influence of drugs on the functions of the organs in the healthy state. Dr. William van Dyck had compiled a well-organized book on this subject. We were amazed at his way of instruction. He made his thoughts clear to us and gave us description which showed his thorough understanding of the subject matter. The cogitation of Dr. Wortabet in physiology was not as clear.

We passed some months of the year before the famous event occurred in the College, during which the medical students unified and demanded their rights. This was the first time that something like this happened in the East.

This event resulted in the exodus of most of the students and their scattering over the world, the change of future for some of them, and the migration of many to Egypt or other places.

---

96. MUNAĞĞID 63 leaves a blank after William, though ms indicates clearly van Dyck as the following word.

97. This word cannot be found in any of the new or older dictionaries. It looks like an Arabization of therapeutics, though this would not fit the meaning Zaidān gives it. Amongst the medical textbooks by G. Post there is included the title *Tarābiyūtiyā* cf. TANIM 303. The book itself was not available.

THE COLLEGE

It consists of sections for science, medicine, theology and others. The Americans had founded it in Beirut. Its head was the great Dr. Bliss.[98] Of all its physicians, Dr. Cornelius van Dyck was the most famous; he was the closest to the people, appeared most frequently in the charitable institutions and displayed the strongest love for the Beirutis. He was a minister, a physician and a professor. He would preach, heal and teach, and receive for this the same salary as the other professors. He was of noble character, magnanimous, generous, very charitable, gentle and sociable. He gained great fame in Syria and the people loved him. In the College he taught pathology and chemistry. Later, Dr. Lewis took over the chemistry from him. The students adored van Dyck; they praised his virtues, merits and kindness. The common people believed that he was the founder of the College, so that some even called it the van Dyck College. He did not claim this, but his fame prevailed over that of his colleagues as a result of his capability.

It appears that this distinction created envy and caused disharmony. An additional reason for this friction was the fact that Dr. van Dyck was a liberal in thought and word and did not mind speaking out frankly about things which his colleagues and others in the group of ministers avoided discussing. Dr. van Dyck was a God-fearing man, his convictions being based on understanding and thought. He cared little for the details and trivialities to which some religious zealots cling and which have absolutely nothing to do with religion. But he held fast to the essentials of the Christian religion, unmindful of its external aspects and its superficialities if they contradicted the principles of science. When a new theory of scientific thought appeared and presumably contradicted

---

98. Daniel Bliss (d. 1916) came as a missionary to Beirut in 1856. He was instrumental in founding the SPC, whose first President he became; Tibawi 167, 168 *et passim*, cf. also F. J. Bliss.

these superficialities, he would nevertheless respect it and examine it from the point of view of scientist as, for instance, the evolutionary theory and similar theories of the philosophy of natural scientists. Perhaps here one finds another reason for the estrangement between the Doctor and some of his colleagues from the faculty of the College, especially Dr. Post. When I entered the College in the year 1881, the faculty consisted of van Dyck, Post, Wortabet, Lewis, Porter, Brigstocke[99] and Bliss, the chairman. Lewis was a young man, liberal in thought and deed. He considered the external religious pretensions unnecessary, even though they were part of the rules of this College. He found it not objectionable to have some wine on the table with his meal or to absent himself, for instance, from prayer from time to time. In his liberal attitude he was very close to Dr. van Dyck, in spite of the difference of age. Usually, when the faculty criticized one of Lewis' deed, van Dyck would back him up.[100]

When Darwin's theory made its appearance, Lewis gave a lecture about it to the students.[101] In no regard did his lecture oppose religion. But this view was altogether new and the men of religion thought it contradictory to the fundamentals of Christianity. They considered this speech a dark stain on Dr. Lewis and complained to the Board of Trustees of the College in America. The Board compelled him to resign, firmly intent on guarding the religious principle for the sake of which they had established this school.

The acceptance of the resignation of Dr. Lewis occurred in the first part of the year we are just discussing. The students loved Lewis and respected him, especially since van Dyck liked him and was close to him. But they used to hate Post, or at least did not like him, because of his violent temper and his attacks against some of them in words and threats for reasons that we mentioned already. The medical students sided with van Dyck and Lewis. They decided unanimously to put forward a plea and a demand to the school for the rights they were entitled to, one of

99. Ritchard W. Brigstocke (d. 1919) a British Missionary who taught at the SPC from 1872-1882; *Catalogue* 81/82. FARAG 77 spells Brickstock wrongly.

100. For a discussion of these tensions, see FARAG, especially 77/78.

101. Lewis gave it in July 1882 as the commencement speech under the title "Knowledge, Science and Wisdom". Text in English in *Annual Reports* 1866/67-1921/22 251 ff. The Arabic text appeared one month after the speech was given in al-Muqtaṭaf VII.

them being that Dr. Lewis should be their chemistry teacher. Amongst the promoters of this issue were Iskandar al-Bārūdī, the teacher, and the late Salīm Ğuraidīnī.[102] They did this to help Lewis and to please van Dyck. They had agreed to protest and I was amongst the protesters. Perhaps more than the others I followed here the lead of al-Bārūdī, convinced that he was doing the right thing — just as every student is convinced by his teacher. He was one of the most active and zealous students, frequently visiting van Dyck's house and that of Fāris Nimr and Ya'qūb Ṣarrūf. They, too, were, of course, siding with the students, because they highly esteemed the capability of Dr. van Dyck who supported them in every literary project especially with regard to their magazine "al-Muqtaṭaf". It was he who had prompted them to found it and he did not spare any effort in tutoring them and helping them in literary matters. He was indeed a living lexicon which they made use of for whatever questions they encountered, or they would look up his writings pertaining to the subjects and he would guide them to their sources — not to speak of teaching and other things. They respected his opinion and supported his views. Their hearts were with the students in this action. But their own good demanded from them neutrality, since they were teaching at the College, even though deep down they were hostile towards the faculty because the latter had not appreciated their capability in terms of promotion and did not pay them the salary they were entitled to. There was much respect and love for the owners of "al-Muqtaṭaf" in the hearts of the students, especially among the younger medical students. This was a help for the unanimous agreement of the medical students on their demands. In the beginning, the more advanced of the science students participated in this — especially Ğibrā'īl Ḥaddād, Na'ūm Šuqair, and As'ad Kalārğī.[103] They attended the first exploratory sessions with the medical students, but then they withdrew, advised by the medical students, lest they should fail and because no benefit would accrue them from this affair.

---

102. Salīm Ğuraidīnī born in Lebanon obtained M.D. degree from SPC in 1883; *Alumni* 13.

103. As'ad Kalārğī Karam (born 1865) obtained a B.A. degree from SPC in 1883, worked later as a correspondent in N. Africa; *Alumni* 14.

But the movement with which the students of the College came to the fore is worth recording because it started a new awakening amongst the students of the schools in the East. The merit for this is again due to the education in this very college, since it educated its students towards freedom of thought and speech and accustomed them to individual freedom and equality of rights, so much so that a student would complain about his teacher to the faculty, *'umda*, if he thought that he had overstepped the proper limits in his conduct. The faculty would establish his right even if he was the weakest student. This spirit distinguished this school from the schools of the East and had a great impact upon the education of the mind of the Syrians during this *Nahḍa*. It was this education which enabled the medical students in this year to complain to the faculty because they were convinced of the correctness of their act.
The protest of the medical students:

The medical students learned that Dr. Lewis had resigned as of the first of December 1882. Some knew of the dispute between him and the rest of the faculty, it became public knowledge amongst the rest of the students and they decided to protest and boycotted the College on Monday, December 4th. There were 45 students, all medical students. They held their first meeting in one of the halls of the Prussian Hospital.[104] All were acquainted with each other and accustomed to meetings in the college itself and in the Society *Šams al-birr*, and some of them in the Freemasons. This helped them towards solidarity and order in their actions — even in their first session, mentioned above. They began to organize their meeting into the form of a society for which they elected a temporary chairman, a speaker, a secretary and a treasurer with the following results: Ǧurǧī Zaidān, Chairman, Iskandar [al-] Bārūdī, Secretary, Ḫalīl Sa'āda,[105] Speaker, Ǧabar Ḥaddād[106] from

104. The Prussian Hospital was founded in 1861 by the Prussian Order of St. John. The staff of the Medical School of the SPC undertook the medical charge, while the Kaiserwerth deaconesses did the nursing; RICHTER 202.

105. Ḫalīl Sa'āda (d. 1934) born in Lebanon, obtained M.D. degree from SPC in 1883. He worked for aṭ-Ṭabīb, lived in Egypt, Sao Paolo and since 1914 in Buenos Aires. Besides as a physician he worked there also as a correspondent for the New York Times; *Alumni* 13, DI ṬARRĀZĪ II 57.

106. Sic in ms. Certainly meant here is the aforementioned Ǧibrā'īl Ḥaddād.

sciences, Speaker, As'ad Kalārǧī from sciences, Speaker, Ǧurǧī Bāz,[107] Treasurer, Fā'iz Šihāb,[108] Assistant Treasurer, Anṭūn Mīlān,[109] Second Secretary, Ibrāhīm Ṣalībī, Reporter, Communicator, Messenger of the absent students. They did this so that their sessions would be organized and their discussions recorded. I was not appointed Chairman of this session because of any particular merit, indeed I was one of the youngest students present. But they established the chairmanship nominally so as to keep order in the session and so that each would speak when it was his turn or after asking permission. They elected me because there was no rivalry between me and any of the students. There was nothing here that called for disagreement or grudges. I was far removed from any issues and was always strongly inclined towards conciliation. I never quarrelled with anybody, even if he wronged me—till this day this has remained my nature. However, they used to elect a special chairman for each session and no importance was connected with this chairmanship. I only mentioned it for the sake of establishing the facts.

This discussion in this session principally revolved around the problem of unity and in another session a statement was put down upon which each student, one after the other, had to give an oath in the following manner, "I swear by God and by my honour to remain faithful to the commitments upon which we decided in this session and to persist faithfully with the group until the end."

Each one gave the oath separately and signed his name beneath the text of this oath in the minutes of the session, which were then in the hands of the Secretary and which are now with me.

In the first session an appropriate course of action was discussed. The talk centred upon a protest against the departure of Dr. Lewis before the end of the year, and upon an inquiry as to who was going to replace him — this was of interest to us since we trusted his work and we had entered the school while he was the professor of chemistry in it. They,

107. Ǧurǧī Rustum Bāz (1861-1956) born in Lebanon, obtained M.D. degree in 1883 from the SPC, worked as medical health officer in Beirut, published a book about the history of medicine and various articles; *Alumni* 13.

108. Fā'iz Šihāb (d. 1923) born in Lebanon, obtained M.D. degree from SPC in 1886; *Alumni* 17.

109. Anṭūn Mīlān (d. 1899) born in Lebanon, obtained M.D. degree from SPC 1883, worked as a physician for the municipality of Nablus; *Alumni* 13.

the students, seized the opportunity to strengthen their protest and put forward demands about issues from which they had been suffering.

Firstly: The diploma of the College was not sufficient qualification to practise medicine in the Ottoman Empire. Without exception its graduates had to go to Istanbul and to take an exam before a committee of professors from the Imperial School of Medicine. The examinations were difficult, because they were detailed. The student would be questioned about every subject separately in consecutive sessions. These exams had been held until that year in Arabic, which was also the teaching language for the students in the College. The students underwent great agony and frequently they would fail or be delayed in their exams and reconsider or abstain altogether from practising this profession. This problem became even more complicated by an announcement, which the College received that year, saying that the examinations of the medical students in Istanbul would not be acceptable any more in Arabic but would take place in Turkish or French. The students raised an outcry when they heard the news. They began to talk about it in an address to the faculty of the school and they took this opportunity to put forward a demand.

Secondly: The committee in Istanbul examined the students of the College in subjects which the College did not teach them, for instance zoology, pathological anatomy, histology and others.

Thirdly: You saw already that the diploma that the College issued did not relieve them [the students] from the exams in Istanbul and were of absolutely no use to them besides confirming that its owner attended the courses of four years and took the necessary exams. These exams, however, were very onerous: each professor examined the students of his class through a short oral exam in the subject that he taught. Frequently, the element of surprise would cause some of them confusion, they would forget the answers and fail the exams. That happened even to many of the bright students, for instance, Nikūlā Nimr and As'ad Raḥḥāl, in our days.

They appointed a committee to write down these demands, together with the protest against the departure of Dr. Lewis. But first they sent a terse statement in which they apologized to the faculty, explaining what made it necessary for them to suddenly boycott the courses. This was its text:

"Considering the present circumstances we are not able at the moment to study and to attend classes. We have other problems which we will present to you at another time. May God protect you."

They sent this statement with a delegation which was directed not to make any statements without permission of the group.

On December 6th, i.e. on the following day, the faculty *'umda*, issued in the Medical School a statement of the following content — after having issued already one before, demanding the return of the students to their classes:

"The professors of the school have noticed with great regret the persistence of the medical students in absenting themselves from their classes and boycotting them. They, [the professors], have no other recourse but to admonish them, [the students], a last time and if they don't follow the advice this time they will be subject to punishment according to the school law."

But we were busy formulating the protest and the other demands in a committee of ours consisting of Ḫalīl Sa'āda, Ilyās Sābā, Ilyās Zahār,[110] and Iskandar [al-]Bārūdī. They wrote a protest and a petition. These are their two texts:

Text of the petition concerning the demands from the faculty of the school:

"We came to study medicine in your school with known professors under fixed conditions according to established rules. We pay money and go to great trouble in order to accomplish what is demanded of us always fulfilling our duties. Meanwhile, it happened that some of the terms under which we entered have been abrogated in spite of the fact that the relations between us and you are defined by these terms and no others. Some have already been abrogated and we are afraid that all might be abrogated. We found ourselves greatly disturbed and stayed away from the required classes because:

1) We entered on the condition that our exam in Istanbul would be held in the language in which we study. Now you have informed us that this has been abolished and we cannot take the examinations

110. Ilyās Zahār (d. 1918) born in Sidon, he was enrolled as a medical student at SPC in 1881 & 82; *Catalogue* 81/82 20.

in this language hereafter. Your diploma has become of no benefit to us with regard to Istanbul.

2) We entered on the condition that our professors would be Dr. van Dyck, Dr. Wortabet, Dr. Post, Dr. Lewis, Dr. William van Dyck and Dr. Brigstocke. This condition also has been abrogated in a strange fashion the like of which has not been heard of — by dismissing one of you from the school while we are in dire need of him, and we worry about the remaining ones.

3) Your diploma, which we attain with our money and effort has no more validity for our government than the required certificates which we obtain with the annual examination. What is the need then to make it dependent upon the intolerably onerous final exam?

As far as our exam is concerned, we demand a limitation, either by confirmation of your diploma by our government or by easing of our exam in Arabic here. Promises and hopes for the future do no satisfy us because our forbearance last time taught us what makes this demand necessary. We don't know anybody besides you to whom we should put forward our demands in this affair.

As far as our teachers are concerned, we came to study only with well-known professors, and for us the school consists of nothing else but these professors. We have learned of the sudden dismissal of our distinguished Dr. Lewis in the middle of the year. You did not notify us of what is happening before we entered the school. We entered the school and completed our requirements with regard to fees and studies based on the assumption that Dr. Lewis would be our examiner in chemistry, signing, as he does, our certificates in medicine and pharmacy and instructing us in all the subjects related to them. Why is it that you repeal all this without informing us before our enrolment? If we hear in the middle of our work about the dismissal of one of our teachers, what prevents then the dismissal of another one tomorrow and a third one after a month? We demand to know who teaches us chemistry and who signs our certificates.

As far as the diploma is concerned: if you make it official and accepted by our government, we are ready for the meticulous exam that you hold, with all its difficulty and seriousness; but, if it is only a declaration with regard to our knowledge and information, it should be made evident, so that we may be known in Istanbul. There is then no need to destroy us with exertion, coercion and the great hardship which we endured last year when preparing for the examination. We are in danger that one of us is asked a simple question [the answer to] which does not come to his mind in the moment of his confusion and fear and you decide to withhold your diploma from him, even though he deserves it. In case this diploma is of no other use, according to our government, than that of the required certificates, we demand its abolishment and the limitation to the required certificates, or an easing of the examination affair — a facilitation which would only be in accordance with the value of the diploma. We suspend our studies while waiting for your answer."

(signed by all the students of medicine and pharmacy)

This is the text of the protest lodged against the dismissal of Dr. Lewis:

"We will only attend instruction by well-known professors. For us the school consists of nothing else but the very professors, and we do not recognize for this school any other responsible authority, *mudabbir*, but them. We have indeed learned that some of you are the cause, undermining the support of our professors. You have decided in favour of dismissing the pious, distinguished Dr. Lewis, accusing him of having offered some wine at the table to which he had invited some Westerners. But we know that he does not deserve such affront and slander of the truth; accusing him of not fulfilling his duties in teaching. That is an outright lie. We, to whom his teaching duties are related, know better. He is more conscientious in his duties than anybody else. He is further accused of making a statement on behalf of the blasphemous ideas of Darwin in his last speech. Nobody who understands his speech and who knows his proper conduct, his virtuous ability and strength as the head of the students' organization of the College and the head of our religious collegiate association,[111] and as leader in charitable activites, will agree with this. You have restrained this distinguished and God-fearing man completely. His esteemed position was not respected and the fact that he served our school and our country twelve years, devoutly and sincerely, was not acknowledged. You have a period of a year at least to wind up his affairs before he leaves his work. You have not informed us as to what happened before our enrolment this year. We enrolled and completed our requirements

111. These two organizations could not be verified. *Ǧam'īyat abnā'i 'l-madrasa* should not be confused with the Alumni Association which was founded in 1910; PENROSE 128, but perhaps it was a precursory organization.

with regard to fees and studies on the assumption that he would examine us in chemistry and sign our diploma and instruct us in all the related subjects. Why is it that you repeal all this without informing us before our enrolment at the beginning of the year? If you put the blame on some people in America, would it not be you who are the slanderous informers? If you say, "Not all of us," would it not be some of you? And you know best upon whom to put the blame. If we hear now in the middle of our studies only that one of our professors had been suddenly dismissed, what is there to prevent us from hearing after two days of the dismissal of somebody else and after a month of a third? What is to be done? We lodge the most severe and strongest protest against those who caused this upheaval and we demand to know who is our professor now and who will sign our certificates, and, if there is nobody, what course of action is to be taken?

(all the students signed this protest)

We sent the protest and the demands with a delegation, which presented them to the faculty on December 6th, 1882. The answer reached us on the following morning. This is its text, signed by Dr. Bliss:

"Our most honourable Children,

Your document reached the faculty, *'umda*, and, after considering it, we answer it as follows:

First: With regard to your examinations — several months ago we established a committee to look into this. The committee determined a change in this matter and this is now the subject of discussion. Once the problem has been settled, we will let you know. No doubt it will be satisfactory to the faculty of the school and to you.

Second: With regard to your examinations in Istanbul — You are certainly aware that we have made the greatest efforts and are still exerting ourselves in this matter and that is the utmost you can demand from us.

Third: With regard to the dismissal of Dr. Lewis from the School — we can understand what chagrin it causes you and we agree with you that you have the right to be notified. But we do not see how this gives you the right to absent yourselves from your classes, as you have done during the last two days. We hope you will be assured of our paternal love for you.

December 5th 1882.[112]

Signature

When the answer of the faculty reached the students they convened on December 6th 1882 under the chairmanship of Ibrāhīm Maṭar to study it. After deliberation, they appointed a committee to respond to it. The following script was formulated and presented to the group. After some amendments it was accepted. This is its text:

"Venerable Sirs, may you live long,

After the proper salutations, we remind you that we have already written about things which we consider more important than our study requirements and our presence in the College. You answered one point, but took no notice of, or reacted upon, the rest which for us is of immense importance. We are, therefore, still waiting for a clear answer, free of all ambiguity and deferment. We asked you to tell us how you decided to handle the exams in Istanbul — we did not receive an answer. We demanded from you the appointment of a professor for us as examiner in chemistry and analytical chemistry — neither did we receive an answer to this. Now we reiterate the demand.

1) Clarification of your determination for clear-cut action related to the exams in Istanbul, as, for instance, the sending of a special representative, or an action of no less value than the sending of a representative. We want to know who is the representative, and when he will go. Patience does not bear fruit for us as it did not for our predecessors. Exaggerated slowness is of no use whatsoever for us, considering that some of us are ready to go to Istanbul upon finishing here.
2) We demand the appointment of a professor for descriptive and analytical chemistry, for geology and natural sciences either by conciliating the venerable Dr. Lewis, our professor, so that he remains here until the end of the year if the hindrance was on his side, arranging what is necessary for him to stay if the objection was yours; or by informing the American Board of Trustees by telegraph, if the objection was theirs; if not, whom are you going to appoint?

112. Sic in ms. It should be at least the 6th of Dec.

3) We also demand an assurance that the professors who are presently on hand remain in their teaching positions at least until the end of the freshman year. We demand to be taught mechanical chemistry, geology, microscopic dissection and to be given training in practical surgery; those are the subjects required of us in Istanbul. Hoping that you are aware how much filial respect we have for you.

The signatures

In this session the members insisted on the duty of each student or member to be presented at the sessions. Whoever was absent was to be fined one *meǧīdī* for each absence. They also ruled that the talk should be calm, and whosoever talked vehemently was not to speak any more. The discussion in this session revolved around persistence for demands of unity. One of the members, Iskandar al-Bārūdī, was appointed to enquire of everyone separately concerning his firmness and if, in case the faculty accepted our demands and contemplated proceedings against one of us, we would remain resolutely together until any harm was removed from that person. Everyone answered individually in the affirmative and they pledged to each other to remain steadfast and persistent until the end.

They re-convened in the afternoon, and in that session they took the above-mentioned oath; every single one bound himself by oath. They then discussed many things. In the meeting on the following day, the seventh of the month, they considered bringing their case to the Board of Managers, *laǧnat mulāḥāẓāt al-madrasa*, which is the highest committee, *al-'umda al-'ulyā*, and consists of missionaries scattered over all parts of Syria for missionary and other work. Their names were mentioned: Mr. Crawford,[113] Damascus; Mr. Dale,[114] Zahle; Mr. More,[115] Jerusalem; Mr. Metheny,[116] Latakia; Mr. March,[117] Zahle; Dr. van

---

113. G. Crawford (d. 1906) arrived 1857 in Syria, worked with Irish Missionaries in Damascus until 1905; FĀRIS, 353.

114. G.F. Dale (d. 1886) worked in Zahle where he had arrived in 1872; he belonged to the Board of Managers 1880-1884.

115. Noel Temple More was British Consul in Jerusalem since 1863; TIBAWI *British Interests* 140.

116. D. Metheny, missionary in Latakia. No further information.

117. F.W. March, missionary in Zahle since 1873. FĀRIS 354.

Dyck, Beirut; Dr. Brigstocke, Beirut; Mr. Bird,[118] Abiyeh; Mr. Nixon,[119] Beirut; Dr. Post, Beirut; Dickson,[120] Beirut; Dennis,[121] Beirut; Eddy,[122] Beirut; Jessup,[123] Beirut.[124]

A committee was formed to check the names of this Board, *'umda*, and to verify their addresses so that a decision was made as already mentioned. Then another committee was appointed to write the appeal. This is its text:

"The school has come to a standstill for reasons which you know, if you want to. Since its welfare concerns you and us all, we ask you to look into its affairs with all possible speed. Friction has occurred between the members of our faculty and we do not consider them able to correct the situation. Because of this we turn to you, hoping that you will look into our affair seriously and promptly, because school will remain interrupted until you have investigated it."

All signed it and passed it on to the committee that had been designed to present it to the members of the Board of Managers, *'umdat al-madrasa al-'ulyā.* The students prepared copies and distributed them all over the City, presenting it to those whom they were able to see (amongst them Brigstocke, Dennis, Eddy and others) and receiving a positive response from them. The students assembled on this day, this being the

118. W.W. Bird (d. 1902) worked in Beirut since 1853; Fāris 354.

119. James Nixon, Esq. Lived in Beirut and belonged to the Board of Managers from 1880-1883; cf. *Catalogue* 80/81-82/83. Munağğid 81 and Fāris 336 have both Nelson. Ms clearly gives Nixon. During these years no Nelson was on the Board of Managers.

120. J. Dickson at the time British Consul in Beirut; *Catalogue* 81/82.

121. J. Dennis, American missionary, came 1869 to Beirut. He became Dean of the Theological School in the SPC. He published several books on missionary activities abroad. He became one of the main opponents to E. Lewis after the latter's speech about evolutionary theory. In the ms. his name appears as Enis and, apparently, he also signed a letter to al-Muqtaṭaf as J. Enis; cf. Fāris 354, Tibawi 201, 246, 283.

122. W. Eddy (d. 1900), American missionary, came to Beirut 1852; Fāris 54.

123. H.H. Jessup (d. 1910), American missionary, came to Beirut 1856. He was instrumental in buttressing the doctrinary inclinations of the SPC in later years; Tibawi 130, H.H. Jessup *Fifty Years in Syria*, N.Y. 1910.

124. In addition to the people mentioned here the following belonged also to the Board of Managers: D. Bliss, President of the Board; J.T. Edgar, U.S. Consul, Beirut; G. Lansing, Cairo; W.M. Thomson, Beirut; C.J. Hardin, Tripoli; T.S. Jage, British Consul, Damascus; G. Mackie, Beirut; John Hogg, Egypt; S. Jessup, Tripoli; *Catalogue* 82/83.

sixth meeting of the association. In this session they deliberated, notifying the dignitaries of the City and its people of rank about their situation. Several delegations were apppointed, each of which went to one of the important people, amongst them Mr. Mott,[125] Rustum *Pāšā*, the British and American Consuls, the teacher Buṭrus al-Bustānī, the Italian Consul, Yūsuf Bey 'Aramān, the Prussian Consulate, Salīm Šihāda,[126] the French Consulate and the American school mistresses.[127] So they went to all these people exposing the injustice, from which they suffered, and those usually encouraged them, approving of their freedom of action, and wishing a just treatment for them.

As for the faculty of the school, a committee was appointed to receive their answer to the latest communication of the students. I was a member of it. They stated that they would answer us orally through the teacher Ya'qūb Ṣarrūf, in an unofficial manner. The teacher Ya'qūb reasoned with us and said that he was not charged with this, but talking for himself, he advised us to return to classes temporarily while the Board of Managers, *al-'umda al-'ulyā*, was convening from all parts of Syria to investigate the case. The return was decided and a committee formed to announce to the faculty of the school that we were returning temporarily until we would see the verdict of the Board of Managers. The students continued to meet as one united association discussing their demands. A committee was appointed to write the text of the complaint which they submitted to the Board of Managers, while it was convening.

The students met in another session on December 10th, which was presided over by Rašīd Qabalān.[128] The complaint was presented here as the committee had written it down. After modifying and editing it in consecutive sessions, the last of which was held on Wednesday the 13th,

125. Mott (d. 1906) British missionary, came to S. Lebanon 1855 moved to Beirut 1861.

126. Salīm Miḫā'īl Šiḥāda (1848-1907) born in Lebanon of Greek Orthodox origin, co-founder of *al-Ğam'īya al-'ilmīya as-sūrīya* in 1868 and its later re-organization *al-Mağma' al-'ilmī aš-šarqī* about 1880. He also taught at the School of the Three Doctors DĀĞIR III 614, ZAIDĀN *Tarāğim* II 230.

127. Meant probably are Miss Nellieh Currah and Miss Eliza Everett, who became head mistress in 1868 of the Female Seminar in Beirut; TIBAWI 179.

128. Rašīd Qabalān (1858-1917) born in Lebanon, he obtained the M.D. degree from the SPC in 1886; *Alumni* 17.

in the anatomy room, it was decided that the text of the complaint should be as follows:

"Revered Sirs,

After salutations we remind you that, in the middle of all our studies, we are suffering great distress: all of a sudden there were internal events in the school, which surprised us and disturbed us very deeply. This preoccupied us and we were ignorant as to how and in what direction the situation at our school would develop. We were no longer able to study and to work. So we wrote a letter to our faculty saying that in view of the disturbances in which the school found itself we have reached the point where we cannot study and recite our lessons any more. We mentioned also that we were determined to present to our professors a detailed statement. On the next day we submitted the following two messages:

(then follows the text of the statement and of the protest)

The faculty responded to us with the following:

(text of the answer of the faculty)

So we wrote them this: (text of the letter)

Whereupon they wrote us the following: (text of the letter)

When we realized that our faculty was in such shape that it would be impossible for us to obtain our right, we notified you without delay, since we know that you are the managers, *mudabbirūn*, who would be interested to look into this whole affair, and who are concerned with the success of our school and the welfare of its students. We presented to you our demands, which we had already presented to our faculty, and we are adding the following:

Does our faculty have the right to dismiss a professor before the end of the year without appointing a replacement for him; or is this not disadvantageous to the students who are hampered considerably by remaining for a time without a teacher? This is the situation in the subjects of chemistry and analysis, upon which the freshman medical students depend for their first two years and the pharmaceutical students for their second.

What are we to do with the new chemistry book, a large part of which we have studied and for which we paid? It is still in the press and Dr. Lewis is not given the opportunity to finish it, even though it is a book necessary for the study of chemistry — we have paid its price and we have nothing in our hands to study from.

We have turned to you, Excellencies, trusting that you will examine the affair exactly and not disregard the truth even if it is sought by such contemptible people as us, because the truth is from God, and he who loves God follows the path of truth, makes it plain and speaks it. We beseech you to examine our appeals and look into our demands. If you so desire, appoint a committee to investigate this with all possible speed. In this way you will have been of benefit to our school and will have treated its students with justice, and will have served the truth as any pious and God-fearing man does. This is what is needed; with respects."

(this is followed by the signatures)

This appeal was written on a long piece of parchment to which we furnished our signatures. On Saturday, December 16th, on the evening of which day the Board of Managers, *'umdatu 'l-idāra al-'ulyā*, was going to convene in order to investigate the problem, the students assembled and decided to add an appendix to the appeal, conveying a complaint against Dr. Post, claiming that he was the cause of these problems. They were prompted to this action when they learned of his rapid efforts with the members of the Board, *al-'umda al-'ulyā*, who arrived from outside, to convince them that the students were rebelling and to turn their opinion against the students. The majority decided to submit a complaint against him and we wrote on the back of this appeal the following complaint:

"Revered Sirs, who are interested in knowing the truth and our opinion. After salutations we suggest that there is no doubt in our minds that we are obliged to present to you an explanation of what caused the vexation and disturbance in the recent times. We say, dear Sirs, you are familiar with the natural irascibility of Dr. Post and you are aware to what such a characteristic leads. We hear, therefore, that outsiders complain — complain bitterly — about his conduct with them.[129] We have experienced the rightness of this complaint ourselves. His severe behaviour towards the students, who were here before us, and towards us, injures our dignity gravely. We feel disturbed and mortified, and we loathe our studies. The disturbance has led all the students to complain about this to the faculty of our school some months ago. We began to realize that all the calamities by which we are surrounded presently in our school originate from him. We took the precaution to turn to the revered principal of our school, whom we used to respect as a father. We had observed him taking the side of the doctor and defending him. After it became evident that it was the President who engineered the dismissal of our beloved and respected professor, the distinguished Dr. Lewis, we arrived at the conclusion that the original source of our difficulties was Dr. Post. We have proof of this, which we will make public upon demand. The President participated with him in this and we, therefore, become worried; our mind is restless and we do not know how we can put up our demands to our faculty and obtain satisfaction.

Here we would like to explain what we have not clearly explained to our faculty and in our preceding petition: our silence about the present teacher in chemistry is not a result of our acceptance of him but of our present adherence to the law. We demand from you the teaching of scientific pharmacology for the pharmaceutics students who presented to the faculty two letters and did not receive an answer to them, and also the teaching of pharmaceutical chemistry, which our predecessors studied with Dr. Lewis. If proof is required from us for the above, we will

---

129. MUNAĞĞID edition 85 differs here slightly from FĀRIS 340. MUNAĞĞID relies here on the ms. while FĀRIS used the original letters sent to the Board. Zaidān had copies or transcripts of all the correspondence between the students and the College. He relied on these transcripts when writing his autobiography (see 183). It is likely that slight variations of the formulation entered Zaidān's transcripts when he made them in the first place. In any case of such variation we have adhered to the version of the ms. In this case MUNAĞĞID 85 following the ms. writes here:

ولذلك كنا نسمع الناس في الخارج يشتكون و يشتكون بمرارة على تصرفاته معهم .

while FĀRIS 340 has:

ولذلك كنا نسمع الناس في الخارج يشتكون و يشتكون بمرارة من تصرفات جناب الحكيم معهم على تصرفاته معهم .

this, however, again varies slightly from the formulation in the original letter which is:

ولذلك كنا نسمع الناس في الخارج يشتكون بمرارة من تصرفات جناب الحكيم معهم .

corroborate it before the commission which you appoint for this purpose. In any case we wanted to make clear what is in our hearts. May God lengthen your life."

All the students signed this complaint with the exception of Iskandar Dabbāk[130] and Ḫalīl Sa'āda; they had betrayed their comrades and returned to the school, and a third student used a similar excuse; we mean Ilyās Sābā, who excused himself saying that he would like to consult with Dr. Wortabet because he was his tutor.

I will never forget our fear on that above-mentioned Saturday evening while the Board of Managers, *al-'umda*, was assembled in the great hall of the College. It served in those days as the church, but now has been converted into the reading room. We were circling the school in expectance of the conclusion of the session. From some of its members we learned at least about the course of the affair, if not the complete verdict. Their session was long and drawn out. Bits and pieces of news reached us from some people stationed close to the hall to the effect that a dispute was blazing and a quarrel arose. Around nine or ten o'clock in the evening we saw the members leaving, each mounting his carriage and going his own way. We sent a couple of people to the house of van Dyck to obtain some information. We learned that the Board, *al-'umda*, was divided into two sections in the course of the deliberation, specially with regard to the complaint about Dr. Post. Dr. van Dyck was assigned the task of reading it aloud, because of the ease with which he read Arabic. Before he had read two lines, one of those present got up and demanded that he should be silenced because it contained a personal defamation. Others objected that this was a complaint to them. A vote was taken and the majority opposed the reading of it. This troubled van Dyck and the fair-minded members, amongst them Nixon and Brigstocke. The discussion then revolved around the other demands and it was decided that the regular faculty of the school, *'umdatu 'l-madrasa al-aṣlīya*, should be charged with looking into them, inspite of their being our opponents. Should this be the highest degree of justice in judgement? They were driven by national fanaticism, *at-ta'aṣṣub al-ǧinsī*, and contempt for the Arabs, *abnā' al-'arab*, as if the latter were overbearing towards them when they

130. Iskandar Dabbāk (1855-1899) born in Damascus, obtained his M.D. degree from SPC in 1884; *Alumni* 14.

raised their voices to complain about the American professors and in spite of the fact that it was the latter themselves who had taught them individual freedom and moral courage.

When Dr. van Dyck realized this, he opposed the decision and demanded that a committee be appointed to look into the demands of the students and to examine what they had to say. If they were wrong they should be sentenced accordingly but, if that was not the case, justice should be done to them. But nobody heeded his remarks. It was learned that the faculty had decided to expel the students from the school and re-admit only those who withdrew their names and retracted their complaint. Van Dyck objected to this, saying that if they insisted upon this decision, he did not want to be one of those pronouncing this unfair judgement, and he left the session infuriated. I had seen him mounting his carriage, his face red with rage.

On Monday, December 18th, the faculty, *'umdatu 'l-madrasa*, affixed an announcement to the blackboard in the hallway of the School of Science with the following text:

"In accordance with the decision of the managers, *mudīrūn*, of the Syrian Protestant College and in accordance with their verdict the students, who presented an improper petition with regard to some professors on December 16th, 1882, are suspended from the College and the Prussian Hospital for one month. After that only those will return who have withdrawn their names from the petition and proclaim their obedience to the rules of the school. For the enforcement of this, the faculty of the school announces hereby the names of those students upon whom the mentioned verdict has been passed. But the rest of the students return to the classes as usual."

(This was followed by the names of the students found on the complaint).

The above-mentioned complaint was furnished with the names of all except six students. Two, Dabbāk and Mīlān, had been afraid, Sābā asked Wortabet for permission, as has been mentioned above. Atanāsiyūs Saiqalī quit with some excuse, as did two others, Anṭūn Naufal and Ḥabīb Kaḥīl.[131] When this announcement was published

131. Ḥabīb Kaḥīl, born in Damascus, obtained his M.D. degree from SPC in 1883; *Alumni* 13.

only Dabbāk and Anṭūn Mīlān returned, then Sābā, and all had anticipated that for obvious reasons. Ḫalīl Birbārī returned, even though he had been one of those who had signed the petition. But Saiqalī, Naufal and Kaḥīl — even though they had not been present — stood fast by the demands still the end and never returned to the school.

When the announcement was made, those who had put it up believed that in no time the students would rush to have their names taken off and to excuse themselves. But they struck upon admirable steadfastness on the part of the students, who did not pay any attention any longer to the school. The latter, however, were aggravated by this tyrannical verdict and wrote a condensed letter to the managers of the school, which they followed up with a strongly worded letter which they made the last communication with them. This is the text of the first letter:

"We point out that we have submitted to you an account of the occurrences in this school and we complained to you with regard to our disaffection and our problems and demanded that you look into this and investigate it, but we never received a written answer from you. But we saw on the school announcement board a statement signed by the faculty which appears to be an ordinance against us, barring us from the school and the Prussian Hospital for a month because we presented a petition dated December 16th, in which something concerning some of the professors is stated. The publication of this verdict does not mention the crime that we have committed nor the law according to which the above-mentioned verdict is permissible. Finally, we don't see any investigation or investigators of the matters which we presented with regard to some of the professors. We hope you will let us know whether this verdict is yours, what the reasons are for which we deserve such a sentence, and according to which regular law this sentence has been issued. We are barred from the School, the Hospital and the dining hall even though we paid money for it all. We consider ourselves wronged and God forbid that you should commit an injustice! We regard it our right to demand from you the reason why you locked us out without any evident crime. We hope for a reply from you upon this communication in the shortest time possible. Salutations."

After some days, without an answer, we wrote the following statement:

"Distinguished Sirs, may God let you remain for ever in the realm of justice. After salutations required by dignity, we address you in the hope that in your wisdom you will hold your judgement of these words until after reading them and examining them. Sirs, it would not have occurred to any intelligent Syrian nor to the sons of the College, your students, that distinguished people like you, who belong to the Land of Freedom, *bilād al-ḥurrīya*, America, would pass a verdict upon a matter without prior investigation, and upon demands and complaints, before having any knowledge of them, that you would refuse to listen to the demands of young people who do not reveal any signs of recklessness in all they are doing but request in all their demands only the truth. Did you retaliate against us because we demanded an assurance that our learned and distinguished professors will remain with us for the whole term, which is required for us? Do you consider this demand a crime? Or did you decide to expel us from the school because we requested those subjects which our Exalted Government, may God strengthen it, ordered us to study? Or are you accusing us because we told you how very much we are interested in planning our diploma in such a fashion that they are acceptable to our Sublime Government? Or was our crime that we explained to you what caused us to present this matter and to appeal about it to you saying that we have a complaint about the judgement of our faculty because one of its members is biased and another one has such a natural disposition that we cannot trust either of them in obtaining our demands. We told you that we have verification for all this. Did you effect the dropping of our appeal after detailed investigation? How was it permissible that you passed a judgement upon us without hearing our petition? Did you appoint a committee to investigate as we demanded and as all laws and rules demand of you?

Sirs, we thought that submitting our demands to distinguished Americans like you and throwing ourselves before God-fearing people, who come to our country proclaiming that they served the truth and the good, and that turning to their open arms to settle our problem would be sufficient to obtain what we requested and to relieve us from all that troubles us. Therefore we returned to our classes and fulfilled all our obligations towards each of the professors of the school in reverence and respect. While we were absorbed in our school duties, having cast our burden upon you and having presented our demands and complaints to you, you arrived from various parts of the country and we took your coming as a good omen. You convened on December 16th, and our hearts were reassured that your meeting would put an end to all problems, making arrangements for each demand. Yet, why on earth did we see you in the one session that you had, when our demands reached you and at the time when they were read to you, why did you rush and hurry to a verdict, following the wishes of the faculty of our school, to expel all the students who had signed the petition for one month and to permit the return of anybody who wants to only after withdrawing his name? You did not listen, you did not investigate and you were not patient as we had been. The President of our school began to dismiss, to threaten, to order and to become violent. Upon his order ropes were brought from the market and our effects and belongings were tied together and he ordered the servants to prevent us from taking what was ours. He dismissed us from the mensa. When we saw all this and looked at those actions our hopes were frustrated and our souls suffered from shock. We obeyed to the fullest and surrendered completely, saying there is no power and no strength save in God and the just amongst his servants. We gave our rights and our complaints a look and your verdict and your lack of investigation another look. Some of you have addressed us orally during the period of expulsion admitting that you did not look into the matter and did not pass judgement after examining it, and that you did not consider the meaning of the statement that we presented. One of you has suggested shortening the time of our lock-out on the condition that we withdraw our names. We told him that we are amazed about this method, as we are amazed about the conduct of the members of the administration towards us. What did we do wrong that we are punished, what crime did we commit? How are we to withdraw our names from a statement which we believe it is our right to make? Every thinking person amongst the local and the foreign people is convinced of this. Then it was said that the faculty would agree that we would withdraw our petition on condition that we would submit a statement of regret signed with our names. But we want to ask your Honours some questions before we sign and if the answers are satisfactory we will do as you say and wish:

1) What is the crime that we committed that we deserve such punishment for it and which law permits this?
2) Do you confirm the professors, whom we met when we enrolled, until the completion of our studies or will you coerce some of them to leave the school?
3) Did you decide to teach the subjects that our Exalted Government demands from us and which you do not teach us and did you appoint teachers for the mentioned subjects?
4) Did you take a greater interest than before in arranging the diploma so that our Government will be satisfied with it?
5) Did you arrange anything that will relieve our worries concerning our studies, that makes our professor, Dr. Post, change some of his characteristics and that convinces us that the President of our school has designs against us?
6) Is it true what we heard that some of you are convinced that we will return to the school and withdraw our names and repent for having demanded our rights and keep quiet about the claim for our material and moral loss and damage-drawing this conclusion from the treachery of Iskandar Dabbāk (whom we call "Arnaut") and Anṭūn Mīlān (whom we call "Softy") and Ḫalīl Birbārī who has not yet been titled appropriately. Is it true that you believe the people of the East, *abnā' aš-šarq,* to be in such conditions as to justify this conduct which you have displayed towards them, and that all the medical student are like Arnaut, Softy and Birbārī? We hope for information from you regarding all these questions, even if it would be damaging for you.

How can we put down our names according to your wishes if you do not answer to this? With all this we see you as the cause of all our loss and damage in our right. This is indispensible, with all due respect to your Honour.

(the signatures)

This is the last that we wrote to them. But the faculty had appointed in the period between its warning and this letter Dr. Wortabet as a mediator in order to conciliate us in a way that Wortabet thought would be satisfactory to us. But we did not find anything else in it save taking off our names. To be precise, one day when most of the students had gone to their home towns and nobody was in Beirut besides me, Iskandar al-Bārūdī and a few others, Wortabet sent for us to come to his house. After a long introduction, which was meant to prove his good intention in this mediation, he said that he had convinced the faculty of a method through which we could be reconciled with them without withdrawing our names from this petition. We asked him what this may be: he drew his hand from his pocket, pulling out a written paper, and said "You only have to sign this paper." We enquired what it was and read it. This was it:

"We regret any word or expression which occurs in our last letter, that implied a lack of respect to his Honour, Dr. Post, and for that reason we withdraw this petition."

We found this grotesque since we did not perceive anything other than what had been worded in the announcement. Dr. Wortabet began to prove to us that it was considerably weaker than that, because the whole secret lay in the word "imply", i.e. we had not intended any insult with our letter but it had implied an insult. However, we were not convinced by his talk and returned.

The faculty tried another approach to conciliate the poor amongst the students. It was known that I paid the school fees only with difficulties. Ṣāliḥ Ṣalībī, the accountant of the school, sent for me and met me in the house of Ibrāhīm Ṣalībī. He began to insinuate to me that if the reason for my not returning to the school was a lack of money, the President would not take anything from me. I gave him an answer that revealed the adherence to the principle with all the vehemence which a young man claims for himself, and he went away. This was our last instance of contact with the Americans and we began to concern ourselves with our future.

This was of greater consequence for my future than for that of all the others. I had entered medical school providing for myself by my own labour. I had hoped that once I entered the third year I could perform simpler treatments in our quarter and could pay back some of the money by which I had been supported. Then, when I could obtain my diploma at the end of the fourth year, I could start officially with a practice and earn my bread. But all my hopes were related to completion of the medical studies.

When we left the school in this manner, I felt as if the thread of my hopes had been cut, and that my effort had become useless. But I had already decided to finish my medical training in *Qaṣr al-ʿainī* School in Egypt, relying upon a letter which we received then from its director through the mediation of *Ḫawāǧa* Mulḥim Šakūr (today Šakūr *Bey*). He was the president in Cairo of the English schools in Faǧǧāla. Amīn Fulaiḥān,[132] one of us medical students, wrote to him. He was a student of the junior year coming from Šakūr's town, 'Ain Zaḥaltā. He enquired in case some students would come from Beirut to finish their medical studies in *Qaṣr al-'ainī*, whether their exams would be accepted and they would be admitted to the appropriate class after their exams. The answer came that they would be admitted to the exam and each would be assigned to his appropriate class.

The medical students who did not return to the College divided into two groups. On the one side the students of the last and final class, on the other all the rest of the classes. The final year students completed their studies with van Dyck at his home. They were furnished with very strong recommendations for Istanbul from the representatives of important centres in Syria so that the government accepted the exams, even though they were not in possession of the diploma of the College. It had been replaced by a certificate from a medical commission composed in Beirut for the examination of the students after they had finished their studies under van Dyck. The above mentioned commission had been constituted under the chairmanship of Murād *Bey*,[133] the Medical Officer of Beirut, with Dr. van Dyck, Dr. Lewis, Dr. Abū Ṭāǧī, Dr. Za'nī,[134] Dr. Brigstocke and Dr. Wortabet. The commission met at Dr. van Dyck's home and gave them an official exam and issued each of them with a printed certificate similar to that of the rest of the schools. Luckily their exam was accepted in Istanbul and they received their diplomas from Istanbul. They practise medicine today, some in Syria and some in Egypt or elsewhere. Amongst them were Dr. Iskandar al-Bārūdī in Beirut, Dr. Ibrāhīm Ṣalībī in as-Salṭ, Dr. Bāḫūs al-Ḥakīm (passed away), Dr. Ǧurǧī Bāz in Dair al-Qamar, Dr. Salīm Ǧuraidīnī (passed away), Dr. Anṭūn Naufal in Cairo, Dr. Ḥabīb Kaḥīl in Egypt, Dr. Ibrāhīm Maṭar in Beirut, and Dr. Ibrāhīm Ṯābit (today in Paris).

---

132. Munaǧǧid here has erroneously Ibn Fulaiḥān.

133. Murād *Bey* al-Bārūdī was at the time the medical officer, *ḥakīmbāšī*, of Beirut Fahmī 657.

134. No additional information could be found about Abū Ṭāǧī and Za'nī.

The other part consisted of those of the other classes. They gave up all hope of making progress outside the framework of the College, and some returned to it. Especially my classmates. All of them returned except me and Atanāsiyūs Saiqalī, head of division in the Office for Public Works. From the freshmen most returned, only Yūsuf Zaḥlūṭ[135] remained, who has now become a famous lawyer, and Nasīb Šiblī (committed suicide in America). From the junior students, only Amīn Fulaiḥān remained, as far as I remember. Perhaps Ḥasan Naṣṣār also remained. He resigned himself to what he had learned or returned and completed his studies. I don't remember.[136]

I and Fulaiḥān decided to go to Egypt to complete our medical studies in the school there, relying on the letter in our hands from the director of the Ministry of Education and upon the help of *Ḫawāǧa* Mulḥim Šakūr. When the medical commission for the examination of senior students, and of some of the junior medical students, was appointed, it was announced that those of the sophomores and freshmen who wanted could take an exam for pharmacy and would receive a diploma of pharmacy. I still have it, even though I never intended to work as a pharmacist.

When Fulaiḥān and I decided to travel to Egypt in order to finish our medical studies, we began to concern ourselves with the necessary preparations. I saw to it to furnish myself with recommendations from some of the holders of higher office in Syria to the *Ḫidīw*[137] or the head of the Medical School, who was then 'Īsā *Bey* Ḥamdī ('Īsā *Pāšā*). I went to Damascus and obtained a reference from the commander of the fifth *orta*[138] for the head of the Medical School, and a letter from the Patriarch of Antakia (Mitwāyūs) for the Patriarch of Alexandria (Aġābīyūs).[139]

---

135. Yūsuf Zaḥlūṭ, no information available. He is not even registered as a student in the *College Catalogue* during these years.

136. He did not return to the College. Interestingly all the above are mentioned in *Alumni* 13 as having graduated in this year. In *Catalogue* 1883/84 and 84/85, their names are not mentioned amongst the graduates. Only in 1913 did the faculty decide to include those who had taken the government examination with the help of C. van Dyck in 1883 as alumni of the College.

137. Title of the ruler of Egypt, Taufīq (1879-1892).

138. I.e. the Fifth Army of the Ottoman Empire.

139. It is not clear to whom Zaidān is referring with these two names. The *Dictionnaire d'Histoire* III 700 indicates Hierothee as Patriarch of Antakia from 1850 to 1885, *ibid.* II 367 gives Sophrone IV as Patriarch of Alexandria from 1870-1899. We are

I also wanted to take a recommendation from the Governor of Syria for the *Ḫidīw*, but he excused himself on the grounds that there were no relations between him and the *Ḫidīw*. My friend Fulaiḥān obtained a letter of recommendation from Rustum *Pāšā*, the *Mutaṣarrif* of Mount Lebanon, for the *Ḫidīw*, pointing out that Syria had the right to send some of her people, *abnā'ihā*, to study medicine on *Qaṣr al-'ainī* free of charge, since the days of Ibrāhīm *Pāšā*.

When the time of the journey drew close I realized that I was lacking the most important requirement, i.e. the money for the trip. I did not have anything, and I was not going to ask my father, knowing how parsimonious he was, since he was the head of the family and had to support it by his exertions. But we had a neighbour next to our restaurant by the name of Miṣbāḥ al-Maḥmaṣānī,[140] who made roasted chick peas and sweetmeats. I had befriended him and had maintained good neighbourly relations with him. I found him to him to be sincere and good natured, so much so that I usually heeded his advice. I do not know how he was aware or observed that I was travelling to Egypt without being provided with any money for the expenditures of the first days in Egypt — until I would enter the medical school. Since once we entered it, all the expenditures for food and all living costs would be taken care of by the school. But when he heard of this he called on me that very day. He advanced gradually in his talk until he forced me to surrender and I told him the truth. He stretched his hand out and gave me six guines, *ǧinīhāt*, saying; "Take it, if it is not enough, I will give you more." I took it and thanked him. I added it to what I had prepared for the journey. I shall not forget this generosity of his. I, therefore, sent it back to him with As'ad al-Ḫašš, who was leaving Egypt for Syria, as soon as I had taken up a job — that is to say one year after this time.

We travelled to Egypt in October 1883, which was the year following the year of 'Urābī.[141] Egypt was hit by cholera, which brought rapidly spreading death. We did not believe that the cases of death had become fewer and the quarantine would be lifted by the time of our journey.

---

indebted for this information to Père Anawati and Père Jomier from the Institut Dominicain des Études Orientales, Cairo.

140. Mentioned on p. 164 as 'Umar al-M.

141. See 33, n. 1.

We went on an English merchant ship, which was the first ship going to Egypt after the quarantine that year. This was the first time that I had travelled by sea. I suffered from seasickness of all kinds, not to mention the smell of the ship, which was a merchant ship carrying sheep and cattle, and not to mention the smell of the dung hills. It was our good fortune that the ship's course was straight from Beirut to Alexandria.

We reached Alexandria in the morning. I remember my view of it from the sea — it was the first city after Beirut that I saw from the sea. How great was my consternation when I went down to the city and roamed through its markets with all the traces of fire and destruction that took place in the time of the 'Urābī events still evident. I had seen the heart-breaking sight of the buildings of Manšīya as piles of heaped up stones unlike the traces of the ghastly fire. We stayed in a small hotel close to Manšīya for several days. When we moved on to Cairo, I and my friend Fulaiḥān, alighted at one of the inns which were rather rare in those days. We rested some days while my companion searched for his compatriot, *al-Ḫawāǧa* Mulḥim Šakūr. We learned that his place was in Faǧǧāla, where the English schools are today. We went to him and he treated us with all honour and hospitality. He exerted himself in order to fulfil our wish. He made us ride in carriages, spent time with us in interviews and assistance. We went from ministry to ministry, from administration to administration — he was on our side. But, unfortunately, we did not succeed in what we had in mind. The reason for that was that.....

The End.

LETTERS

Cairo, Nov. 12, 1908

My friend,

After writing the last page I received your letter from the 9th of the month, and I was very pleased. How nice to receive your letters continuously; indeed, it is almost half as good as seeing you.

Your decision to learn Turkish made me very happy. It is the language of our government; after the gloom of tyranny has been dispersed, after knowledge has prevailed over ignorance and after the constitution has been proclaimed, our time has come to demonstrate to the other nations that we are a living nation who know to gather and to unite and that we help our Government with our tongues, pens and words. The election of our friend, Sulaimān al-Bustānī,[1] for instance, is one of the victories of knowledge over ignorance. The rise of the committee of Union and Progress[2] and its victory over the old despotic party, is a sign of the prevalence of knowledge over ignorance, because the men of that party were ignorant, greedy and despotic people, while the members of the committee of Union and Progress are all philosophers, poets and educated people. The former shed blood, the latter avoid it. The victory of al-Bustānī's party in Beirut is a proof for the supremacy of knowledgeable people. That is the only hope for the realization of the constitution. Indeed, the educated youths are the hope of the

---

1. Sulaimān al-Bustānī (1856-1925) born in Lebanon. Poet, writer, journalist, and translator of the Iliyad into Arabic. He was elected 1908 as representative of Beirut to the Ottoman Parliament. Later he became a member of the Senate and was made Minister of Trade in 1913. During World War I he went into exile to Switzerland because of his opposition to Young Turk policies; Dāġir II 189, dī Ṭarrāzī II 159 ff.

2. Committee of Union and Progress formed itself towards the end of the 19th century as an underground opposition to the regime of Abdülhamid II. Most of its members were exiled but continued their agitation from Europe. After the Young Turk Revolution it became the main political instrument for the Ottoman policies of the Young Turks, Berkes 325-337 et passim, Lewis 194 ff.

nation, *al-umma.* It is to be hoped that they will guard over the freedom which they obtained with the constitution. I cannot tell you how great my joy about this is.

I told your Uncle Mitrī to send you all the novels — those that are part of the series and those that are not — and to give me the invoice. You will continue to collect the money and keep it with you as I told you before. [Mrs.] Yasmīn will deposit for you the tarbush and the jam with the pharmacy Matar. I wrote to you that she will leave it with the son of our aunt, Luṭfallāh Ṣabbāġ; ask for it from him. I sent you in the last letter some French Oriental stamps. If you can use them, do so, if not return them together with some Ottoman stamps. We have none right now. If we get any I shall send them to you. Regards to the teacher Ǧabr Ḍūmiṭ.[3] Tell him that I received his letter and thank him...

Greetings.

Ǧurǧī.

Cairo, Jan. 7, 1909

Dear Emile,

I received your two last letters on the fifth of the month. Today is our Christmas.[4] Visitors are coming continuously and since the morning I have been on my feet. Nevertheless, I do not want the mail to leave without having written to you. We shared your happiness about the visits and the decision of the kind Lady Mīlīyā. You did well to mention all kinds of food, because our ladies like to talk about this subject. I sent you some newspapers, but the Islamic newspapers are still not appearing. Perhaps today they will come out for the first time. Enclosed is a letter from your Uncle Mitrī. At the occasion of the feast I called upon many friends and they all asked me about you. Tell me your grades in algebra even though I believe that you will have no problems. Sufficient proof of this is your statement "I think I am in the clear". This thought is for us tantamount to confirmation, because usually you understate your own case.

3. See 24, n. 41.

4. i.e. the Greek Orthodox Christmas.

I wish you a happy Christmas and pray for your success and progress and that you may continue to enjoy health and well-being. Concerning your question whether we accept subscribers even after the beginning of the year, the answer is that nothing prevents the subscriber to start in any month. But for the subscriber himself, it is most desirable to subscribe at the beginning of the year of "al-Hilāl", i.e. at Oct. 1, so that he should have all parts of the serialized articles — as you know very well. But as from our side, there is no objection as to when the subscription starts.

Asmā is angry with you because you sent in the last two letters two postcards to Šukrī. They are not written to her, and you do not even mention her, even though she loves you very much and would sacrifice herself for you, *tamūt fīka.* Write her a special letter. I have asked her just now to write to you but she said, "He will not answer to the letter I write!"

Your mother is preoccupied with visitors and has not the time to write to you. If it was not for my agility, *ḫiffat al-kaʿb,* I would not be able to write this. But I did not want to change my habits. Give Professor Ǧabr [Ḍūmiṭ] my best regards and to all the other friends. The mentioned bundle of newspapers will be sent with this together. It reached me from Paris on behalf of Iskandar Muṭrān.[5] You will understand, when reading it, that the Arabs or Syrians are the ones who started the break-away from the Turks, even though the Turks approached them amicably. They [the Arabs] fear them, are on their guard against them and think badly of them. I consider publications like these damaging to all the Ottomans, *al-ʿuṯmānīyūn.* These activities express only their perpetrator's desire for empty fame. They do not care whatever the sequence of their actions should be. It is my opinion that the Syrians and the other Ottoman elements, *al-ʿanāṣir al-ʿuṯmānīya,* ought to think only in terms of

5. Probably Rašīd Muṭrān, brother of Naḍra M. from a Greek Orthodox landowning family in central Syria. Rašīd Muṭrān founded in 1908 in Paris a *Comité Central pour la Syrie* which openly demanded autonomy for Syria and appealed for European intervention. See M. Hartmann "Der Islam: 1908" *MSOS* XII (1909) 56.

In December 1908, a petition was circulated in the Middle East written by Rašīd Muṭrān in Paris in which he demanded a "Comprehensive measure of self government" for Syria but "it met with no favourable response... except a counterproclamation signed by eight or ten leading Muslims in Damascus protesting against the circular sent from Paris, disapproving of Muṭrān's conduct and calling him a traitor to his country..." *Times* (London), April 13, 1909, p. 6.

Ottoman unity. As for administrative independence, *al-istiqlāl al-idārī*, there will come some other time for it. It will become a necessity at a suitable time, i.e. after the Ottoman people, *al-umam al-'uṯmānīya*, have progressed and have learned their rights and duties, and after the political viewpoints have changed in Europe. At this moment division is only harmful.

My regards and may you be in good health for the sake of your loving father.

Ğurğī.

Cairo, Oct. 12, 1910

Dear Emile,

In this letter you will read quite some news which will amaze you. The details you will read in the newspapers. But they will not provide the full truth. I am referring to the university question. I had written to you already in my last letter about the fear of some people here that in my lectures some sentence or passage may emanate from me which some illiterate Muslims might understand as an insult or offence and that they might publicize it for the sake of disturbance or something of that kind. Some people fear a rumour may spread that the university intends to demean Islam and that then the interest of the wealthy to support it will diminish. As I told you, I assured the people that I would avoid everything they were worrying about. But on the very day (Thursday) "al-Mu'ayyad" published a report that the university felt it to be improper for a Christian to be the professor for Islamic history and had, therefore, decided to replace me and to compensate me — as you will find it written in "al-Mu'ayyad" and other papers enclosed in this letter to you. On the same day a reporter from "al-Aḫbār" [6] came to me and asked me whether the news of my dismissal were true. I told him that I had no information about it. He wrote down his interview with me and you will find it in "al-Aḫbār" of Friday. Through all this I realized, however, that the administrative board of the university was discussing the subject.

6. Al-Aḫbār, daily newspaper founded 1896 by *Šaiḫ* Yūsuf al-Ḫāzin; DĪ ṬARRĀZĪ IV 170.

In view of the fact that Ibrāhīm *Pāšā* Nağīb[7] was the one to promote my appointment and the first to talk to me about it, I thought it right to go to him and to ask him not to defend me, because I am in no need of this work. My tasks are already too many as to permit it, and I would not want to inconvenience him. So I went to his house and learned that he was in a special meeting of the university, I understood that the meeting had not yet finished and I went home, expecting a decision. Then I deemed it right to go back again to Ibrāhīm *Pāšā* Nağīb to explain my thoughts to him. He might have finished with the meeting and I would hear from him what happened. I found him at his home at noon. I told him that I had come to plead with him not to exert himself on my behalf because I was in no need of this position. He said the discussion concerning me got heated and that he had been on the verge of resigning — similarly also.....[8] *Pāšā*. The appeal was then postponed to another time. To my question he answered that the majority was against us and that the university had decided to compensate me and that it had sent a delegation to me to conciliate me and to apologize to me. I returned home. The delegation had been there already while I was absent. So I sent a message that it should come at four o'clock in the afternoon. I waited for them and they came. They were four: 'Abdallāh *Bey* Wahhāb,[9] Murqus *Bey* Ḥanā,[10] 'Alī *Bey* Bahğat[11] and Lūzyānā *Bey*.[12] They said that two others were coming but were late. I welcomed them. One of them began

---

7. Ibrāhīm *Pāšā* Nağīb, he had various positions in the Egyptian administration. Since 1908 he was on the General Committee for the Establishment of the Egyptian University, later he was vice chairman of the administrative committee of the university; Budair 24.

8. Illegible in ms.

9. No information available. Not mentioned in Budair.

10. Murqus *Bey* Ḥanā, born 1872 in Egypt of Coptic origin. Studied in France 1892-98, served in the government of Egypt, then opened a lawyer's practice. Since 1905 member of the National Assembly, protagonist of women's education. He collaborated with Muṣṭafā Kāmil, later became a member of the *Wafd* party and eventually Minister of Public Works. Since 1906 member of the General Committee for the Establishment of the Egyptian University, since 1908 on the administrative committee, later he taught at the university. Fahmī 212-219.

11. 'Alī *Bey* Bahğat (d. 1924) Member of the administrative committee of the university since 1908; Budair 61, az-Ziriklī, 2nd ed., V 74.

12. Sic in ms. Here is meant the lawyer Luznīyā *Bey* of Jewish-Egyptian background. He was since 1908 on the General Committee, on the administrative committee and the program committee of the university; Budair 24, 25, 61.

to apologize that, in view of the sentiments of the uneducated Muslim common people, the university thought it proper to turn to a Muslim professor to lecture about the history of Islam. That was the essence of their talk and I answered them that it did not matter for me to resign from this position because my other tasks did not leave me any time. From the beginning I had accepted the proposition only with hesitation and out of the desire to serve the fatherland, *waṭan* — as I had been told [was the case]. At the time I had been pleased that the university had dared to engage in something that nobody else had dared — I mean the religious tolerance it showed in choosing a Christian to teach the history of Islam. The news had already spread amongst my friends and I had heard praise of the university especially concerning this aspect. I would now resign from lecturing about the history of Islam with great ease. However, I would never accept to come back to it even if I was paid 2000 guineas. There was no doubt in my mind that there would be much written about the reasons of my joining and the manner of my resigning from the university. Should I declare that the reason for my leaving was the fact of my being Christian? This was of no interest for my own sake but I was concerned about the name of the university that it might not sink in the esteem of the people to a point of an accusation of fanaticism. Certainly there would be a way to guard over its reputation.

It must be admitted that the purpose of the address of the delegation was to conciliate and satisfy me. The delegates swore that every single one of the members of the commission, regardless of differing political and religious affiliation, agreed that I was the only person suited for this position and subject. In short, the discussion between us stretched over two hours and I left nothing unsaid. They believed my words and eventually asked me for a solution to this problem. I told them the best would be if they proposed to me to teach a subject other than Islam and I would then refuse. The disrepute of this would be less. When I told them this they seized upon it and asked, "But, truly, you would like to offer another subject. Which one would you like?" I answered, "Choose what you want and propose it to me. If it is agreeable to me. I will accept it." So they left with the understanding that the administrative board of the university would convene today and would inform me as to what the final decision was.

True is the saying, "Do not hate anything, perhaps it is for the better".[13] Indeed this commotion was a benefit for me in every aspect, especially inasmuch as the newspapers discuss the question. The rashness of "al Mu'ayyad" in what it wrote intensified the attack upon the university. They had felt small in front of me since the man of truth is master — especially when I told them that I had been the first to oppose openly my appointment claiming that I am a Christian and that there are amongst the Muslims persons suited for this subject. But they had not agreed and had taken a wrong decision. I am pleased by the event and I tell you so. It is obvious that they will propose to me to give a class in Arabic literature and history before Islam, or in philosophy of history or something similar. I am inclined to accept under the condition that the number of lessons be less because I am not prepared for them. Your mother would like me to refuse. But since I saw you being happy about this professorial position, I decided to accept teaching a course other than the history of Islam. The truth is that any other subject is easier for me than this history in view of the troubles which I fear will occur — especially after I have observed how people are full of envy and fanaticism against me because I as a Christian teach the history of Islam. I believe you will agree with me on this.

I have taken your time with my explanations but I know you would like to know the details that nobody else but you will know. I wrote you in a few words what passed between me and the delegation, although they requested me to keep our discussion secret until a final decision is made by the board today. They are deciding as to what to write to me and this evening I will get their answer containing the new proposal. It is likely that I will accept it but on the condition that the number of classes will be reduced, instead of 40 only 30 or 20. The reason for this is that it will demand preparation in addition to the time spent preparing the course in the history of Islam. Today's result will be better than the earlier one. We have obtained publicity, *reklām*, and benefit.

---

13. Zaidān writes here:

لا تكرهوا شيأً لعله خير

He probably was referring to the *Sūrat al-baqara* 216.

وعسى ان تكرهوا شيأً وهو خير لكم

"It may happen that you hate a thing which is good for you."

Everybody here is content and people in the markets, at gatherings and in the clubs speak of nothing else but Zaidān and the university, as to what happened and will happen. This has created fervour and a solid defence amongst many, because the university erred in accepting me and then changed its decision for the only reason that I am a Christian. The moral of it all is "Do not hate anything, it may be for the better".

Asmā yesterday made an attempt in Arabic composition and she excuses herself for her weakness. When she did it I found many mistakes in it. But I realized that she has an inclination for composition like you and I encouraged her to continue writing.

I end now with kisses and greetings.

Ǧurǧī.

Cairo, Nov. 10, 1911

Dear Emile,

Today your uncle went down to the printing press; thanks to God, he has recovered. I have returned to my work on the [book *The History of*] *Literature in* [*the Arabic*] *Language*. It seems that this part of the book will be longer than the preceding one, because it will contain the learning and literature of the Abbasid period. This is the most important period in our history, from 122 — 606 A.H. I want neither to cut short the discussion of it nor do I want to leave part for the third volume. I believe that, therefore, the present part will be voluminous.

Enclosed is a bank cheque in your name for twenty guineas. We here, thanks to God, are all happy and hope for you the same. Nothing is of interest to the people here except the news from the war.[14] They hope very much for an Ottoman victory, regardless of the fact that it is a distant hope. But God is almighty. In any case I may mention for what the Ottomans are being praised; they are showing firmness, courage and independence. Nothing better can be expected under the circumstances. It is not unlikely that they will defeat the Italians, even if it takes a while.

14. The Italian invasion of Bengazi and Tripoli 1911/12 and colonization of these Ottoman provinces.

Proof of their judiciousness and high-mindedness is that they were able to send the elite of their commanders into Tripolis at a time when the approach from the sea was closed off. This Enver[15] publishes in Bengazi pamphlets against the Italians. This Raḥmānī, Niyāzī and Nišāt[16] and other members of the Ottoman Army goad the Arabs towards unity with as-Sanūsī,[17] who is now in Bengazi — all this shows their high-minded aims. May God grant them eventual victory. If this war ends in a defeat of the Ottomans, it will pain me very much; it would grieve me to see the aggressor triumph. If you could see how your brother Šukrī is a loyal supporter of the Ottoman cause. Reading the newspapers keep him from his homework. He wakes up in the morning and asks about the news and reads them. When he comes home at noontime I usually have prepared for him some newspapers of interest to him regarding news about the victory of the Ottomans. At noontime he will, rather than repeating the questions of the morning, ask for the whereabouts of the newspaper. If he reads any news of Ottoman victories, he will sing out in joy. He begins to praise the courage of the Arabs and proclaims that the Europeans, *al-afranǧ*, despise the Arabs, but they should come and see the Arabs or read about their history and contributions to civilization, etc. Frequently meetings are organized in school to discuss which side is victorious: the Arabs or the Italians. I am truly happy about his support of the Ottomans. This is what his patriotic duties demand. I wish to God that the Ottoman Government emerges triumphant from this war and gains thereby [?] an important position amongst the other governments. But I digressed from the personal to the political. Today at four o'clock your uncle Ibrāhīm is going to Alexandria to bring his

---

15. Enver *Pāšā* (d. 1922). Graduate of the War College in Istanbul. He joined the Young Turks and participated in the revolution 1908. 1913 he was made Minister of War. Together with Ǧamāl *Pāšā* and Ṭal'at *Pāšā* he held virtually dictatorial powers until the collapse of the Ottoman Empire in 1918. LEWIS 221.

16. Aḥmad Niyāzī. Attended the War College, became a member of the Young Turk movement and played a decisive part in the Young Turk Revolution in 1908; LEWIS *passim*. Nišāt one of the Ottoman Officers ABBOT 89.

17. A descendent of Sidi Muḥammad as-Sanūsī (1791-1859) founder of the puritanic Islamic religious order as-Sanūsīya in Cyrenaica. During the 19th century the order spread all over Tripoli. When the Italians occupied Tripoli in 1911-12 they met with unexpected resistance from the population, whose religious fervour let them maintain their loyalty to the Ottoman Caliph; ZIADEH *passim*.

cousin to her home. He will return Monday morning. He charged Mulḥim to take his place in the office and no doubt I, too, have to go there for this purpose. Before that I have to go to the printing press to substitute for your uncle Mitrī since I ordered him to go every day at two o'clock to the oases because of the pure air there.

In short, I end this letter with a kiss and greetings.

Your father,
Ǧurǧī.

Cairo, March 28, 1912

Dear Emile,

I received your letter just now. It came on time, i.e. Thursday morning. I am very pleased that you enjoy good health and benefit from your being President of the Society. No doubt this is to your benefit. It is of use for the future because the Society resembles a constitutional government and a political or commercial society. Above all I am pleased with your patience. This is also, as you know, my approach in associating with people. I believe that the most forgiving people are the wisest — to a certain limit, of course. It seems that the president still wants to employ you for teaching and you did well to refuse. Surely you explained to him your decision in the light of [your] service to the school in other aspects. It is indeed true, that serving the Syrian Protestant College is a service to the whole nation and a service to freedom and the constitution, because it prepares people for it.

I was astonished about your enquiry for the third time about the name of the German book. I answered you already twice — and this is the third time — that the title which you asked for is vague. The name of the author must be specified or the topic of one of the book's sections must be narrowed down in order to search for it. Then we can send it to you. Yesterday we received a note from your friend. He asked for the letter from the school (I think it is Šuwair) concerning the subscription to "al-Hilāl". He also remarked that he had asked you to enquire about the German book and did not receive any answer, and I will write him that we cannot buy the book without specification of the author and a very good description of the subject of the book.

I read "al-Manār" and saw, what you, too, saw. Grief prevailed over all other feelings in me. Not because this foolish criticism had any influence upon me! Indeed, the station of "al-Hilāl" is too lofty as to be hit by such tasteless slander. But I was grieved by the deterioration of the character of our writers to such a level, that even from an-Nu'mānī, the greatest scholar of India, emanate phrases that even the rabble would be ashamed to use. With all this we were friends for twenty years and our relations were amicable. When I read his criticism I wrote him a letter, reproaching him in very strong terms. A copy of it you will find enclosed. Return it to me after you have read it, so that I can save it! Don't you think that he deserves such severity? As for the owner of "al-Manār", he is excused by his exasperation with "al-Hilāl", the success of our books, our fame and with the proposition of the university, that I should teach. I think the last issue that angered him was the letter of Prince Muḥammad 'Alī[18] to me in which he praises my work and which was published in "al-Ahrām"[19] without my suggestion. And.....[20] affected the envious people. All this does not interest me either. But it weakens my determination to exert myself in the service of this nation, *umma*, the history of which was lying dead. I brought it back to life and I indeed say without boasting it was I who revived the Arab literature by what I wrote and by the influence my books had upon the envious feelings of the writers, inducing them to compete. Before the appearance of "al-Hilāl" nobody mentioned the history of Islam. Those who composed works about it copied only from the ancient authors. Today they begin to write in a reflective and explanatory manner. All this they got from my works. They tried to imitate me in writing historical novels about Islam and were unsuccessful. The first to fail was the owner of "al-Manār"[21] since he announced already seven years ago that he had

---

18. Prince Muḥammad 'Alī, born 1872, brother of 'Abbās II. He studied in Switzerland and travelled widely. He belonged to the same Free Mason Organization as Zaidān. He supported and directed various welfare and learned societies in Egypt. FAHMĪ 95 ff.

19. Al-Ahrām, first major daily newspaper in Egypt, founded in 1876 in Alexandria by the Syrian immigrant, Salīm Taqlā; DĪ TARRĀZĪ IV 215.

20. Illegible in ms.

21. i.e. Rašīd Riḍā.

asked Šaiḫ ʻAbd al-Ḥamīd Zuhrāwī[22] (who was then in Egypt) for help to compose a series of historical novels about Islam because "nobody' had written about this subject in Arabic"!! Regardless of the fact that my novels fill his library and he has read all of them. If this did not change his irritation, how can we blame him that his vexation increased when he started with this project and did not even finish the first novel. Other deeply envious people strove for this and intended to obliterate the light of truth even though it shines like the sun. There are other examples of their intent to extinguish this light. There is a certain Muḥammad Masʻūd[23] — one of the Muslim writers of the old school, owner of a newspaper, and now employed in the office of press and information. He began to be interested in translating Le Bon's book about the history of Arabic civilization into Arabic. When he announced his decision, the Islamic newspapers and others began to encourage him. Some began even publishing eulogies full of lies, namely, that no book dealing with Arab and Islamic civilization was available in Arabic. They also regretted that none of the Arab writers was encouraged to write on this subject in spite of its importance. Therefore, Muḥammad... Masʻūd is forced to translate this topic from the French. Imagine this delusion and how it proves the extremity [of their position]. But Dr. Fayyāḍ Bin al-Iskandar wrote to the newspaper "al-Ahālī",[24] which had published this praise, pointing out the existence of my book *Ta'riḫ at-tamaddun al-islāmī*, and reproached the newspaper for this eulogy. His letter was published.

Some days later I met the above-mentioned Muḥammad Masʻūd. After greeting him I enquired about his book and he told me that he was now busy printing it. I asked him, "Why did you leave us open to rebuke and criticism with your translation of this book from the French? Would it not have been preferable that you yourself write a book about

22. ʻAbd al-Ḥamīd az-Zuhrāwī (1871-1916) born in Homs, in 1902 went to Egypt where he worked for al-Mu'ayyad and al-Ǧarīda. 1909 he became representative of Homs in the new Ottoman Parliament. 1913 he presided over the first Arab Congress in Paris. He was a member of the Decentralization Party and wrote about Islamic reform and Arab nationalism. He was executed in 1916 by the Ottoman government in Syria; DĀĠIR II 427, DĪ ṬARRĀZĪ III 28.

23. Muḥammad Masʻūd (1872-1940) born in Egypt, was a writer, translator and journalist. As a friend of ʻAlī Yūsuf he worked for al-Mu'ayyad. Later he edited various magazines and newspapers; DĀĠIR III 1206.

24. Al-Ahālī. Newspaper founded 1894 by Ismāʻīl *Pāšā* Abāẓah; DĪ ṬARRĀZĪ IV 168.

this topic, especially since you often told me that you were engaged in such a project even before me?" Can you imagine his answer? He claimed that if he translated if from the French he would increase the trust of the public in the presented material. At this point I shouted at him, "Until when [shall we indulge in] this cowardice and weakness. If *you* say that, how about the others? Why don't we ourselves write about this topic? We are the people most capable [to deal] with it. This book of mine, even though its author is an Easterner, has been translated by the Europeans and others into five languages, and others of my works have been translated." He did not utter a word in response and went away embarrassed.[25]

I have prolonged my talk about this subject to you and actually it is not so important. I have broached the subject in response to your question. Rest assured that the cunning of the envious people makes us only firmer and more successful. The nation, *al-umma*, however — and I mean its educated members — appreciate our work and its true value. I have encountered groups of them during all this time at different occasions. They all laud my work and challenge all the critics. One educated man told me, "Don't get angry, my friend, if some irascibles do not know the value of your work and do not recognize it. Jean-Jacques Rousseau said that the seed of science bear fruit ondy after a hundred years have passed." I told him that I enjoy already, thanks to God, the fruit of my past travail and that I see the literary fruits in the contemporary intellectual movement.

If it was not for the praise and the truthful recognition which I have heard from some educated people, I would have given up writing about Islamic topics and turned to more general subjects. In any case my determination to engage in this subject is weakened. I shall direct my energy to other general or Syrian topics and the like, preferably about society and other sciences. We shall discuss this when we see each other.

As for the money, I have sent for a cheque to be issued for ten guineas, if it comes in time I shall put it in this letter.

I am longing very much to see you and we, left behind here, pray for your and are proud of you.

Ǧurǧī.

25. Illegible in ms.

APPENDIX

BIBLIOGRAPHICAL NOTES

A. THE WORKS OF ǦURǦĪ ZAIDĀN

Ǧurǧī Zaidān was a most prolific writer. His published works include various studies on history and literature, twenty two novels and twenty two years of his monthly magazine "al-Hilāl", which he authored almost exclusively himself.

Since, with very rare exceptions, his works are not available in European languages it seems worthwhile to give short outlines of content, to describe the organization of material and to discuss the sources upon which Zaidān drew. Two of his projects, to wit, the historical novels and the magazine "al-Hilāl" seem of special importance. The interest in them arises not from their volume, which is considerable, but rather from the appeal they had for the Arabic reading public, and the popularity they enjoyed. It would be difficult to underestimate the role they played in popularizing knowledge, be it of Arab history or of matters concerning modern civilization. Generally speaking they contributed greatly to the development of a taste for secular literature amongst Arab readers. From these points of view their impact was certainly greater than that of the scholarly works Zaidān put out.

1. Scholarly Studies

Zaidān's first efforts as an author were directed towards scholarly works. From the beginning two topics attracted his special attention, history in general and the history of language and literature in particular. His first three books that deal with historical topics appeared between 1889 and 1890.

In his *Ta'rīḫ al-māsūnīya al-ʿāmm* he attempted to correct the misconceptions of ignorant people about the Freemasons. Zaidān used for his work the standard European works about Freemasonry and the information he gathered from former heads of lodges in Syria, Egypt and Palestine.

Taking similarity of phenomena in history as a proof of their related continuation throughout history rather than as a sign of similar human needs and social circumstances, Zaidān was able to trace the precursors of Masonry to the Egyptian Pharaohs and to date its definitive organization to the time of the Roman king Numa Pompilius.

The *Ta'rīḫ miṣr al-ḥadīṯ* was primarily addressed to the Egyptian student. The book was indeed later used as a textbook in schools.[1] Rather arbitrarily Zaidān declared that the history of Egypt after the Muslim conquest was the richest period of Egypt's history and, therefore, the worthiest to describe. This was the period he meant by *Ta'rīḫ miṣr al-ḥadīṯ*. He, therefore, restricted the description of pre-Islamic Egyptian history to a summary of some seventy pages and gave roughly six times the space for the Islamic period. The first edition of this work was organized strictly according to the sequences of rulers and governments. In the enlarged second edition, which appeared twenty-two years later, Zaidān added topical chapters concerning social and economical questions, such as the reforms of Muḥammad ʿAlī or the *Nahḍa* of the Arab world.

The ambitious project of a "general history", *at-Ta'rīḫ al-ʿāmm*, never got beyond its first part, which included "the history of the ancient and modern kingdoms of Asia and Africa". The treatment of this vast subject is very unbalanced or, to be more exact, rather culture-centric. In the section about Asia some fifty pages deal with the history of Biblical times, relying for its narration exclusively upon the Bible itself. Some pages are given to the Persian and Chinese empires and some more to the first appearance of Islam. A timetable of the most important events from the Tower of Babel to Beirut's being made a *vilayet* in 1888 concluded this part. The part of Africa consisted of two pages of general introduction and a 120-page history of Egypt from its beginnings to the present.

Again, the main purpose was to provide a textbook in an easily understandable style for schools in this case. Each chapter was followed by a questionnaire. With the help of these questions the student could check his comprehension of the preceding chapter.

---

1. *Letters, Madrasat al-qaḍā' aš-šarʿī* to Zaidān, Cairo July 2 1910.

During the following ten years Zaidān's preoccupation with his newly founded magazine seems to have left him time only for some hasty compilations dealing with the history of different Western nations. Amongst other publications we find also one of rather dubious value about physiognomy, *'Ilm al-firāsa*, which relies heavily upon the works of Lavater and Samuel Wells[2] from whose books he even took most of his illustrations.

By 1900 the work for "al-Hilāl" had been better organized and settled into a certain routine. Since 1901 Zaidān eliminated the issues of August and September and distributed to his subscribers each year one of his scholarly works as a substitute. The books mentioned in the following were all originally distributed in this fashion. These new arrangements permitted Zaidān to return to his interest in history and literature. His scholarly endeavours in these fields were from this time on almost exclusively concentrated upon the Arabs and their civilization.

In the years 1901-06 he published the five volumes of his *Ta'rīḫ at-tamaddun al-islāmī*. The five volumes deal roughly with the following subjects: 1) history of political and military institutions from pre-Islamic times to the fall of the Abbasids and general political history of that time; 2) finances, taxes and wealth of the caliphs, the state and the cities; 3) Arabic and non-Arabic branches of knowledge and science, and the impact of non-Muslim sciences upon the Islamic culture; 4) political history including the Fatimid dynasty and the "Second Arab Period", meaning the petty states in the Fertile Crescent which rose after the Seljuq Turkish unification of the empire had broken down. This volume also includes some sociological and ideological aspects of the Umayyad and Abbasid periods. 5) Cultural aspects and social structure of the Muslim empire until the fall of the Abbasids.

Zaidān had made during the preceding years many preliminary studies for this work which were often published in essay form in "al-Hilāl". The composition of his historical novels had made it necessary

2. J.K. Lavater (1741-1799). a Swiss clergyman who played a certain role as a patriotic author against the French. He became famous for his *Physiognomische Fragmente* in which he tried to establish a scientific relation between facial structure and character. S.R. Wells (1820-1875) was the editor of the Phrenological Journal and Life Illustrated. He also wrote a book dealing with the relations between physical features and psychological characteristics.

for him to familiarize himself with the historical background. More inspired by Western scholarship than by the traditional Muslim historiography, Zaidān attempted to write a history organized according to subject matters using systematically nonliterary evidence and critical comparative investigation of sources to establish the veracity of the historical account. According to his own statement, Zaidān read more than a hundred books for the subject, and he named twenty-five Arabic and seven Western sources.[3] The work was called a *History of Islamic Civilization* but in reality, as one can see from the above list of contents, it concentrated upon that period of Islamic history in which the Arab element prevailed or at least was visible in the person of the Abbasid Caliphe. That the Arabs and not the other people of Islamic civilization are Zaidān's main concern, was also shown by the fact that two years later he published a book, *al-'Arab qabla 'l-islām*, in which he tried to stretch Arab history back to the time of Hammurabi.

Another book, this time dealing with the very recent history of the Middle East, was compiled by Zaidān in 1907, *Tarāǧim mašāhīr aš-šarq fī'l-qarn at-tāsi' 'ašar*. The vitae of more than one hundred personalities are collected here. The first part of the book contains the biographies of the members of the family of the *Ḫidīw*, kings and rulers of the East, commanders, ministers and administrators. The second part concentrates upon founders of the *Nahḍa* — publishers and journalists, men of science and *adab*, and poets. The large majority of the people dealt with are Arabs, but some Westerners of importance for the cultural history of the Near East in the 19th century are mentioned; prominent teachers of the Syrian Protestant College and French advisors to the government of Muḥammad 'Alī. The inclusion of three Japanese and Chinese personalities, though somewhat *déplacé* here, constituted probably an attempt to include all of Asia as part of the one entity called "East". The book remains till today a valuable source for biographical information especially for Egypt and Syria in the 19th century. But in spite of his precocupation with history Zaidān never lost his interest in Arabic language and literature, the historical aspect of which remained of decisive importance for him. In 1904 he published *Ta'rīḫ al-luġa al-'arabīya bi'tibārihā kā'in ḥayy ḥāḍi' linămūs al-irtiqā'*. It is an elaboration on his very first work *al-Alfāẓ*

3. *Ta'rīḫ at-tamaddun* IV 14.

al-ʿarabīya wa'l-falsafa al-luġawīya which had appeared nineteen years earlier. In the first book he had made the attempt to describe in evolutionary terms how language developed from animal sounds into the abstraction of speech. In the second book the emphasis shifts to the development of Arabic itself.

By far his most important contribution in the field of the history of Arab literature in its widest possible meaning, is his *Ta'rīḫ ādāb al-luġa al-ʿarabīya*, the four volumes of which appeared during the years 1910-1914. Early essays on the subject had already been published by Zaidān in "al-Hilāl" during 1894-95. Zaidān believed that he was the first to have coined the expression *ta'rīḫ ādāb al-luġa*[4] and defined it as a general intellectual history, *Geistesgeschichte*, including not only literature but all branches of learning and knowledge in the sciences and humanities considering their history as the basic explanation for the reasons of the rise and the fall of a nation. Zaidān considered European scholarship to have been the first in setting a pattern for the writing of such intellectual histories. He himself was the first to make the attempt to produce something equivalent in Arabic. Quite clearly Zaidān made great use of Nicholson's and Brockelmann's works. Probably very much of the bibliographical information and some of the biographic information were taken more or less directly from Brockelmann's *Geschichte der Arabischen Litteratur*.

But while Brockelmann's interests were predominantly of a biographical and bibliographical kind, Zaidān wanted both to introduce the Arab readers to their cultural and literary heritage within its proper historical context and to give his readers a tool with which to help themselves continue their education in this subject. Thus, these four volumes constitute a mixture of a collection of cultural-literary essays and an encyclopaedia of names of writers, poets, philosophers, historians, theologians, scientists, etc.

The general periodizing of literary history along political events into a pre-Islamic, early Islamic, Umayyad, several Abbasid, a Mongol and an Ottoman period is more or less the same as Brockelmann and Nicholson offered it. But Zaidān subdivided the pre-Islamic period into a first and second period of ignorance, *ǧāhilīya*. In the first the codifications of Hammurabi and the Book of Job were cited as the first evidence

---

4. *Ta'rīḫ ādāb* I 8.

of Arabic culture. The second *ǧāhilīya* covers the period usually described as pre-Islamic to which much space is given in Zaidān work. Already here he considered it appropriate to introduce special sections for sciences, such as medicine, veterinary medicine, meteorology, etc. In striking contrast to the extensive discussion of Arabic literature and culture during the pre-Islamic period, Zaidān did not need more than a dozen pages to deal with the period of early Islam until the rise of the Umayyads. After talking about the Umayyad period mainly in terms of its poets and poetry, Zaidān dealt at great length with sciences, literature, theology and philosophy during the reign of the Abbasids, which period he subdivided into four sections. He introduced this part with a short survey of Greek, Persian and Indian literature and culture and their impact on the Islamic culture. Throughout all parts of the book each section is opened with an introduction giving the general historical and social background. A list of the most important people during the particular period and their works follows. Here, of course, Zaidān lacked the comprehensiveness of Brockelmann's work, but for the people Zaidān did mention in these lists he often gave more detailed information.

For the Western reader familiar with the works of Brockelmann and Nicholson, the first three volumes of this work offer relatively little additional information. The fourth volume constituted Zaidān's most original contribution to the study of the history of Arab literature and culture. It deals with the modern period under the impact of modern Europe, a period which is hardly mentioned in Brockelmann's work and in Nicholson's book on a few pages only.

Zaidān dealt with the phenomenon of the Arab *Nahḍa* of the 19th century by describing all those factors that in his opinion constituted the cause and the means for this new development. The following institutions, their development and their representatives seemed to him of importance: schools; printing press; journalism; scientific, literary and other cultural societies; libraries, European oriental studies; the translations from European languages into Arabic and, finally, all that had been orginally written in Arabic prose or poetry during this time. Again, much of the material that Zaidān compiled in this volume is today, sixty years later, outdated, but together with L. Cheikho's works in this field, it remains one of the most important Arabic sources on the literary and intellectual life of the Arab world in the 19th century.

Still engaged in composing this work, Zaidān published in 1912 a book on ethnology, *Ṭabaqāt al-umam*, the title of which he took from Sa'īd b. Aḥmad al-Andalūsī's book written in the 11th century. But as far as its content is concerned, it is a close adaptation of Keane's *The World's People*. The book dealt with the scientific description of all people, their physical appearance, their habits and mores, their intellectual development, and their arrangement on a scale of human development and evolution starting with the Negro on the lowest and the Caucasian on the highest step of development.

The subject of this book might indicate a certain shift of Zaidān's main interest during his last years away from Arab and Muslim matters towards universal subjects, and from history to social sciences, an impression which is corroborated by the change of topic and section in the last volumes of "al-Hilāl".

Zaidān's voluminous studies of Arabic history and literature are today of little scholarly value. Much of their content was an adaptation of the works of Western orientalists. Already his contemporaries were aware of many mistakes and superficialities in his works. The main merit of these works at the time was to have introduced Western scholarship and concepts to Arab historical studies. In our context works have been used mainly as a primary source to extricate Zaidān's concepts of Arab national identity and of his historical consciousness. Two works, however, should be excluded from the above judgement. The fourth volume of his *Ta'riḫ ādāb al-luġa al-'arabīya* and his two volumes of *Tarāǧim mašāhīr aš-šarq fi'l-qarn at-tāsi' 'ašar*, provide till today valuable information about the Arab *Nahḍa* movement in the nineteenth century.

2. The Magazine "al-Hilāl"

In September 1892 Zaidān launched probably the most important project of his career — the magazine "al-Hilāl", the Crescent. In the opening statement for the magazine he explained the reasons for the choice of the name: to indicate the monthly appearance of the magazine; to gain the blessings of the Ottoman Crescent wich is the symbol of the Ottoman Empire and to imply by comparing it to the waxing moon the intention of the magazine to grow like the moon towards a full, strong light.

He proposed organizing the content of the magazine in five sections:

1. A section of the most famous events and the greatest men which would give him a free hand to choose any subject from history and discuss it in the magazine.
2. A section for articles. Articles would be written either by him or other contemporary writers.
3. A section for novels in which he wanted to serialize historical novels as "examples of the habits of the Easterners and their history according to their taste, void of foreign events and expression".
4. A section of monthly events which would bring news summaries from the best newspapers concerning the world and especially Egypt and Syria.
5. A section of selected news, eulogies, criticism. This section would mainly deal with contemporary literature.[5]

The magazine was to appear in monthly issues of about forty pages, but the composition of the magazine was not to be as rigid as this plan may suggest. Zaidān noted in the opening statement that it would be a main task of "al-Hilāl" always to please the readers and to cater to their wishes. This would demand many changes over the years. In the third issue of the first year he added a new section for "Letters to the Editor". *Bāb al-murāsalāt,* usually dealing with general topics such as women's rights. From the second year on "al-Hilāl" appeared twice monthly, its size somewhat reduced. During this and the following year the section for novels did not appear but was reintroduced in the fourth year and became a great success. A new section was added in the second year, "Questions and Suggestions", *Bāb as-su'āl wa'l-iqtirāḥ,* in which Zaidān wanted to answer the letter from his readers who asked him about practically any subject, and by no means always concerning topics dealt with in the magazine itself. New also in the third year was the section "Scientific News", *Aḫbār 'ilmīya,* dealing with scientific discoveries, inventions and technology in general.

Until its tenth year "al-Hilāl" offered these ten sections with great regularity. The size of each issue varied between 32 and 40 pages. The last two issues of each decreased in size and were often combined. From the ninth year onwards only twenty issues of "al-Hilāl" were published.

5. I 1-2.

Between the tenth and fourteenth year (1901-02/1905-06) a whole range of new sections was introduced. Some disappeared again soon, such as the "Section of Kings and Rulers of the East", *Mulūk aš-šarq wa-umarā'uhū*, which was continued only for three years. Others appeared somewhat irregularly such as the "Health of the Family", *Ṣiḥḥat al-'ā'ila*, the first section of which was written predominantly by authors other than Zaidān himself; or "wonders of Creation", *'Aǧā'ib al-maḫlūqāt*, which probably emanated from the scientific news but brought mainly *curiosa*, such as the man with the longest beard in the world, or the habits of kangaroos. Of rare appearance were the sections "The Circumstances of States", *Aḥwāl ad-duwal*, and "Strange Habits", *Ġarā'ib al-'ādāt*. Only the section for "New Publications", *Maṭbū'āt ǧadīda*, introduced in volume X appeared in each issue. In the same years two existing sections were slowly phased out: "Monthly Events" and "Eulogies and Criticism". With the beginning of volume XIII in October 1904 the magazine appeared only once monthly ten months a year with about 80 pages to each issue.

Size and frequency of the sections remained very unbalanced. With the doubling of space per issue almost all the sections mentioned were presented with some regularity. Probably because of Zaidān's occupation with the Young Turk revolution and its meaning and implications, most sections faded away again beginning with volume XVI (1908-09). During the next three years the magazine usually consisted of one main article which in most cases analyzed the background of contemporary events followed by one or two articles of general interest not assigned to any particular section. The only sections that were regularly given space were "New Publications", "Scientific News" and "Questions and Suggestions". Only in volume XXI did a greater variety of sections, for instance "Health of the Family", "Wonders of Creation", return. A new section "Social News", *Aḫbār al-iǧtimā'īya*, appeared rather frequently; demographic information, technological events that were of impact upon society, and developments in society were reported here. In volume XXII, the last one that Zaidān himself published, he attempted a basic reorganization of the magazine, which was enlarged to 96 pages. A large part of each issue was reserved for articles on various topics which were not put under a specific section. Almost all the other sections which had been partially neglected appeared again in each issue, but usually very little space was assigned to them.

Not only size and frequency of the sections varied, but throughout the years their content and emphasis changed. Perhaps one of the most interesting sections in that respect was "Monthly Events". It was intended as a summary of the most important news of each month, condensed from daily newspapers. This section started with the very first issue of the magazine. It is noteworthy what the section was usually subdivided into Egyptian, Syrian and foreign events. The latter, *Ḫāriǧīya*, dealt with European news; also often found there was a subdivision for Japanese and Chinese news. More important, Zaidān published the events from other parts of the Ottoman Empire under the heading of foreign events. Political and cultural news were reported, ranging from the opening ceremony for a new railway line to a visit of a Russian naval unit in Toulon, and from the printing of new stamps for the Ottoman mail to earthquakes in Greece. Reports from the royal court were regularly included in the Egyptian news. Also, news from the Eastern churches found their place here. Included sometimes were news from the world of sciences until they found their own section in volume III.

During the first eight years or so the trend towards cultural and social news was emphasized more and more. Often the "Monthly Events" consisted of one or two lenghty articles about a person or a certain issue. The section lost increasingly its "news" character. From volume VI the "Scientific News" appeared before the "Monthly Events", while the former increased in size, the latter decreased. Eventually it appeared only irregularly, and in volume XIII, even though the size of the issues had been doubled, it was not mentioned any more. Only nine years later in the last year of Zaidān's editorship did the same section reappear, focused more than ever on news of general cultural and social relevance.

Of central importance in terms of size and placement seemed to be the section of "Most Famous Events and Greatest Men", which was always the first part of each issue and, with some exceptions in volumes V and VI, also provided the subject for the cover picture of the issue. This section appeared with great regularity during all 22 years, with the exception of volumes XI to XIII where it was repeatedly replaced by the section "Kings and Rulers of the East", which in fact could be part of the former. In the last years the name of the section was dropped, but the front article kept the same character. Because of its importance and its very wide range of possible topics, this section seemed rather representative of the spirit of the magazine and worthy of being investigated somewhat more closely as to characteristic trends and developments of "al-Hilāl".

The usual ratio between articles dealing with topics or people from the Western world (almost exclusively Europe) and articles dealing with the East (predominantly the area of Islamic culture) appeared to be between 1: 4 and 2: 3 in each volume; only once was there no article dealing directly with the West at all: volume XVII (1908-09) which was filled with the events of the Young Turk revolution. Twice Western topics constituted slightly more than half of all the articles: volume IX which deals with the Boer War in South Africa, and volume XVI which at the eve of the Young Turk revolution brought out extensive articles about the French Revolution and the war of independence of the American colonies against England.

Two-thirds of all the articles were built around a person, his actions, inventions, or thoughts with some *exposé* of the historical, scientific or intellectual context in which he appeared. Even in articles which contained, for instance, the general description of a country, the title of the article would usually mention the ruler of the country, and a considerable part of the article would dwell on the personal history of the ruler and his private life. But a clear trend can be seen over the course of time that an increasing amount of articles were built around a subject matter rather than using the life description of an outstanding personality as the main structure of an essay.

Of the roughly one hundred articles dealing with the West, fourteen took their subject from antiquity (mainly from Greek culture) and only five dealt with the European Middle Ages. Three of those articles, the articles about Charlemagne, Richard the Lionheart and Frederick II had clear relevance for the Islamic world. Obviously the European Middle Ages were of no interest to Zaidān. By far the largest space taken by the articles concerned the modern West.

About two hundred articles dealt with Islamic countries and culture. One-quarter of them pertained to the classical period of Islam. By far the majority of these articles appeared in the first half of the 22 volumes. Here, as with the articles concerning Western topics, we may recognize a predominant interest in modern times, a trend which even increased with the years.

The non-Islamic Eastern cultures were fairly evenly represented with one to two articles in each volume and with an exceptional accumulation of articles in volume XI and XII after Zaidān introduced the new section of "Kings and Rulers of the East", declaring the need for a more balanced knowledge of European as well as Eastern states and governments. In the first volumes the emphasis was on old Near Eastern cultures such as Pharaonic Egypt, the Chaldaeans and Assyrians. Later "al-Hilāl" was mainly interested in non-Western, non-Islamic cultures of contemporary importance, such as China, Japan and India.

In spite of Zaidān's marked interest in modern times, he did not consider it as the task of "al-Hilāl" to report about the current political events or to give pronounced political opinions concerning such events. He was mainly concerned to give in these articles a general historical background to such events and persons as caught the headlines of the daily newspapers. Good examples of this kind of journalism can be found in volume IV (1897-98) with articles about the Sudan, its geography, its people, its history at a time when its re-conquest was in full swing; or in volume XVII (1908-09) which dealt in its main articles exclusively with the Young Turk revolution, the history of the Ottoman Empire and constitutionalism in other Eastern countries. Very often the main article would also have as a topic a famous person either on the occasion of his death or when he was involved in important contemporary events.

The magazine "al-Hilāl" remains an invaluable treasury of information about contemporary society and about Zaidān himself.[6] Not only does it give somewhat of a chronology for the development of Zaidān's concept and ideas but Zaidān here is also much more outspoken, as far as his own opinions are concerned, than in his scholarly studies.

6. An index to al-Hilāl is being prepared by the American University in Beirut.

3. Historical Novels

Altogether Zaidān wrote 22 novels,[7] only one of which *Ǧihād al-muḥibbīn*, is a novel about contemporary society. All others are called by Zaidān historical novels, *riwāya ta'riḫīya*. He started out with *al-Mamlūk aš-šārid* in 1891, a novel taking place in Egypt and Syria in the time of Muḥammad 'Alī. Two more novels set in a comparatively recent historical background followed. The fourth historical novel, *Armānūsā*, the second to be serialized in "al-Hilāl", turned to classical Islamic history. While writing this novel (1895-96) the idea occurred to him to encompass the whole Islamic history from its beginning in a sequence of novels.[8] Zaidān held fast to this project and after writing in 1896-97 a novel dealing with Muslim history before the conquest of Egypt, he continued to publish every year, serialized in his magazine, another historical novel, each dealing with a consecutive period of Islamic history. Thus he covered in seventeen novels from 1895 to 1914 Islamic history from its beginnings until the time of the Ayyubid rule in Egypt. Only once did Zaidān interrupt this chain when he offered his readers a novel in 1910-11 about the Young Turk revolution.

The clumsiness of the plot in Zaidān's novels and the tediousness of their descriptions are not only the result of a lack of tradition and experience in novel writing in Arabic literature, but they are even more a sign that Zaidān's ambitions were mainly that of an educator and historian rather than that of a novelist. A certain set of persons appear in most of his plots. There is the hero and the heroine, a young girl well educated and intelligent, who is in love with the hero. She is supported and protected by an equally well educated and intelligent mother. A totally devoted male or female servant generally completes the list of representatives of the good element. On the evil side we find usually the father of the girl who is cruel, uneducated and tyrannical and tries to force his daughter to marry the villain of the plot, who does not love the girl but wants to marry her for his own personal advantage. This checker-

7. Some sources indicate 23 novels. This error occurs when an English historical novel about Muḥammad 'Alī, translated and published by Zaidān, is counted among his own novels; see for instance Ḥasan 98, Badr 95, GAL Suppl III 190, which may be the source of the mistake.

8. V 24.

board of relations is not always necessarily the same, but the clear-cut division between the evil and good elements is always there. In extension, these elements are affiliated loosely with historical personalities and events which may belong to either side but remain usually in the background.[9] Sometimes, however, a historical personality will be actively involved in the plot.[10] The personalities of the characters of the narrative remain one-dimensional and stereotyped. We do not find any development of character in the course of the narrative. Psychological analysis is lacking. The good element is pitted against the evil element. In order to set the action of the narrative into motion and to compensate for the lack of psychological motivation and development Zaidān had to introduce elements of intrigue, conspiracies, secrets, confusion and coincidences. We find similar plots with variations in each novel providing in general happy ending in which the good vanquishes the evil.

No attempt has been made here to evaluate the literary function and value of Zaidān's novels in the development of the modern Arab novel. It should only be pointed out that until today the novels are widely read in the Arab world and that they go continuously through new editions. Their popularity was even greater in Zaidān's own time.

4. Unpublished Material

In addition to the published works of Zaidān there exists a collection of his private papers, which is now in the archives of the American University in Beirut. The collection contains the manuscript of a history of Ottoman Egypt, *Miṣr al-'uṯmānīya* which he had prepared as a lecture course at the Egyptian University in 1910; several notebooks which Zaidān used for his own research, the manuscript of his autobiography, which has been discussed in the introduction to the translation and finally a multitude of letters to and from Zaidān. A large part of these letters consists of business correspondence concerning the publication of books or exchanges with European scholars. Especially to be mentioned here is a set of some 125 letters written by Zaidān to his son Emile between

9. For instance Saladin in the novel *Ṣalāḥ ad-dīn al-ayyūbī* or 'Urābī and General Gordon in the novel *Asīr al-mutamahdī.*

10. For instance Abdülhamid in the novel *Al-inqilāb al-'uṯmānī* takes an active part on the evil side.

1908 and 1912, while the latter was studying in Beirut at the American University. These letters provide insight into the personality of Zaidān, his relations with his family, his feelings about contemporary events, his social life and his relations with other members of the educated class in Egypt. The few letters chosen here for translation are not necessarily the most representative for the general tone and content of the correspondence with Emile, but are particularly relevant for the subject of this study.

BIBLIOGRAPHY OF ZAIDĀN'S WORKS

We have always indicated here the year and place of the first editions. If another edition has been used in this study the quoted edition is given in parentheses. There exist some collections of articles of Zaidān which originally appeared in "al-Hilāl" and were published posthumously as books. Those books are not mentioned here.

a) Works on History

Ta'rīḫ al-māsūnīya al-'āmm Cairo 1889

at -Ta'rīḫ al-'āmm Cairo 1890

Ta'rīḫ al-yūnān wa 'r-rūmān Cairo 1899

Ta'rīḫ ingilterā Cairo 1899

Ta'rīḫ at-tamaddun al-islāmī 5 vols. Cairo 1901-1906 (1958, ed. Mu'nis, Ḥusain). Vol. IV transl. into English by D.S. Margoliouth *Zaidan's Umayyads and Abbasids* Leiden 1907. For quotations from this volume its English translation has been used.

al-'Arab qabla l-islām Cairo 1907 (n.d. ed. by Mu'nis, Ḥusain)

Miṣr al-'uṯmānīya unpublished ms. in the collection of unpublished papers at AUB.

b) Works on Language and Literature

al-Alfāẓ al-'arabīya wa'l-falsafa al-luġawīya Beirut 1886 (*al-Falsafa al-luġawīya* ed. by Kāmil, Murād, Cairo 1969)

Ta'rīḫ al-luġa al-'arabīya bi'itibārihā kā'in ḥayy ḫāḍi' lināmūs al-irtiqā' Cairo 1904 (*al-luġa al-'arabīya kā'in ḥayy* ed. by Kāmil, Murād Cairo 196?)

Ta'rīḫ ādāb al-luġa al-'arabīya 4 vols. Cairo 1910-1913 (196? ed. by Ḍaif, Šauqī)

c) Works on Other Sciences

Muḫtaṣar ǧuġrāfīyat miṣr. Cairo 1891

Ṭabaqāt al-umam Cairo 1912

'Ilm al-firāsa Cairo 1901

d) Bibliographies

Tarāǧim mašāhīr aš-šarq fi'l-qarn at-tāsi' 'ašar 2 vols. Cairo 1907 (1922)

e) Autobiography

Muḏakkirāt ǧurǧī zaidān ed. by Munaǧǧid, Ṣalāḥ ad-Dīn, Beirut 1966

"*al-Madrasa al-kullīya*", second part of the Autobiography, ed. and annotated by Fāris, Nabīh Amīn in "al-Abḥāṯ" XX (1967) 323-255

f) Magazine

al-Hilāl vol. I - XXII (1892-1914). References to this Magazine are indicated in the footnotes only by volume number and page.

g) Novels

In this study the latest edition, Cairo 1966, has been used.

al-Mamlūk aš-šārid Cairo 1891

Asīr al-mutamahdī Cairo 1892

Istibdād al-mamālīk Cairo 1893

Ǧihād al-muḥibbīn Cairo 1893

Armānūsa al-miṣrīya Cairo 1896

Fatāt ġassān 2 vols. Cairo 1897/98

'Aḏrā' quraiš Cairo 1899

17 Ramaḍān Cairo 1900

Ġādat Karbālā' Cairo 1901

al-Ḥaǧǧāǧ ibn yūsuf Cairo 1902

Fatḥ al-andalus Cairo 1903

Šārl wa-'abd ar-raḥmān Cairo 1904

Abū muslim al-ḫurāsānī Cairo 1905

al-'Abbāsa uḫt ar-rašīd Cairo 1906

al-Amīn wa 'l-ma'mūn Cairo 1907

'Arūs farġāna Cairo 1908
Aḥmad ibn ṭulūn Cairo 1909
'Abd ar-raḥmān an-nāṣir Cairo 1910
al-Inqilāb al-'uṯmānī Cairo 1911
Fatāt al-qairawān Cairo 1912
Ṣalāḥ ad-dīn al-ayyūbī Cairo 1913
Šaǧar ad-durr Cairo 1914

h) Unpublished Papers

Collection of unpublished papers in the archives of the American University of Beirut. Letters that are to be found in this collection have always been referred to in this study as *Letters*.

B. SECONDARY SOURCES

Looking at the secondary sources dealing with Zaidān and his work one is struck by the relative scarcity of such sources. A rather curious work should be mentioned here first, which appeared during the lifetime of Zaidān. It is called *Riwāyat al-baṭalain.* The author behind the pseudonym *D̲āk* has been identified as Nasīb 'Abdallāh Šiblī al-Lubnānī, who apparently was a classmate of Zaidān.[11] He set out to write a novel, the two heroes of which are Ǧurǧī Zaidān and Gordon *Pāšā,* who was killed in Khartoum by the troops of al-Mahdī. We can only guess why the author chose to juxtapose the life of these two persons in one book. Indeed throughout the novel the two figures are brought into no relation whatsoever. The purpose was obviously to write two morally edifying biographies, which could serve as examples for the reader. As far as factual information is concerned, the book neither adds to nor contradicts the information of the autobiography. Only the description of Zaidān's travel to the Sudan is missing from the autobiography. Zaidān himself never mentioned this book by *D̲āk* and we do not know his opinion about it.

Soon after the death of Ǧurǧī Zaidān his son Emile published a collection of essays about his father which are strictly eulogistic. Also in *al-kitāb ad̲-d̲ahabī* published for the 50th anniversary of the magazine "al-Hilāl" one finds only articles of laudatory character. Of similar

11. 'Īsā Iskandar al-Ma'lūf identifies *D̲āk* as Nasīb 'Abdallāh Šiblī al-Lubnānī, AL-MA'LŪF p. 474. He calls him a friend of Zaidān and claims that he wrote this novel in co-operation with Salīm Sarkīs. Zaidān mentions in his autobiography a Nasīb Šiblī as one of the fellow students participating in the strike of the Syrian Protestant College, see p. 204. The letters of protest sent on Dec. 13 and 16, 1882, by the students to the faculty of the SPC were signed also by a Nasīb 'Abdallāh, cf. facsimiles of the two letters in FĀRIS, 330, 346. For the discussion of the strike at the SPC see p. 17-24. It seems highly probable that the Nasīb Šiblī of the autobiography and the Nasīb 'Abdallāh of the letters are identical with the Nasīb 'Abdallāh Šiblī al-Lubnānī, whom Iskandar Ma'lūf mentions. Nothing more is known about this person other than that he lived later in the U.S.A. where he committed suicide, see p. 204.

quality are a number of articles that appeared after his death. Laudatory in character they usually contribute nothing but a factual biography of Zaidān. The most complete list of articles until 1956 is to be found in Yūsuf A. Dāġir's *Maṣādir ad-dirāsā al-adabīya,* II, 442-448.

Alman Arasili's article is restricted to a discussion of the historical novels and limited in its analysis by its Marxist approach. Boudjemeline's paper is of a very narrow literary scope.

Ṭāhir aṭ-Ṭanāḥī's essay *Ǧurǧī Zaidān* appeared in a collection of biographies of self-made men and he dwells lengthily on this aspect of Zaidān's life without, however, providing any critical treatment of the subject.

Three books published between 1966 and 1970 show a reawakened interest in the person of Zaidān in the Arab world. They are written by Ǧuzīf Ḥarb, Muḥammad 'Abd al-Ġanī Ḥasan and Anwar al-Ǧundī. All three books are of apologetic character and totally unanalytical in their approach. Only Ǧ. Ḥarb is somewhat more critical in his evaluation. But he tries to establish Zaidān as a wholesome, unblemished representative of Arab nationalism. In the same group should be mentioned a recent doctoral dissertation from the University of Cologne by Hamdi Alkhayat. The author identifies too much with the subject of his study. The result is an uncritical apology with a considerable number of mistakes.

Two Ph.D. dissertations have recently been written in the U.S.A. about Zaidān. The first was written by this author. The present study emanates partially from this dissertation. The second thesis is by L. Ware. His is an anlytical study, which relies heavily on the unpublished letters (with the exception of the last mentioned two dissertations, no other study seems to have made use of Zaidān's unpublished papers) of Zaidān and on his novels. Ware's emphasis is on a psychoanalytical approach to the person of Zaidān. This method is certainly legitimate. But we have hesitated to make much use of it because we feel it to be severely limited by the amount of psychologically relevant information that can be gathered about people who lived in the past. Even such insights as the letters and the autobiography give us are more often than not wide open to differing interpretation.

BIBLIOGRAPHY OF SECONDARY SOURCES

The sources are quoted in this study by the name of the author only. If more than one work by the same author has been used, the additional works are quoted by the name of the author and the beginning of each title.

ABĪ RAŠĪD, Ḥanā: *Dā'irat ma'ārif al-māsūnīya*. 2 vols. Beirut 1961.

ABBOT, G.F.: *The Holy War in Tripoli*. London 1912.

ALKHAYAT, Hamdi: *Ǧurǧī Zaidān. Leben und Werk*. Cologne 1973.

ALUMNI ASSOCIATION BEIRUT: *The American University of Beirut. Directory of Alumni 1870-1952*. Beirut 1953.

AMĪN, Aḥmad: *Ǧurǧī Zaidān al-mu'arriḫ wa 'l-adīb*. In *al-Kitāb aḏ-ḏahabī*. Cairo 1942.

ANTONIUS, George: *The Arab Awakening*. New York 1964.

ARASILI, Alman: *Ǧurǧī Zaidān wa 'r-riwāya at-ta'rīḫīya fī 'l-adab al-'arabī*, transl. from the Russian by YŪNIS, Muḥammad. Baghdad 1969.

BADR, 'Abd al-Muḥsin Ṭāhā: *Taṭawwur ar-riwāya al-'arabīya al-ḥadīṯa*. Cairo 1963.

BARTHELEMEY, A.: *Dictionnaire Arabe-Français. Dialectes de Syrie*. Paris 1935.

BERQUE, Jacques: *L'Egypte: impérialisme et révolution*. Paris 1967.

BLISS, F.J. ed.: *The Reminiscences of Daniel Bliss*. New York 1920.

BLUNT, W.: *Secret History of the English Occupation of Egypt*. London 1906.

BOUDJEMELINE, Mohamed L.: *La vie et l'œuvre littéraire de Djirdji Zaydan*. Mémoire de Diplôme d'Etudes Supérieures. Université de Paris 1960.

BROCKELMANN, Carl: *Geschichte der Arabischen Litteratur*. 2 vols. Leiden 1943, 1949, 3 supplement vols. Leiden 1937-1942 (Quoted as *GAL*).

BUDAIR, Aḥmad 'Abd al-Fattāḥ: *al-Amīr Aḥmad Fu'ād wa-naš'at al-ǧāmi'a al-miṣrīya*. Cairo 1950.

BURTON, Richard L. Transl.: *The Book of the Thousand Nights and a Night*. 16 vols. Benares 1885-1888.

AL-BUSTĀNĪ, *Muḥīṭ al-muḥīṭ*. Beirut 1870.

AL-BŪSTĀNĪ, Fu'ād, A.: *Dā'irat al-ma'ārif*. Beirut 1956.

— : *Muḏakkirāt rustum bāz*. Beirut 1955.

AL-BUSTĀNĪ, K.: *Amīrāt lubnān*. Beirut 1950.

CACHIA, P. *Ṭāhā Ḥusain. His Place in the Arab Literary Renaissance*. London 1956.

Catalogue of the Syrian Protestant College 1880/81-1884/5. Beirut 1881-1885.

CHEIKHO, Louis: *al-Ḫulāṣa al-māsūnīya*. Beirut 1885.

— : *as-Sirr al-māsūn fī šī'at al-firmāsūn*. Beirut 1909.

— : *al-Ādāb al-'arabīya fī 'l-qarn at-tāsi' 'ašar*. 2 vols. Beirut 1908, 1910.

CROMER, E.: *Modern Egypt*. 2 vols. New York 1916.

DĀĠIR, Yūsuf: *Maṣādir ad-dirāsa al-adabīya*. 3 vols. Beirut 1955-1972.

DEMOLINE, E.: *A quoi tient la supériorité des Anglo-Saxons?* Paris 1897.

DESORMEAUX, C.: *L'Œuvre de Georges Zaidan*. In: Revue du Monde Musulman IV (1908) 837-845.

Dictionnaire d'Histoire et de Géographie Ecclésiastique. 3 vols. 1912, 1914, 1924.

DĪ ṬARRĀZĪ, Filīb: *Ta'rīḫ aṣ-ṣiḥāfa al-'arabīya*. 4 vols. Beirut 1914.

ḎĀK: *Riwāyat al-baṭalain*. Beirut 1889.

ENDE, W. *Arabische Nation und Islamische Geschichte. Die Umayyaden im Urteil arabischer Autoren im 20. Jahrhundert*. Beirut 1977.

Encyclopaedia of Islam. 1st edition 4 vols. Leiden 1913-1934. 2nd edition 3 vols. Leiden 1960-1971 (quoted as EI[1] and EI[2] respectively).

FAHMĪ, Zakī: *Ṣafwat al-'aṣr fī ta'rīḫ wa-rusūm mašāhīr riǧāl maṣr*. Cairo 1912.

FAKKHAR, R.: *Al-Hilal: La pensée progressiste en Europe*. Cairo 1959.

FARAG, Nadia: *The Lewis Affair and the Fortunes of al-Muqtataf*. In: Middle Eastern Studies VIII (1972) 72-83.

FĀRIS, Nabīh, A.: *al-Madrasa al-kullīya*. In al-Abḥāṯ XX (1967) 323-255.

— : *Ṣaff 1883 fī 'l-madrasa al-kullīya*. In: al-Abḥāṯ XXI (1968) 39-55.

GABRIELI, F.: *The Autobiography of Mikhail Nu'aima*. In: TIKKU G.L. ed. *Islam and its Cultural Divergence*. Chicago 1971.

GENDZIER, I.L.: *The Practical Vision of Ya'qub Ṣanu'*. Cambridge 1966.

GIBB, H.A.R. & LANDAU, J.M.: *Arabische Literaturgeschichte*. Zürich 1968.

AL-ǦUNDĪ, Anwar: *Ǧurǧī zaidān munšī' al-hilāl*. Cairo 1968.

— : *Tarāǧim al-a'lām al-mu'āṣirīn fī'l-'ālam al-islāmī*. Cairo 1970.

HAIKAL, Ḥusain: *Fī auqāt al-farāġ*. Cairo 1924.

— : *'Ahdī bi'l-hilāl*. In: *al-Kitāb aḏ-ḏahabī*. Cairo 1942.

HAIM, Sylvia: *Arab Nationalism*. Los Angeles 1964.

— : *The Arab Awakening: A source for Historians*. In: Die Welt des Islams (New Series) II (1952) 237-250.

HANDJERI, A. *Dictionnaire Français-arabe-persan et turc*. Moscow 1841.

HANF: *Erziehungswesen in Gesellschaft und Politik des Libanon.* n.p. 1969, published by Bertelsman Verlag.

ḤARB, Ǧuẓīf: *Ǧurǧī zaidān riǧāl fī raǧul.* Beirut 1970.

ḤASAN, Muḥammad ʿAbd al-Ġanī: *Ǧurǧī zaidān.* Cairo 1970.

HINZ, Walter: *Islamische Maße und Gewichte.* In: SPULER, B.: *Handbuch der Orientalistik, Ergänzungsband* I. Heft 1, Leiden 1955.

HOURANI, Albert: *Arabic Thought in the Liberal Age.* London 1962.

ḪŪRĪ, Y.: *ad-Duktūr Kurnilīyūs fān Daik.* Unpublished M.A. dissertation AUB. Beirut 196?.

ḤUSAIN, Ṭāhā: *Zaidān kamā ʿaraftuhū.* In: al-Hilāl XLVII 964 ff.

— : *Aṯar al-hilāl wa-munšiʾihī.* In: *al-Kitāb aḏ-ḏahabī.* Cairo 1972.

— : *al-Ayyām* Cairo 1929; Transl. into English by PAXTON, E.H.: An Egyptian Childhood. London 1932.

JESSUP, S.H.H.: *Fifty Three Years in Syria.* New York 1910.

KEANE, A.H. *The World's People.* New York 1908.

KEDDIE, Nikki: *An Islamic Response to Imperialism.* Los Angeles 1968.

— : *Sayyid Jamal ad-Din al-Afghani: A Political Biography.* Los Angeles 1972.

KEDOURI, Elie: *Afghani and Abduh.* London 1966.

KERR, Malcom: *Islamic Reform.* Los Angeles 1966.

al-Kitāb aḏ-ḏahabī. Cairo 1942; published in the *Dār al-Hilāl.*

KÖCHER, E.: *Untersuchungen zu Ǧamīl al-Mudawwar's Ḥaḍārat al-islām fī dār as-salām.* Berlin 1958.

KRACHKOVSKY, I.I.: *Der Historische Roman in der neuren arabischen Literatur.* In: Welt des Islams XII (1930) 51 ff.

— : *Avec les Manuscrits Arabes.* Alger 1954.

— : *Jurji Zaydan.* Encyclopaedia of Islam. First Edition.

LANE, E.W.: *An Arabic English Dictionary.* 8 vols: 1863-1893.

LEWIS, Bernard: *The Emergence of Modern Turkey.* London 1961.

LUṬFI AL-SAYYID, Afaf: *Egypt and Cromer.* London 1968.

AL-MADANĪ Amīn al-Ḥulwānī: *Nabš al-haḏayān min taʾrīḫ ǧurǧī zaidān.* Bombay 1890.

MAKĀRIYŪS, Šāhīn: *al-Ādāb al-māsūnīya.* Cairo 1895.

AL-MAʿLŪF, ʿĪsā Iskandar: *Fāǧiʿat al-quṭrain.* In: al-Āṯār III (1913-1914) 469 ff.

MARLOWE, J.: *A History of Modern Egypt and Anglo-Egyptian Relations.* Connecticut 1965.

MOOSA, Matti: *Ya'qūb Ṣanū and the Rise of Arab Drama in Egypt.* In International Journal of Middle Eastern Studies V (1974) 401-433.

MUBĀRAK, 'Alī: *al-Ḫiṭaṭ at-taufīqīya al-ǧadīda.* vols. Cairo 1886-1889.

MŪSĀ, Salāma: *Tarbiyat salāma mūsā.* Cairo 1947; transl. into English Schuman, L.O.: *The Education of Salama Musa.* Leiden 1961.

NAĞM, M.Y.: *al-Qiṣṣa fī 'l-adab al-'arabī al-ḥadīṯ.* Beirut 1961.

PENROSE, S.B.L.: *That they may have Light.* New York 1941.

PHILIPP, Thomas: *The Role of Jurji Zaidan in the intellectual Development of the Arab Nahda.* Los Angeles 1971; unpublished Ph.D. thesis.

— : *Language, History, and Arab National Consciousness in the Thought of Jurji Zaidan (1861-1914).* In International Journal of Middle Eastern Studies IV (1973) 3-22.

— : *Approaches to History in the Work of Jurji Zaydan.* In: Asian and African Studies IX (1973) 63-85.

POLITIS, A.G.: L'Hellénisme et l'Égypte moderne. Paris 1928.

Presidents' Annual Reports to the Board of Managers. Syrian Protestant College. 1866-67/1901-02 (quoted as *Annual Reports*).

REID, M.: *Syrian Christians, the Rags to Riches Story and Free Enterprise.* In: International Journal of Middle Eastern Studies I (1970) 358-367.

— : *The Syrian Christians and Early Socialism in the Arab World.* In: International Journal of Middle Eastern Studies V (1974) 177-193.

RICHTER, J.: *History of Protestant Missions in the Near East.* London 1910.

RIḌĀ, Rašīd ed.: *Kitāb intiqād kitāb ta'rīḫ at-tamaddun al-islāmī.* Cairo 1912.

— : *Ta'rīḫ al-ustāḏ al-imām aš-šaiḫ Muḥammad 'Abduh.* Cairo 1931.

ROSENTHAL, Franz: *A History of Muslim Historiography.* Leiden 1952.

— : *Die Arabische Autobiographie.* In: Studica Arabica I (1937) 1-40.

SĀBĀT, Ḫalīl: *Ta'rīḫ aṭ-ṭibā'a fī 'š-šarq al-'arabī.* Cairo 1966.

SALIBI, K.S.: *The Modern History of Lebanon.* New York 1965.

SAMARAN, C. ed. *L'Histoire et ses méthodes.* Bruges 1961.

SCHAENDLINGER, A.C. *Osmanische Numismatik.* Braunschweig 1973.

SCHREGLE, G.: *Deutsch-Arabisches Wörterbuch.* Wiesbaden 1965.

SEIGNOBES, C.: *History of Contemporary Civilization.* London 1923.

SMILES, S.: *Self-Help.* London 1958.

SMITH, W.C.: *Islam in Modern History*. Princeton 1957.

STEPPAT, Fritz: *Nationalismus und Islam bei Muṣṭafā Kāmil*. In: Welt des Islams IV (1955) 241-341.

— : *Eine Bewegung unter den Notabeln Syriens*. In: Zeitschrift der Deutschen Morgenländischen Gesellschaft 1969 Supplementa I Vorträge Teil 2 640 ff.

AṬ-ṬANĀḤĪ, Ṭāhir: *al-Hilāl fī niṣf qarn*. In: *al-Kitāb ad-ḏahabī*. Cairo 1942.

— : *Ǧurǧī zaidān*. In: ABŪ ḤADĪD, M.F.: *'Iṣāmīyūn 'uẓamā' min aš-šarq wa'l-ġarb*. Cairo 194?. The second half of the book is a transl. of Bolton. S.K.: *Lives of Poor Boys who became Famous*. New York 1947.

TANIM, Suha, ed: *Bibliography of AUB Faculty Publications 1866-1966*. Beirut 1967.

TIBAWI, A.L.: *American Interests in Syria 1800-1901*. Oxford 1966.

— : *British Interests in Palestine 1800-1901*. Oxford 1961.

— : *History of the Syrian Protestant College*. In: SARRUF, F. ed.: *AUB Festival Book*, Beirut 1967.

TIGNOR, E.L.: *Modernization and British Colonial Rule in Egypt*. Princeton 1966.

VON GRUNEBAUM, G.E.: *Nationalism and Cultural Trends in the Arab Near East*. In: Studia Islamica XIV (1961) 121 ff.

— : *Medieval Islam*. Chicago 1962.

WAHRMUND, A.: *Handwörterbuch der Arabischen und Deutschen Sprache*. 2 vols. Graz 1970.

WARE, Lewis: *Jurji Zaydān: The Role of Popular History in the Formation of a New Arab World View*. Princeton 1973; unpublished Ph.D. thesis.

WELLS, S.R.: *How to Read Character: A New Illustrated Handbook of Phrenology and Physiognomy*. New York 189?.

WENDELL, C.: *Ahmad Lutfi as-Sayyid and the Concept of an Egyptian Nation*. Los Angeles 1967; unpublished Ph.D. thesis.

ZAḤŪRA, Ilyās: *Mir'āt al-'aṣr fī ta'rīḫ wa-rusūm akābir ar-riǧāl bi-miṣr*. Cairo 1897.

— : *as-Sūriyūn fī miṣr*. Cairo 1927.

ZAIDĀN, Emile ed.: *Ǧurǧī Zaidān*. Cairo 1915.

ZEINE, N. Zeine: *The Emergence of Arab Nationalism*. Beirut 1966.

ZIADEH, Nichola: *as-Sanūsīya*. Leiden 1958.

ZOLONDEK, L.: *aš-Ša'b in Arabic Political Literature of the 19th Century*. In: Welt des Islams X (1965) 1 ff.

INDEX OF NAMES